# RENEWING
# THE WORLD

HOWARD L. HARROD

# RENEWING THE WORLD

Plains Indian Religion
and Morality

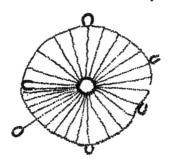

The University of Arizona Press
Tucson

The University of Arizona Press
© 1987 The Arizona Board of Regents
All rights reserved

www.uapress.arizona.edu

Library of Congress Cataloging-in-Publication Data
Harrod, Howard L., 1932-
Renewing the world.
Bibliography: p.
Includes index.
1. Indians of North America—Great Plains—
Religion and mythology. I. Title
E78.G73H36    1987    299'.798    87-5010
ISBN 0-8165-0958-1 (alk. paper)
ISBN 0-8165-1312-0 (pbk)

*To Lee Ann and Amy Ceil*

# Contents

# Illustrations

# Preface

TRIBAL PEOPLES POSSESSING COMPLEX CULTURES flourished on the Northwestern Plains at the beginning of the nineteenth century. This book seeks to recollect aspects of the lives of these tribal predecessors, many of whose descendants still live on reservations in the region. The time frame of the analysis is from about 1850 to the turn of the century. Studies of these peoples, from the point of view of many disciplines, have illuminated the nature of their diverse cultures. The contribution of this work lies in its focus upon religious and moral traditions as these are embodied in symbolic forms and mediated through ritual processes.

This task is difficult because we seek to understand peoples and cultures which are different from contemporary American culture and which are distant in time. The narrative which arises out of this effort is informed by many sources: historical, linguistic, ethnographic, sociological, and archaeological, as well as by a guiding theoretical perspective. If the interpretation is successful, it will approximate a single goal which motivates and lures the analysis: to allow readers to see something of the world as these distant peoples saw it and, more deeply, to apprehend how very different these world experiences are from our own, while at the same time glimpsing something which speaks across social time and cultural space.

The interpretative perspective which informs this work focuses attention upon basic dimensions of human existence: the nature of human social worlds and how these are constituted, the way human experience is rich and multidimensional, the nature of symbolic forms and their connection with transcendent horizons of meaning, the importance of ritual processes in human communities, and the way religious and moral experiences may be interpreted. The central notion which binds these dimensions together is the idea of *meaning*. Human beings are understood as creatures who generate and interpret meanings.

The task of interpretation becomes that of exposing the meanings that constitute individual experience and, when shared, form social worlds. The task of the interpreter becomes that of providing an exposition of the specific meanings which give sense to individual and social life. This interpretation will expose those fundamental meanings that form a people's apprehension of the sacred, showing how these experiences are intimately connected with an understanding of their moral universe.

These tasks are complex and have their obvious problems. But the adequacy of any interpretation is judged by how accurately it reflects meanings which the human beings who are the subjects of interpretation actually share. The fit between the interpreter's point of view and the people's point of view will never be completely adequate. And getting at a "people's point of view" can never mean a perfect reproduction of their cultural meanings. Rather the task is *interpretative,* which involves the construction of ideal types on the basis of specific cultural materials. Through this process are built up the outlines of the social worlds which characterized peoples on the Northwestern Plains. When these matters become clear, then a picture of their religious and moral experience emerges.

This book is not only about the past. It is also motivated by concerns for the way non-Indian Americans relate to and understand contemporary descendants of Northwestern Plains tribes. At a basic level there is a concern that both Indian and non-Indian peoples come to a greater appreciation of the religious and moral traditions which form a rich heritage too often ignored or forgotten. Forgetfulness, ignorance, or romantic misinterpretation are characteristics more likely to be present among non-Indians, however. For many descendants of tribal groups on the Northwestern Plains, there will be flashes of recognition in what is presented in this book; and for some there will be deep familiarity with the oral traditions discussed, since many of these traditions continue, though not in unmodified form, down to the present. For these people my hope is to represent with as much accuracy as possible the rich religious and moral heritage which is theirs. For non-Indians my hope is that greater understanding and appreciation of these traditions will lead to a new vision of what our common life might become. These traditions reveal not only worlds that are past but also worlds that continue in the experience of many persons. These are worlds from which we may learn as we grope, for better or worse, toward the twenty-first century.

HOWARD L. HARROD
North Fork of the Flathead
Montana

# Acknowledgments

A NUMBER OF PERSONS made contributions to the argument of this book. Colleagues who read the entire manuscript and made helpful comments include Sam Gill of the University of Colorado at Boulder, Peter Paris of Princeton University, and Ed Farley, Walter Harrelson, and Doug Knight, all of Vanderbilt University. Carling Malouf of the University of Montana read the first chapter and contributed helpful insights; and Volney Gay of Vanderbilt University commented on chapter three. Thanks are also due to Daniel Patte and to the members of the Seminar on Structuralism and the Humanities at Vanderbilt University for reacting critically to portions of the manuscript. David Barton made an essential contribution toward illuminating the context of the argument.

Graduate students at Vanderbilt who contributed comments include Jack Johnson-Hill, Paul Kong, Viki Matson, John Reiman, and Charles Johnson, who helped with the final preparation of the manuscript; students in other seminars and classes also made illuminating remarks.

I am grateful to Bill Hook for typing the manuscript and for introducing me to the mysteries of word processing. Paula McNutt provided the map showing approximate tribal locations and assisted with the index and the final proofreading. Tom Ventress provided the line drawings that appear at the beginning of each chapter.

Institutional support was provided by fellowships from the American Council of Learned Societies and the Vanderbilt University Research Council. Through the good offices of Jim Flanagan, work space and other institutional support at the University of Montana were generously provided.

An essential contribution was made by my colleague, Bob Funk of the University of Montana, who made available a place for reflection on the North Fork of the Flathead River during the summers of 1982 and 1984. Over the years another North Fork colleague, my friend Ray Hart, has provided both rich intellectual stimulation and personal support.

I should also like to express appreciation to Joseph Epes Brown of the University of Montana. I have learned much from him and his work, and for that I am deeply grateful.

As always, thanks go to Annemarie for her support at the most fundamental levels.

Finally, it seems appropriate to remember with gratitude those predecessors on the Northwestern Plains, many of whose names are unknown, who created the rich symbols and evocative ritual processes that are the subject of this study.

# CHAPTER 1

# Retracing Time

THE CENTRAL FOCUS OF THIS STUDY is upon religious and moral traditions of tribes living in historic times on the Northwestern Plains. Rather than assuming the form of sacred texts or holy canon, these traditions were preserved, reinterpreted, and mediated through elaborate ritual processes. By participating in these ritual processes, powerful religious and moral sensibilities were evoked in the experience of the people. Basic in this context are root symbolic forms which encode the fundamental meanings borne in the oral traditions and enacted in ritual processes. The basic thesis to be explored is that a study of these symbolic forms and their attendant ritual processes provides some clue to the shape of religious and moral attitudes, dispositions, and sensibilities among peoples of the Northwestern Plains. Although not a study of behavior, inferences may be drawn from this study as to how certain of their moral and

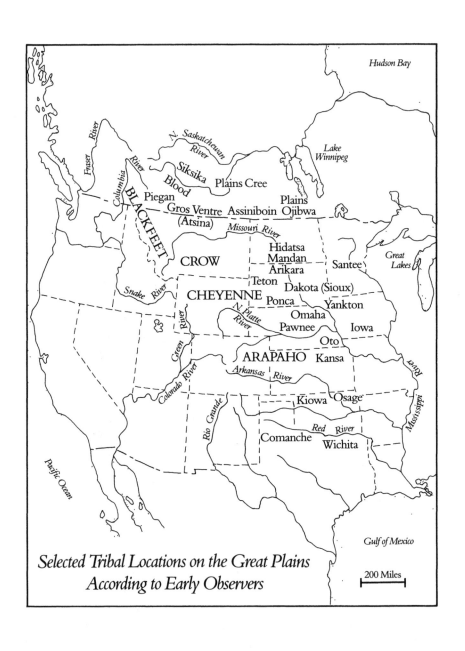

Hudson Bay

Fraser River

N. Saskatchewan River

Lake Winnipeg

River

Columbia

Siksika

Blood

Plains Cree

BLACKFEET

Piegan

Gros Ventre (Atsina)

Assiniboin

Plains Ojibwa

Missouri River

Great Lakes

CROW

Hidatsa
Mandan
Arikara

Santee

Snake River

Teton

Dakota (Sioux)

CHEYENNE

Ponca

Green River

N. Platte River

Yankton

Omaha

Pawnee

Iowa

Oto

ARAPAHO

Kansa

Colorado River

Arkansas River

Rio Grande

Kiowa

Osage

Mississippi River

Red River

Comanche

Wichita

Pacific Ocean

Gulf of Mexico

*Selected Tribal Locations on the Great Plains*
*According to Early Observers*

200 Miles

religious attitudes, dispositions, and sensibilities may have informed action. At a more fundamental level, what may be discerned is the way these peoples apprehended their world and, in this light, how their responses to their environment and to other beings, human and nonhuman, were shaped.[1]

The traditions of central interest were powerfully articulated in ritual and symbolic form about the middle of the last century. Their expression in 1850 was the product of a long process of social change, reinterpretation, and creative adaptation. At the turn of the century, these traditions were still alive in the experience of peoples otherwise scarred by conquest, disease, and exploitation. In the early years of the present century a massive descriptive record of these traditions was laid down as a consequence of the work of anthropologists, ethnographers, and other interested observers. Despite its inherent difficulties, this record forms the background of the present study.[2]

Attention will be focused upon four major groups: the Blackfeet, Crows, Cheyennes, and Arapahoes. A comparative study of their rituals and symbolic forms will deepen our insight into the complex religious and moral sensibilities which characterized the experience of these peoples.[3]

In order to understand the religious and moral sensibilities of the historic Plains tribes, some effort must be expended on tracing their emergence in time and space. Only in this manner will we be able to deepen our grasp of these traditions as they appeared in 1850. If we begin with our present experience, it may be possible to work gradually back to an understanding of the context within which these traditions emerged; at the same time, it may be possible to develop a more adequate image of these historic peoples, as well as some view of their prehistoric predecessors.

It requires an act of the imagination to visualize what the vast region known as the Northwestern Plains must have been like to our own predecessors. Driving west across Kansas, traversing eastern Colorado, there to turn north at Denver, modern travelers are isolated from extremes of heat and cold, dangerous wind currents, and driving rain or snow. Their trip is smoothed by ribboned super highways, their sense of vast distances dulled by the speed of

[3]

powerful automobiles or sleek jet airplanes. The spiny cordillera dividing the continent may inspire momentary awe in the hearts of tourists to these regions; but, for the most part, experience is domesticated by the signs and symbols of a mass economy and its institutions. Even in the most remote of areas there are now signs which indicate the ubiquitous presence of the Holiday Inn, replete with comforts of television, restaurants, and convenient shelter from the vastness of surrounding space. Occasionally nature rises up and brings modern movements to a brief halt, as in the case of floods or massive winter storms. But routine activities soon appear again, and a sense of the undomesticated face of nature fades into the recesses of memory.

As compared with the tourist, many residents have also achieved an attitude of familiarity with the Northwestern Plains. Tracts of land, though immense, are often fenced; water rights, though sometimes acrimoniously debated, have historical and legal depth; small cities and towns, though sparser than in other regions, are evident; and state lines, though not visible as children sometimes suppose, mark off the land at deep psychic, political, and economic levels. All of these factors indicate the fabric of a culture which has most recently draped itself upon this sometimes harsh and always beautiful environment.

Being creatures of historical consciousness, most reflective Americans know that it was not always so. There is the dim perception that others were there before us and that change marks the face of the Plains. We may have a more or less clear image of immediate predecessors—those settlers who pioneered the country, who marked the trails, who cleared the timber, and who later irrigated the soil and made the land agriculturally productive. Beyond this our understanding may be clouded by romantic images often informed by movies and television.

Problems of interpretation become more complex when we seek to envision the cultures of aboriginal inhabitants of the Northwestern Plains. Three reasons, among others, account for this complexity.

First, if we attempt to bring into view the cultural horizons of prehistoric peoples, we are confronted immediately by an interpre-

[4]

tative opacity. Very little is known about the institutions and life-ways of early residents on the Plains. At this level, we shall have to be content to throw as much light as possible upon the material horizon of these cultures by appealing to the archaeological evidence. On the basis of this evidence, we shall seek to infer something of the cultural flavor of these peoples. It will become manifest, however, that the picture is unclear, that it is debatable in many of its important details, and that we know less than we would like about even the most fundamental of matters.

Second, most tribes which inhabited the Northwestern Plains during historic times were themselves migrants into the region. Some came from a horticultural background which included a mixture of planting and hunting. The interpretative problem of origins is always difficult and often shrouded in mystery; this problem generates difficulties at the point of determining the historical depth of the traditions we are seeking to interpret. There is sufficient evidence, however, to allow us to form adequate images of the migrations of these peoples onto the Plains. This picture will of necessity be a dynamic one, reflecting the creativity and the adaptability of the oral traditions themselves.

Third, there is the problem of our own cultural images of these Plains peoples, images that have been funded by dime western novels, romantic accounts of travelers and of missionaries, and, more recently, by movies and television. The historic roots in literature and art of the "white man's Indian" have been traced by others (Berkhofer 1978). The importance of these analyses is that they have the potentiality to liberate us from grosser forms of cultural bondage, enabling us to begin the task of confronting Indian institutions and cultural patterns on their own terms and not simply as extensions of our own interpretative views.

Why, one may still ask, is it necessary to spend so much time seeking to trace the context—natural, prehistorical, and historical—if our interest is in religious and moral traditions? The answer to this question lies in the view that moral and religious traditions, wherever they appear, are inextricably a part of the culture that is the subject of interpretation. This point seems obvious. Further, however, culture is related to surrounding ecological conditions;

[5]

morality and religion, as parts of culture, also reflect the influence of the ecological context (cf. Hultkrantz 1981, chaps. 7–10). This view does not lead to a materialistic or deterministic theory of religion and morality, or even of culture itself. The emphasis is rather upon the mutual interaction between culture (and thus religion and morality) and nature as it is constituted by culture.[4] From this point of view, culture is more than a filter for our experiences of nature; culture is rather a force which images what we experience as *nature* in fundamental ways.

In the light of these considerations, it is impossible to abstract the study of religion and morality from surrounding natural and cultural contexts. A study of the religious and moral traditions of Plains tribes is intended to expose some of the fundamental apprehensions of human beings, natural processes, animals, and other beings which constituted their world. If successful, the analysis should provide deeper insight into the vast differences between their apprehensions and our own; and this expanded vision may lead to a deeper and more sympathetic understanding of these peoples and their social worlds.

## The Great Plains as a Cultural Context

The Great Plains as a whole has aptly been characterized as a land of "sun and wind and grass" (Wedel 1974, p. 24; cf. Webb 1981). The nature of this terrain, its climate and its forms of plant and animal life, provided a set of possibilities out of which human cultural responses arose. When combined with an understanding of changing Indian technologies, an analysis of this context will deepen and enrich our subsequent understanding of cultural values and religious experience. Even though the climax period of Plains cultures in the mid-nineteenth century has been viewed as the consequence of a flowering not many centuries old, it is still probable that the institutions so characteristic of these cultures had more ancient roots. This argument is made more plausible when we understand that the ecology of the Plains region is of considerable geo-

[6]

logical age and that cultural responses have tended to have a certain continuity.

The area of the Northwestern Plains may generally be defined to include a portion of the western Dakotas, the present states of Wyoming and Montana, and an area north into Canada for at least 150 miles. This part of the Plains shades off gradually to the east, as precipitation rises, on a line running roughly north and south through the eastern parts of the Dakotas, Nebraska, and Kansas. In Canada, the Plains end on the east where we confront stands of coniferous forest in the park belt. On the west, the Northwestern Plains terminate at the Rocky Mountains, extending somewhat farther to the Continental Divide in the state of Wyoming (Wedel 1974, p. 240).

However we choose to explain the formation of this region in geological time, since its formation it has exhibited certain climatic features which have shaped in important ways the cultural possibilities of human habitation. Of prime importance is the arid character of the region, annual precipitation normally not exceeding 15 inches, dropping sometimes to 10 inches along the International Boundary and to 6 inches in the Bighorn Basin. Given these conditions, trees requiring deep ground moisture disappear, except in the river valleys, and the environment is dominated by short grasses, sage, and other varieties of desert plants. Because water is at such a premium, the cultural importance of rivers, creeks, and springs in the region becomes obvious. For prehistoric and historic tribes, the river valleys provided supplies of water, wood, and forage for animals, as well as some shelter from the rigors of winter.

Climatic conditions placed severe limitations, given native technologies, upon the development of sedentary patterns associated with agriculture.[5] As a culture area, the Northwestern Plains were characterized by the development of subsistence patterns which depended primarily upon hunting. The main food staple for the historic tribes was the buffalo, and this great animal penetrated deeply into their religious and moral sensibilities.[6] This primary dependence upon a single animal does not mean, of course, that aboriginal peoples failed to depend upon the other rich animal, vegetable, and berry resources of the region. Among these vegetable and berry

[7]

foodstuffs on the Plains were service berries, choke cherries, wild rhubarb, wild potatoes, onions, bitter roots, camas, and wild turnips (McClintock 1968, pp. 529–30). Animal resources other than the buffalo were also abundant. Pronghorn antelope, mule deer, white-tailed deer, and elk were plentiful, as were wolves, coyotes, kit foxes, and jack rabbits. Black and grizzly bears ranged over the area, as did smaller fur-bearing animals, such as beavers, otters, minks, and raccoons. Fish were abundant in the streams, although they were not a major source of food for the tribes under consideration. Bird life was also rich, and included geese, ducks, and other water birds, as well as grouse, prairie chickens, and sage hens. Bald and golden eagles, as well as great horned owls, were numerous and assumed importance in the ritual life of the people.

The animal that preeminently dominated the cultural life of peoples on the Northwestern Plains was the buffalo (Roe 1970, pp. 601–70). This dependence is so well known that only a few remarks at a general level are necessary as background for later analysis. As many observers have pointed out, the buffalo provided not only the major food resource for the people but also yielded material for clothing and for covering the conical tipi. Tools and other implements were fashioned from the bone, and from the skin were constructed rawhide bags and other household articles. Almost all of the products of this animal were put to some use, and there were persons quite skilled in preserving the meat for future use (Ewers 1958, pp. 72–87).

The kinds of tribal institutions which developed upon the Plains also reflected the interrelationship between humans and buffalo. On the level of tribal organization, for example, a single illustration will suffice. Tribal life was characterized by a rhythm of uniting in the summer months and dispersing during the winter months. During the summer months the buffalo moved in great herds across the Plains. Corporate hunting was required during this period if a food supply sufficient to last throughout the winter was to be gathered. Likewise, larger numbers of people were required to dry the meat, prepare the skins, and fashion needed utensils and implements. Thus evolved the tribal hunt and tribal division of labor in preparing the products of the chase.

During the winter the buffalo dispersed along the creek banks and valleys, which were sheltered from the winter winds and snow. Tribal groups were constituted as small, mobile hunting bands. These bands were large enough to provide for protection against enemies but small enough to sustain themselves through the winter on previously prepared food and on what hunting could be done given the availability of game (Wissler 1911, pp. 20–21). Interpreters have pointed out the influence of the buffalo hunting economy upon the general social structure: "It seems probable that the conditions of Plains life favored a rather amorphous and mobile type of social organization which could vary to meet changing conditions" (Eggan 1955, p. 48; cf. Oliver 1962). Subsequent analysis of particular parts of the social structure, such as the kinship system, will be important for understanding religious and moral experience.

Two other animals, the dog and the horse, are important to mention at this juncture. There is evidence to show that the domesticated dog was critical to the culture of prehistoric hunters on the Plains (Wedel 1974, pp. 302–3). These animals bore the burdens of the camp when movement was required and also transported the products of the hunt when a kill took place at some distance from the permanent camp. Given the carrying capacity of the dog, it is probably true that the number of possessions and the size of the tipis were smaller in prehistoric pedestrian times than was later the case.

The diffusion of the horse during the seventeenth and eighteenth centuries radically transformed the life of Plains tribes. Previous methods of hunting, such as the surround, driving animals over cliffs or into corrals, and perhaps the fire drive, were replaced by hunting animals on horseback. The mounted hunter, especially when equipped with a gun, could kill more efficiently and with greater ease than could his pedestrian predecessors. Not only did the horse transform subsistence patterns, but changes also reverberated elsewhere throughout the social structure. Gradually the horse became an important standard of wealth, giving rise to processes of social stratification which generated the need for continual acquisition of horses. A consequence of this impulse may have been the emergence of widespread patterns of horse raiding. In addition,

[9]

intertribal conflicts may have been heightened owing to the greater possibilities for mobility introduced by the horse. The horse also became, in many cultures on the Plains, an animal of sacred significance and power. This animal, along with the gun, produced innovative and expansive, as well as destructive, effects within Indian cultures (Roe 1955; Wissler 1914; Ewers 1955, 1969, 1975).

As we contemplate the general picture of developments up to this point, it would appear that social change is an important, if not primary, theme. This is indeed the case, especially upon the Plains.[7] As indicated above, most historic tribes are believed to be migrants, some settling on the Plains more recently than other groups. Their movement from a cultural background that often included agriculture or a mixture of agriculture and hunting involved the creation of social worlds and patterns of moral and religious significance which characterized, in historic times, typical Plains cultures. An elaboration of some of the evidence relating to these migrations will deepen the interpretative context.

## Migrations of the Historic Tribes

The Blackfoot[8] confederacy is composed of the Piegan (Pikuni), Blood (Kainah), and Northern Blackfeet (Siksika). These peoples presumably migrated onto the Plains at some distant point in time. When first contacted by whites, the Blackfeet were probably residents of the lands of the Canadian park belt. Memorial traditions seem to support the view that these people were, at some time in their history, forest dwellers (Curtis 1911, pp. 3–4, 6). There is little evidence in either memory or tradition which would suggest that the Blackfeet had recent agricultural roots (cf. Kehoe 1981, p. 279). Indeed, on the basis of linguistic evidence, it has been argued that the Blackfeet, along with the Arapahoes, may have been "ancient occupants" of the Northwestern Plains (Kroeber 1939, p. 82). This argument is based upon the fact that both tribes are of Algonquian linguistic stock but that their languages are highly divergent from the parent body. Such divergences are not characteristic, so the argument goes, for languages that have remained in close geographical proximity with the parent stock. Thus, the conclusion that the Blackfeet and Arapahoes must have migrated away from their linguistic roots a long time ago (Kroeber 1939, p. 81).

Others have argued, to the contrary, that the Blackfeet are more recent migrants. This argument relies upon traditions reported by David Thompson in 1787 to the effect that the Blackfeet were residents of the Saskatchewan Plains as late as the early eighteenth century. On the basis of this evidence, one may conclude that it was not until after the reception of the horse, and perhaps the gun, that the Blackfeet migrated west and south to their traditional homeland (Ewers 1955, p. 300; 1967, p. 170). In either case, it seems probable that the Blackfeet did migrate to the Plains from the eastern woodlands at some time in their past. Even if that migration was more recent than the view which holds that they were "ancient occupants," it is still true that they developed institutions and traditions that finally enabled them to flourish on the Northwestern Plains.

Precisely when the Arapahoes arrived on the Plains is also difficult to determine (Kroeber 1902, p. 4). Some evidence in Arapaho traditions indicates that they were once an agricultural people living east of the Plains (Oliver 1962, p. 35). They were first observed above the Missouri River on the northern Plains in 1789. After this time a part of the tribe moved south and west, while the group remaining north of the Missouri became known as the Gros Ventres or Atsinas. Later these people moved farther west and became closely associated with the Blackfeet (Eggan 1955, p. 36; Kehoe 1981, pp. 279–81). By historic times, however, the Arapahoes reflected few traces of their previous cultural roots and had become full-scale nomads, following the great buffalo herds. The transformations of their social world that must have occurred as a consequence of this shift from agriculture to hunting were surely vast, but there is no detailed evidence which allows a specific description of this process. By the time they are met by whites, the Arapahoes had developed a social world and moral and religious sensibilities which were similar to their neighbors on the Plains. These moral and religious traditions, despite their similarities with other tribes, possessed unique contours. It is in describing the special features of these dimensions of cultural meaning that we will be able to understand the nuances of the Arapaho social world.

More is known about the early migrations of the Cheyennes than of the Blackfeet and Arapahoes. Like the Arapahoes, the Cheyennes were of Algonquian linguistic stock. If interpreters of early records are correct, the Cheyennes were living in the area of the headwaters of the Mississippi River in the year 1680. Whether they came from somewhere else, or had lived in this vicinity for a long time, is not known. In any case, the Cheyennes were at this time probably village dwellers who subsisted on a diet of wild rice supplemented by small game. They may also have done some gardening during this period (Hoebel 1978, pp. 4–5). The Cheyennes were dislodged from their eastern woodlands home by the better armed and more numerous Crees, Assiniboins, and Woodland Sioux. As a consequence of these pressures, the Cheyennes moved westward toward the prairies.

By 1750 the Cheyennes had reestablished themselves in the area of the Sheyenne River in South Dakota. Adapting themselves to the new conditions, the Cheyennes improved their agricultural techniques, cultivating crops of maize, beans, and squash. They also spent part of the year hunting buffalo and other game animals. In addition to these food supplies, the country was abundant with wildfowl and fish. At this time the Cheyennes further developed their village life-style, living in earth lodges similar to those of the Arikaras, Mandans, and Hidatsas. Again the patterns of adjustment to new conditions must have influenced their moral and religious traditions, although little is known about how these changes actually occurred (Hoebel 1978, pp. 6–9; Wedel 1974, pp. 214–15, 242–43; Kroeber 1939, p. 83; cf. Mooney 1907, p. 361–63, and Grinnell 1972, vol. 1, pp. 1–46). We will identify, in subsequent analysis, echoes in the oral traditions which seem to reflect their earlier agricultural roots.

Intertribal hostilities again disturbed the Cheyennes, producing additional migration and social change. Their sedentary villages, though prosperous, were easy targets for mobile warriors on horseback. In addition, these villages were increasingly prey to diseases such as measles and smallpox. Instead of being exterminated by disease, as almost happened to their neighbors, the Mandans and Hidatsas, the Cheyennes migrated again. Having acquired the horse around 1760 and having integrated this animal into their culture by 1780, the Cheyennes were prepared for their future life as Plains nomads. Pressured by warfare and disease, they gradually abandoned their village lifeways, and by the beginning of the nineteenth century they had become a typical nomadic hunting tribe on the western Plains. During their westward movement, the Cheyennes met and assimilated another Algonquian-speaking tribe, the Suhtais. These people may have been buffalo hunters for some time, and from them the Cheyennes must have learned much (Hoebel 1978, pp. 9–11; Wedel 1974, p. 215; Oliver 1962, p. 29).

The pattern of social change illustrated by the Cheyennes is significant. Rather than experiencing a total destruction of their social world, the Cheyennes evolved new cultural responses and generated patterns of meaning appropriate to each new environment. These adjustments must have affected their lives in quite pervasive ways, but they survived through a process of creative adaptation. These complexities are emphasized by consideration of the fact that the Cheyenne migrations, as probably was also the case for other tribes, did not occur as a consequence of a single mass movement. Moves probably took place in smaller groups. While the general trend of the migration was westward, some groups probably passed other groups who had moved before them. Thus, the drift onto the Plains was complicated by the very way in which the migrations occurred (Grinnell 1972, vol. 1, pp. 21–22). Given such conditions, it is easy to imagine how dynamic the evolution toward Plains life forms must have been and how this movement was probably marked by considerable cultural pluralism.

Another example of creative adaptation in the face of social change is provided by the Crows, a people of Siouan linguistic stock. Once associated with the Hidatsas, who lived in the area of the upper Missouri River, the Crows began their drift toward the Northwestern Plains and, as had other groups, adapted themselves to life as mobile buffalo hunters (Eggan 1966, p. 65; Kehoe 1981, p. 279). While the dates of their migration are not known with precision, the actual pattern of their cultural evolution may have been much like that of the Cheyennes (Lowie 1954, p. 186). They too created patterns of meaning appropriate to their new life circumstances. What is interesting in their case is that they preserved evidence of their previous agricultural existence in the social structure. Crow traditions, for example, memorialize both their kinship with and their separation from the Hidatsas (Lowie 1918, pp. 272–75).

Many other groups, whatever their previous social organization, adapted themselves to Plains life by means of a loose social structure. This form was not determined absolutely by the principle of kinship, but rather exhibited considerable fluidity. The Crows, by contrast, preserved a clan system of social organization, a form which reflected their previous existence as an agricultural people (Oliver 1962, p. 32). Even this pattern was thought, by some interpreters, to be changing "from a more highly organized kinship system to a more diffuse type represented by the Cheyenne and Arapaho system" (Eggan 1955, p. 74). In the chapters that follow we shall explore the relation between Plains kinship systems and patterns of religious and moral experience.

The general picture of migration to the Northwestern Plains characterizes the experience of other groups, such as the Plains Crees, the Gros Ventres, the Assiniboins, the Dakotas, and the Shoshones (Wedel 1974, pp. 242–43). The dynamics of social change must have exhibited similar features for all of these groups since they all generated social worlds and patterns of religious and moral significance which came to typify Plains cultures in historic times. These social worlds, despite their continuities, must also have preserved a great variety of memorial traditions which related to their previous experience either as agricultural people or as people who depended upon a combination of hunting and agriculture. Also, each group finally developed moral and religious responses which were shaped in terms of the history of their experiences as a people. Thus, the Northwestern Plains, as an area, continued to be characterized both by a general institutional and cultural continuity and plural social worlds, each possessing its dimensions of uniqueness.

The picture of migration will be clearer if we bring more sharply into view the influence which the settlement of the continent by Europeans had upon indigenous peoples. The harbingers of change, the horse and gun, had already altered the Pre-Columbian balance of power before the actual population pressures were felt. Tribes that had the gun could and did drive those without the gun from their settlements, as we have seen. And sedentary villages, such as in the Cheyenne case, were increasingly threatened by the activities of mounted warriors. In addition, there was increasing pressure as Europeans populated the eastern part of the continent and began their westward movements. Such pressures displaced the tribes, forcing them to move westward. According to some interpreters, this created a kind of "chain reaction," culminating in the expulsion of populations from their homelands east of the Mississippi River and forcing them onto the already crowded Plains (Weltfish 1971, p. 201). Understood in this way, the development of Plains lifeways and social worlds must be partly interpreted within the context of American continental development rather than viewed as a frozen slice of history which relates to the story of stone age Plains dwellers (Weltfish 1971, p. 203).

The cultural portrait of Northwestern Plains tribes may further be clarified by general reflection upon the nature of human traditions. Human traditions, whether in oral or written form, are a sedimentation of the experiences of the groups which generate them. Whether sedimented in text or story, these traditions form a context within which each succeeding generation achieves a sense of identity and a vision of destiny. No human tradition, however conservative, is completely static. Change comes to all traditions in the process of their mediation; the process involves a teaching function, on the one hand, and an interpreting function, on the other. The elders who mediate a tradition interpret that tradition in the light of new circumstances, and those who receive the tradition do so by means of a process of interpretation. This continuous process of interpretation, whether the subject of interpretation is written or oral, introduces the possibility of change as an essential ingredient of any human tradition. In times of rapid social change or crisis, human traditions tend to be reinterpreted, often radically, in response to changing environmental or cultural circumstances. The outcome of such a process may be cultural transformation, as we observed in the case of the tribes which migrated to the Plains.

Plains cultures thus emerged as a consequence of creative reinterpretation by the peoples who generated them. Fundamental to this understanding is that the process of reinterpretation and eventual transformation of traditions occurs within the structure of unfolding generations. Thus, unless identity and group destiny are completely forgotten, new interpretations of tradition will more than likely build upon the previous experience of the people. Some things about the past are gradually forgotten, but not immediately; and that which is remembered will be reinterpreted in a selective manner in order to conform to new cultural needs. If we had more information about the ancient traditions of the historic Plains tribes, we could trace the course of their cultural evolution in a more precise fashion.

## Predecessor Cultures on the Plains

Archaeological evidence expands our understanding of human habitation on the Plains. Contrary to a view expressed at the turn of the century, that the Plains may have been a prehistoric uninhabited territory (Wissler 1908, p. 201), there is now reason to believe that habitation in this region is very old indeed. This evidence allows inferences to be drawn concerning culture patterns which were adopted by the historic tribes. The archaeological evidence may be summarized at a very general level (Wedel 1974, pp. 247ff.; cf. Frison 1978, pp. 20–22).

The oldest evidence of human habitation on the Northwestern Plains comes from the period of the big-game hunters, who lived between 5,000 and 10,000 years ago. The material remains of this early habitation are in the form of stone artifacts, such as spear points, and items relating to the processing of the hunt, such as knives, scrapers, and chopping tools. Evidence that would reveal the nature of these early cultures in terms of their social life, values, or religion is non-existent. It seems reasonable to infer, however, that these populations were small and sparse and that they ranged over a wide area in search of food. It may also have been the case, given the harshness of the winters, that these peoples moved during colder weather into regions where they had some shelter, wood, and water (Wedel 1974, pp. 249–50). There is also some evidence, from about 8,500 years ago, to show that these early hunters possessed a social organization which allowed a very efficient division of labor in hunting and processing the kill (Wheat 1967; cf. Frison 1978, pp. 301–16). Beyond these indications, the early period remains opaque.

For the period from about 2500 B.C. to A.D. 500, similar artifacts have been found on the Northwestern Plains relating to processing the hunt, although the nature of the projectile points changes. In addition, it is hypothesized that a change of weather may have occurred between about 4500 and 2000 B.C. During this period the climate may gradually have changed until the region became characterized by very hot and dry conditions. If such a change in climate occurred, it must have had radical effects upon the types of plants and animals which could survive in the region. Furthermore, subsistence patterns would have had to change, given this hypothesis. There is evidence, for example, that around 1500 B.C. devices for grinding seeds and other vegetable products made their appearance, as well as pits probably used for roasting roots. In addition, the bones of animals smaller than the buffalo have been found in the archaeological sites. The way of life characteristic of this period is presumed to be that of small, mobile groups who foraged for whatever food was available (Wedel 1974, pp. 250–54).

Evidence from the period after A.D. 500 has yielded a horizon of material artifacts which related to processing the hunt, some grinding implements, and some evidence of the bow and arrow. For this time there are also evidences that pottery appeared on the Northwestern Plains. All of this suggests the presence of a richer culture, which may indicate a change in climate from the semi-desert environment of the forager period to a moister climate more favorable to the buffalo and other large game animals (Wedel 1974, p. 256; cf. Gilbert 1980, pp. 8–15).

Other artifacts which appear from this period are the circles of stone, commonly known as tipi rings, which some presume were used to hold down the covers of skin lodges (Kehoe 1958; Kehoe 1960; Malouf 1961). Medicine wheels, formed in great circles with spokes radiating from the center, have also been found. Given the importance of the symbolism of the center and the circle for the tribes of historical times, these stone structures are fascinating but their meaning is still unclear (Simms 1903a; Grinnell 1922; Kehoe 1954). Structures that may have been used for the purpose of fasting during a vision quest are also evident (Wedel 1974, pp. 265–66), as are sites for quarrying stone and petroglyphs and pictographs on the walls of canyons and rock ledges (Wedel 1974, pp. 271–77; Frison 1978, pp. 403–19). All of these artifacts are interesting and suggestive of the shape of human habitation, but most of them are still clouded in interpretative ambiguity. What we can say with certainty that human habitation on the Northwestern Plains is very old indeed.

Is it possible to infer more than this? Some observations may be made concerning the possible continuity of Plains social structures by appealing to documents from the Coronado expedition of the sixteenth century. It is true that these Spanish observations concern the southern Plains and thus cannot be extended with confidence to the entire region. The evidence is, however, extremely suggestive. When the Coronado expedition reached the southern Plains, it met a nomadic people whose economy was centered almost entirely upon the buffalo. Like the later Plains tribes, these people, believed to have been the Plains Apaches, used dogs as draft animals, lived in portable conical tipis, had extensive knowledge of skin working, and stored food through the techniques of drying meat and making pemmican. What is interesting here is that there is no essential difference in form between the knives, scrapers, choppers, and other implements found in sites that date from 6,000 to 10,000 years ago and the implements used by the historic tribes. All of this suggests that there may have been considerable continuity on the Plains at the level of cultural adaptation. If this is true, the conclusion of one interpreter becomes more convincing. With the coming of the horse in the seventeenth and eighteenth centuries, we have an event which was expansive, to be sure, but which also "gave a last colorful fillip

[18]

to a mode of life old when the first Conquistadores set foot on the Great Plains" (Wedel 1974, p. 306). The fundamental point is that migrants to the Plains may have adopted traditions and institutional forms that were rooted in a long past. There are persistent traditions among the Blackfeet, for example, which speak of a time when the people had no horses and used dogs as beasts of burden (Ewers 1958, pp. 17–18). If the people Coronado observed in the sixteenth century had migrated from the north (Wedel 1974, p. 302), it is possible that the Blackfeet assimilated Plains lifeways from tribes already occupying the area before their migration. These pedestrian Plains cultures would perhaps not have had such institutions as the Sun Dance as a part of their ritual life. But there is reason to believe, at least for the Blackfeet, that certain sacred bundles existed during dog days and that the people relied upon the communication of power from special animals and birds (Ewers 1958, pp. 17–18).

Absolutely clear evidence of the shape of social life, forms of polity, cultural values, and religious institutions is not present in the horizons illuminated by archaeology. We have produced some evidence, however, supporting the view that the Plains way of life is older than some observers thought (Kroeber 1948, p. 823). Still we know very little directly concerning the subjects of central concern for this study—namely, dimensions of religious and moral meaning. Is it possible to draw any inferences at all about these matters, or must we simply work with what we know of the historic tribes? It is possible, I believe, to make some observations at a very general level which will illuminate later analysis.

Recall that with the exception of the medicine wheels, structures perhaps used for fasting, and the cave art, there is almost nothing in the form of artifacts which illuminates the nature of the religion and morality of ancient dwellers on the Plains.[9] And there is little in the traditions of the historic tribes which sheds light upon such artifacts (Wedel 1974, pp. 266–70). An exception to this generalization appears among the Blackfeet, who apparently constructed medicine wheels to mark the graves of outstanding chiefs (Dempsey 1956). These traditions, however, are of relatively recent origin.

We can speculate that the religious and moral sensibilities of prehistoric peoples must have been deeply conditioned by their apprehension of natural phenomena and animal life. These motifs appear as well in the traditions of the historic tribes. From what is known of human cultures generally, it is not unreasonable to suppose that responses to the mysteries of the growth of vegetal foods, the presence or absence of life-giving rain, the succession of the seasons, and the centrality of phenomena of the sky would be reflected in the morality and religion of planting and hunting peoples alike. In addition to these elements, animals were perhaps occasions for the apprehension of sacred powers for hunting peoples—an ancient theophany (Paulson 1964, p. 219). This argument would tend to the conclusion that the revelatory power of nature and animal life in the experience of the people in historic times may have quite ancient roots and may have been reflected as well in the experience of their predecessors.

Given the way migrations probably occurred in small groups, it is reasonable to suppose that those entering the Plains area later in time would assimilate institutions and lifeways present among the more ancient residents. Although the more recent migrants would naturally preserve elements of their previous culture, there would also be the tendency, over generational time, for an integral culture to emerge. This new culture would arise as a consequence of the creative contribution of many diverse peoples. Indeed, something like these social processes must have been responsible for the emergence of what has been called the "typical Plains culture." These institutions and lifeways surely arose as a consequence of a long evolutionary process.

In the final analysis, however, we do not need to know with certainty the age or the evolutionary trajectory of the traditions which we confront in the mid-nineteenth century in order to appreciate their depth and symbolic power. Indeed, we will come finally to see that the richness and complexity of religious and moral traditions on the Plains are specific instances of what is primordial and pervasive in human experience.

One of these features of human experience is the capacity for transcendence, a capacity which is rooted in the symbolic nature of the human being. Experiences of transcendence are given content through the capacity of humans to imagine—to create worlds of meaning and to populate these worlds in various ways. On the Plains, important experiences of transcendence occurred through vision. The content of such experiences reflects the richness of the social worlds and the imaginal capacities of the human beings who created them. A description of some of these worlds and their content forms the substance of the chapters that follow.

CHAPTER 2

# Experiencing the Sacred

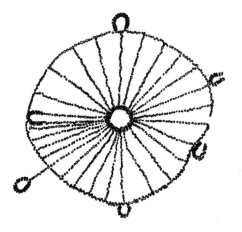

AMONG THE HISTORIC PLAINS TRIBES, individual experience was an important locus for the appearance of transcendent meanings. This experience cannot finally be abstracted, of course, from the shared meanings of the social world which support and reinforce the sensibilities of persons. Also such experience must be seen in its intimate connection with ritual forms. The particular focus of this chapter, however, is the vision experience which mediated a sense of transcendent power to Plains peoples. The notion of vision may be distinguished in two forms: the dream-vision and the waking-vision. This distinction represents a classification which is not superimposed but which is recognized by the people themselves. For the most part, description will focus upon the form of the vision experience, leaving more complex discussions of the content of such experiences for later chapters. It is an overriding conviction, however, that an initial analysis of the vision experience will provide a clue to basic religious and moral apprehensions of Plains peoples.

In approaching traditions that embody vision experiences, it is well to begin with a description of some of the general features discussed by early twentieth-century interpreters. The best place to start is with reported views of the general nature of transcendent power which irrupts in human experience. We have to move with care at this point, precisely because we are seeking to interpret the views of those who were themselves observers. We will be seeking to discern in their views basic motifs that illuminate the religious and moral experience of the people.

## Visions of Power

If we begin by seeking to understand Blackfoot sensibilities at this level, we seem to be in the presence of a paradigmatic "people of the sun." The material representation of perhaps the most important of transcendent sky powers was a life-giving, solar reality:

> the Blackfoot theory is that there functions in the universe a force (natoji = sun power) most manifest in the sun but pervading the entire world, a power (natoji) that may communicate with individuals making itself manifest through any object, usually animate. (Wissler 1912, p. 103)

It is doubtful that Blackfoot metaphysics was as abstract as this description indicates. It will become clear, however, that this basic solar imagery was central to the constitution of their religious and moral experience.

Even more interesting in this context is the claim that the sacred power pervading the universe reveals itself to humans by means of speech (Wissler 1912, p. 103). The being who speaks may be an object, such as a rock, or an animal form; or the being who speaks may take first the form of an animal and then become transmuted into a person; or the process may begin with a person who is transmuted into an animal. Speech also should be expanded to include not only speech-acts as they would normally be understood, but

[23]

also communicating by means of song. It is, however, at the moment of speaking or singing that the being who appears in vision becomes a source of power.

Crow experiences of transcendence also involve the view that there is a power, a sacred source, which manifests itself in particular forms (Lowie 1922, p. 315). It is difficult to identify this power as exclusively represented by the sun, however. The reason for this lies in what interpreters perceived as an ambiguity in Crow traditions between a culture hero/trickster figure and the sun. Old-Man-Coyote, the Crow culture hero and trickster, was identified by some with the sun, but others vacillated at this point, making a distinction between these two figures (Lowie 1922, pp. 318–19). The next chapter will deal at greater length with the relationship in tradition between culture hero, trickster, and creator figures. Each of these figures was probably of considerable antiquity. But in the judgment of one interpreter, the sun "must have been an ancient constituent of aboriginal religion" (Lowie 1922, p. 319).

The importance of speech as a vehicle for revelation is characteristic of Crow experience in the nineteenth century. Animal visitants appear and, as in the Blackfoot case, are often transmuted into human form; humans may also assume the form of animals at certain points (Lowie 1922, p. 326). These motifs appear in Arapaho religious experience (Kroeber 1907, pp. 419, 428), as well as in the experience of the Cheyennes (Grinnell 1972, vol. 2, p. 113). Later chapters will demonstrate the importance of solar motifs in these traditions, but at this point we must reflect generally upon the meaning of what has been introduced.

The cultural importance attached to vision in Plains experience has been treated by many interpreters, some of whom have produced quite detailed analyses (Benedict 1922). What must be exposed at this point is how such experiences seem to be constituted in human cultures generally. Whether we are speaking about Plains cultures or of experience in contemporary cultures, human beings seem everywhere to exhibit the capacity to migrate among several worlds or dimensions of meaning. Plains peoples shared a sense of a common, largely taken-for-granted everyday world. This world was constituted by a common language, common objects of perception, particular classes of persons, and common social projects. In addition to this world, there were other possibilities for human experience. Humans migrated regularly into dream worlds of various sorts, they imagined worlds of meaning and sought to embody their imaginings in the everyday world of work and play, and they had traffic with worlds of religious meaning that were populated with beings who transcended and also who related to the human world in particularly important ways. These elements Plains cultures share with other human groups. All human beings, or so it seems, transcend the limits of their embodiment through such migrations.

In the experience of Plains cultures, however, the "accent of reality" was granted so powerfully to transcendent orders of meaning that the everyday world was often subordinated to and shaped by the vision experience. There was such a thing as ordinary experience, to be sure; and persons were not trapped in illusion or fantasy. Rather, individuals granted such a normative role to vision experiences that they came to constitute the ground upon which other, more ordinary experiences were interpreted. Persons lived out of their vision experiences and sought to enact them in the everyday world of common affairs. Later chapters will seek to show how such experiences gave shape to the moral attitudes and dispositions of the people.

Migrations in experience between the everyday world and realms of transcendent meaning are made possible through symbols. In its briefest definition, a symbol may be understood as anything that evokes in experience one or more levels of transcendence. Symbols form the passageways between the world of ordinary experience and worlds of transcendent meaning. An object, event, or person in the everyday world may perform a symbolic function in experience, evoking a sense of transcendent realms of significance. Clusters of symbols in story, song, or ritual may also perform such a function. But what is symbolic for a person or culture is known only through investigating the particularities and history of the specific group or individual. Such investigations usually reveal the presence of paradigms of symbolic form which evoke in the experience of many people a common sense of transcendence. The remainder of this chapter will deal with the structure given to multiple levels of experience in Plains cultures, reserving a more specific treatment of symbolic forms for subsequent discussion in chapters dealing with ritual.

On the Plains great social value was placed upon experiences of vision which transport the individual into transcendent realms of meaning. Among the Blackfeet of the mid-nineteenth century, individuals of proven leadership and wisdom probably spent great effort seeking, interpreting, and trying to embody in the world the experiences that occurred through vision (Wissler 1912, p. 101). The incidence of such experiences was also rather widely distributed, and individuals of all stations waited with expectation for the vision world to open up before them. An observer of the Blackfeet, Alexander Henry, vividly describes this phenomenon among the Piegan division of this tribe at the close of the eighteenth century:

> If a Piegan dreams something particular, on awakening, he instantly rouses his wife, makes a speech about his dream, and begins to sing, accompanied by this woman, and sometimes all his wives join in the chorus. . . . During my short stay here I have frequently been awakened by such speeches and songs in the dead of the night. (cited by Wissler 1912, p. 101)

Four modes of access to worlds of vision seem generally to characterize many Plains cultures. Two of these modes appear at the level of the immediate experience of the individual, the dream-vision and the waking-vision. Two other modes are the transfer of power and the inheritance of power. An elaboration of these forms will fill out and deepen our understanding of their importance for Plains cultures in the nineteenth century.

# Dreams and Waking Visions

An example of a dream-vision drawn from Blackfoot experience is a convenient place to begin. Succeeding chapters will describe many such experiences, not only among the Blackfeet, but among other tribes as well. The illustrations at this juncture, and subsequently in this chapter, are designed simply to indicate something of the flavor of these experiences in a preliminary fashion.

A typical dream-vision is reported by a Blackfoot man who fasted and prayed for seven days on a lonely mountain. Dressed in old clothes, he cried continually for the sun to take pity upon him. Finally the sun appeared, taking the form of an old man. Taking pity upon the man, the sun gave him a drum and a song. The drum and song were powerful and enabled the man to control the rain. The following year, the same man had a dream in which the sun again appeared in the form of an old man with white hair. Sun transferred to the man another drum and a new song. This time the power of the drum and song was more extensive, giving the man powers not only over humans but also over all living things, even beings of the plant world (Wissler 1912, p. 72). This account, told by a medicine man, would not stand as true simply in the reporting, without empirical confirmation. Thus the man claimed that at the Sun Dance of 1902, during a hard rain, his drum kept the water out of his tipi. In addition, he used the power of the drum to flood the tipi of a rival shaman. Such appeals to evidence would have to be acknowledged by the group, of course, in order to be socially effective.

Such dream-visions seem to be distinguished by the Blackfeet from vision experiences that might occur during sickness. These types of experience, while granted their own reality, are more likely to be viewed as prehensions of the future life rather than as dreams of power. And at the turn of the century, both the dream-vision and the vision during illness were distinguished from those experiences endured under the influence of alcohol. Early in the present century, these latter experiences were not accounted among those of true revelatory power (Wissler 1912, p. 101).

The Crows also made distinctions among dream experiences, granting some greater value than others. On the lowest level of significance was the ordinary dream, to which no special revelatory significance was attached. A second level of dream had to do mainly with visions of the coming of the seasons, or other states of affairs. These dreams seemed to embody the person's wish that he or she might live to experience the next spring or summer, or the events envisioned. A third level of dream was specifically related to the desire to acquire property. Finally, there was the dream of power, the most highly valued, in which a being appears to the person and a transfer of power takes place (Wildschut 1960, pp. 5–6). The dream motif in its various forms was apparently an ancient constituent of Crow cultural experience, and it is a dimension that continues in certain forms down to the present time.[1]

The intrusion into experience of the waking-vision is also generally characteristic of Crow experience, as it is among the Blackfeet, Arapahoes, and Cheyennes (Lowie 1922, pp. 328–29; Wissler and Duvall 1908, pp. 85–87; cf. Wissler 1912, p. 101; Kroeber 1907, p. 450; Grinnell 1972, vol. 1, pp. 80–85, 196–97; Grinnell 1972, vol. 2, pp. 112ff.). Although this type of experience may not be universal, it was certainly widespread on the Plains. Essentially what seems to be involved here is a powerful burst of imaginal content which displaces the sense of everyday experience and brings into clear focus a world of vision into which the person enters. While the dream-vision may be more common, it is still the case that the waking-vision is often equally as powerful, opening up revelatory dimensions in the lives of persons.

An example of such an experience among the Crows was reported by Gray-bull, who recounted his grandfather's waking-vision (Lowie 1922, pp. 328–29). This experience involved the appearance of a bird with a white head who came one day into the lodge of Gray-bull's grandfather. After settling itself opposite the grandfather, the white bird was transmuted into a man whose face was painted in a certain manner and who wore on his head the skin of the bird that had initially appeared in the lodge. The bird-man sang a song and told the grandfather that he would come again the next day with his wife and would grant him some of his power. The next day the bird-man and his wife came to the lodge of Gray-bull's grandfather and his wife. In a transfer ritual, the bird-people adopted the two humans and revealed to them sacred songs and objects. These sacred things were powerful for activity on the warpath, and not long afterward Gray-bull's grandfather related his vision experience to others; in the fall of the year he counted coup on an enemy and in time he became a chief among the Crows.

# The Transfer of Power

The dream-vision and the waking-vision, as described up to this point, are immediate in the sense that they occur within the experience of a person. Power is mediated, of course, by the being or beings who appear in the vision. This notion of "transfer" is of central importance in the vision experience. Without the transfer, humans would not come to share in the power that is available through the medium of transcendent beings who appear in vision. Among the Crows, and also among the Blackfeet, the transfer of power is a matter of establishing a particular relation between humans and sacred sources of power. This relationship is more one of kinship than it is an economic relationship, which the notion of transfer might initially suggest. Indeed, among the Crows, the formula of relationship between humans and sacred vision-beings is expressed in the language of adoption: "You . . . my child I will make," says the transcendent being to the human visionary (Lowie 1922, p. 326; cf. pp. 333, 336). The vision-being is then addressed as "father" or "mother" and the human's self-understanding is that of a "son" or "daughter." Although the formula does not appear among the Blackfeet in such an explicit manner, the relationship established between humans and the world of vision-beings is finally one of kinship (Benedict 1922, pp. 13–14).

This pattern seems to be generally present within the cultures of the Northwestern Plains. Among the Cheyennes and the Arapahoes, for example, kinship terms are extended to aspects of nature, such as the sun, earth, and sky, as well as to certain animals. At the level of the individual, appearances of sacred beings in visions are interpreted in the language of kinship (Eggan 1955, p. 48). Experiences of such kinship relations are evident in the Arapaho view of the sun as Grandfather, since it is ". . . so distant and old yet so near and attached to us" (Eggan 1955, p. 54). In subsequent chapters it will become clear how important was this view of kinship for religious experience, as well as for the development of moral attitudes and dispositions.

Distinguished from the irruption of power within the

immediate experience of persons is the mediation of power through another transfer process. Highly developed among the Blackfeet, this form of transfer involved the mediation of power that had been received initially in the experience of another person. We shall discuss this form of mediation along with the second form, mentioned above, which was transfer through inheritance.

The first form of mediated or secondary power transfers was one in which the relationship and obligations between humans and vision-beings established in the original vision experience are transferred to another person. When the ritual and songs associated with the original vision experience are transferred, the power inherent in the initial vision becomes active in the experience of the receiving person (Wissler 1912, p. 103). This transfer opens up into a general pattern which is significant for understanding the Blackfoot social world. This world is one in which an originating vision experience, with its obligations, ritual forms, and essential power, may be successively transferred through social time. The movement through the experience of a number of individuals must have added new elements to the ritual, in some cases. But at any point in time the ritual, its associated sacred objects, and its power may be understood as the latest stage in a process of ongoing transfers.

It was also understood among the Blackfeet that a faithful reproduction of ritual acts was actually a recapitulation of the original experience. Its reality is thus contemporaneous with the experience of individuals. Unlike experiences which receded in the past, to be recovered only through memory, such experiences of sacred power may be renewed through the media of ritual and symbolic forms. In the transfer of such power, the assumption seems to be that the individual who occupies a relation, through ritual transfer, to a being of power in the present is in the same or fundamentally similar relation to that being as were his or her predecessors. For this reason, one interpreter of the Blackfeet concluded that it was "impossible to tell from the form of the narrative whether the narrator himself had the experience or not" (Wissler 1912, p. 103).

There is little doubt that among the Blackfeet of the late nineteenth century the ritual transfer of power had significant implications for the social status of individuals and family groups. Not only was a great deal of property actually exchanged in the course of such transfers, but honor accrued to persons with a long history of the ownership of various sorts of sacred power (Wissler 1912, pp. 276–87; cf. Albers and Parker 1971). The acquisition of social status and honor is not so clearly "economic" as some have made it, however. The elements of reciprocity in the transfer context are clearly evident, and there seems to be no profit motive that would correspond to the economic processes of modern societies. Indeed, the exchange of property may have been motivated more by gratitude than it was by a desire for gain in a strictly economic sense. Thus, even though social status, honor, and economic advantages may attach to such transfers, it seems to be the spiritual significance of the relation to transcendent power which was primary and which gave meaning to the entire social process.

This indicates something about the configuration of cultural meanings in the Blackfoot social world. High value was placed upon experiences of transcendence, and those who had such experiences, either for themselves or through transfer from another, were honored by the group. Certainly this system must have evolved over time, and it may have been subject to secularization as a consequence of experiences with western culture. The motives of economic gain and social prestige may have become primary in the experience of some persons (Benedict 1922, p. 17). Still, such evidence should not obscure the fact that the normative relationship seems to have been otherwise and that the social or economic advantages that may have accrued were believed to presuppose the prior spiritual relationship. There is certainly no reason to go so far as did one interpreter who, in discussing Crow transfers, argued that secularization had so deeply penetrated the social structures that the acquisition of sacred objects through transfer was a process almost totally devoid of spiritual significance (Lowie 1922, p. 317).

Although the Blackfoot system of transfer was apparently nonhereditary in form, there are evidences of such a principle operative in other groups. Among the Crows, for example, there seems to be a system both of patrilinear transmission and, in some cases, of matrilinear transmission (Lowie 1922, pp. 330, 335). Among the Arapahoes there were practiced both the pattern of free transfer to relatives and the pattern of transfer by purchase (Kroeber 1907, p. 450). The following description of the relation between an Arapaho elder and one of his relatives illustrates a transfer between kinspersons which also involved an exchange of property.

> A young man might pray to an old man for his power. Then, instead of going out on the hills and suffering hardships to acquire it, he received his power by instruction. He paid the old man for each sitting with him. He learned the old man's medicine-roots and their uses, his way of painting, his songs, and so on. By the time the old man was dead, the young man had his power. (Kroeber 1907, p. 436)

Whether mediated in experience, transferred from another, or inherited, power and its reception clearly preoccupied the energies and attention of individuals in the mid-nineteenth century.

## The Pursuit of Vision

Given the cultural importance of vision among the Plains tribes, it is understandable that such experiences would be actively sought. The pursuit of vision was also accompanied by various forms of action which would qualify the individual to come into the presence of sacred powers. These forms of action involved types of ritual cleansing and sometimes patterns of sacrifice and deprivation. Self-torture was not uncommon, although some tribes did not associate this motif with the pursuit of vision. For example, self-torture was apparently not associated with the quest for vision among the Blackfeet and Arapahoes, preparation taking instead the form of isolation and fasting (Benedict 1922, p. 4). The typical form of such deprivation involved retreating to a lonely place, often the summit of a hill, there to fast for a number of days, usually from four to seven. If the person was fortunate, a vision experience would occur (Wissler 1912, p. 104; Kroeber 1907, pp. 419ff.).

Other ritual acts often accompanied preparation for fasting and possible self-torture in pursuit of a vision. Among the Crows, for example, vision seekers were careful to purify their bodies in preparation for spiritual experience. Such purification involved a thorough cleansing of the entire body, even to the nails of the fingers and toes. Then the person would enter a sweat lodge, where water was poured over hot stones, causing intense heat. After purifying the body further with incense from the smoke of pine needles, the person would begin a fast, abstaining from both food and water, the odors of which were believed to be offensive to the spirits sought in vision (Wildschut 1960, p. 7).

A case of Cheyenne self-torture in pursuit of vision will illustrate what is involved in this form of preparation for traffic with transcendent powers. In this instance, a young man was prepared for his ordeal by an older man. At the place of suffering, a pole was sunk into the ground. A rope was tied to the pole and at the end of the rope were tied pieces of sinew. The breasts of the supplicant were cut, and small skewers inserted; then the skewers were attached to the pieces of sinew. The young man was instructed to walk around the entire day in a sunwise direction; at the same time he was to throw himself back, stretching the rope and attempting to tear the skewers from his flesh. The report of his suffering is vivid:

> Each time I came to the end of the rope I threw myself back against it and pulled hard. The skin of my breast stretched out as wide as your hand, but it would not tear, and at last my chest grew numb, so that I had no feeling in it; and yet, little by little, as I threw my whole weight against the rope, the strips of skin stretched out longer and longer. All day long I walked in this way. The sun blazed down like fire. (Grinnell 1966, p. 80)

At the end of the day, the older man returned and released the young man by cutting the flesh loose from the skewers. Taking the strips of flesh in his hand, the older man made movements toward the sky and the cardinal directions. After praying to the sun and the powers of earth and air, the older man buried the sacrificial skin at the foot of the pole. The young man remained at the lonely place and, late in the evening when exhaustion had given way to sleep, he dreamed. In his dream a wolf appeared, granting him power and instructing him in its appropriate use (Grinnell 1966, pp. 81–82).

Similar incidents of self-torture appear among the Crows. For example, an individual who had lost his relatives sought a vision of power. He went to a mountain and began to fast, crying for a vision. He chopped off a finger joint with his knife, and holding it up to the sun, prayed: "I am poor, give me a good horse. I want to strike one of the enemies and when I go on a good road I want to marry a good-natured woman. I want a tipi to live in that I shall own myself" (Lowie 1922, p. 337). Lying down to sleep, the vision came, and later in this man's life all that he had cried for came to pass (Lowie 1922, p. 338).

Given the importance attached to vision in Plains culture, one might conclude that there would develop tendencies to limit the benefits of such experiences to a select few. That is, one might expect rather clear distinctions to develop between persons who have had experiences of power and persons who have not, and that such distinctions might develop into social differentiation between a priestly or shamanistic class and a class of lay persons. While such differentiation may be observed among the Dakotas and the Pawnees (Benedict 1922, p. 12), the motif which characterizes the Plains generally is a sort of "democratized shamanism," a wide distribution of experiences of transcendence among different levels of the social structure. Even though there was a tendency for such experiences to be more apparent among mature individuals, as compared with being associated with puberty rites (Benedict 1922, pp. 2–3), it is still true that among the Crows, for example, even young boys fasted for visions (Lowie 1922, p. 332).

One might also expect that experiences of transcendence would be more characteristic of male as compared with female experience. Nothing could be further from the truth, for both at the level of the quest for vision and the level of ritual participation, women occupied places of prominence. In the case of the pursuit of vision, such experiences were actively sought by both men and women in Blackfoot society (Wissler 1922, p. 104). And for the Crows, one interpreter says, "There was no limitation either as to age or sex, so far as seeking a vision was concerned" (Lowie 1922, p. 332). This position is qualified somewhat by the fact that it was not usual for young girls to seek such experiences, but when they were older they did. Finally, there are evidences among the Arapahoes that experiences of power came to women as well as men (Kroeber 1907, p. 434).

Another theme which does appear on the Plains has to do with the appearance of a special helper, or guardian spirit, within the context of the vision experience (Benedict 1923). Among the Cheyennes, for example, such experiences would usually occur after a person was twenty years old. In such cases, the experience might qualify the person as a prophet or seer, and it secured him or her a special position in society (Grinnell 1972, vol. 2, pp. 112–17). It was within the broader context of the pursuit of vision that such experiences are to be placed in Plains cultures, since the migration into dimensions of transcendent meaning could and did occur within many contexts that did not involve the acquisition of a special helper or guardian spirit (Benedict 1923, p. 29).

It is also true that there seems to be a distinction drawn between different types of power, such as the power to control rain or to have success on the hunt, and the power to heal diseases. The first type is more often possessed by a shaman, while the second is more characteristic of a doctor (Wissler 1912, pp. 71–72). Of course shamans may be doctors and vice versa, and every person has presumptive access to such powers, although not all in fact do become doctors or outstanding shamans. And those who do so acquire prominence in the social structure. Despite these comments, it remains a characteristic of Plains cultures for such experiences to be very widespread and not absolutely confined to the functions of priestcraft or the activities of a religious elite.

The oral traditions on the Plains gave rich cultural backing for experiences of transcendence, especially when those experiences occurred through the agency of animals. Indeed, the social worlds of Plains peoples were filled with tales of such encounters. A Crow narrative may be taken as illustrative of motifs that are widespread (Lowie 1918, pp. 158–61). This story centers upon an anonymous young man who desired to visit the country of the birds. The young man fasted, and on the fourth day a meadow lark offered to adopt him (grant him power). He refused this offer, as well as offers from all the other birds who returned in the spring. After this Seven Cranes appeared, six of whom were as large as humans while the seventh was even larger—the Chief of the Cranes. After much pleading the cranes agreed to take the young man to bird country. Riding on the back of a crane, the young man could see the camps of his people stretched out far below. When all the birds came to the place where the sky meets the earth, Crane Chief lifted the corner of the sky with his pipe and all the birds passed over into their own country. To his surprise the young man saw that all of the birds lived in tipis painted in the same colors as their bodies. After sojourning in this strange land, the young man migrated back to Indian country with the birds, flying on wings which were made by the cranes. When they came to the place where the sky touches the earth, Crane Chief gave the young man his pipe. After singing a song the young man lifted the sky so that the birds could pass through. The cranes then transferred some of their power to the young man and he became a great warrior among the people. Such narratives motivated persons to seek similar experiences.

Because the cultural expectation that vision experiences would occur was so powerful, a certain conventionality appeared in the types of experiences that were reported. This is not surprising, given the deeply shared meanings which constituted the social worlds of most tribes. Structures of shared meaning in the social world commonly produce continuities at the level of individual experience. In addition, a social process of interpretation of vision experiences was operative. For those who had little experience with transcendent powers, or for those who were young, there was the elder or group of elders who were sought out to render an interpretation of vision experiences. Out of such social processes, an additional level of continuity in experience is achieved (Wissler 1912, pp. 101–2). This does not mean, of course, that such experiences can be reduced in their spiritual significance simply because they are routinized at a certain level. To be routinized means that the basic symbols of a culture are deeply shared and thus have power to shape the experience of individuals in a similar manner.

In this chapter we have shown how Plains cultures place normative importance upon experiences of transcendence which occur in dream- or waking-vision, as well as through transfers. The center of these experiences is the individual rather than the priestly class or the sacramental institution. Such experiences are mediated through the central imaginal capacities of the human being, which we have discussed in an introductory fashion. Although we have illustrated the content of such experiences briefly, we have dealt mainly with their formal aspects located in the migratory capacities of humans. We have seen how the everyday world is breached by vision, and how powerful were the cultural expectations that such experiences would occur. We have also indicated, in a preliminary manner, that such experiences of transcendence were normative for the self-understanding, the identity, of persons, as well as having implications for their social location within the group. What we shall seek to show in subsequent chapters is how such essentially religious experience forms moral attitudes and dispositions. We will move increasingly toward a demonstration of how, through ritual enactment, religious and moral experience is constituted and shaped at both the levels of the individual and the social world. At the level of the social world, we will be speaking of religious and moral traditions which are mediated and interpreted through social time; at the level of the individual, we will be speaking of how these traditions are symbolically evoked and how their powerful horizons of meaning give shape to the moral and religious sensibilities of persons. The following chapter provides a preliminary understanding of human social worlds within which moral and religious traditions are shaped and carried, and within which human beings experience various forms of transcendent power.

# CHAPTER 3

# Forming the World

HUMAN SOCIAL WORLDS have a number of general characteristics, despite their diversity at the level of cultural forms. One of these general features, pointed out in the previous chapter, was the multiple levels of meaning that constituted social worlds. We showed that these levels were ordered in particular ways by different groups, that they were reflected in individual experience in concrete ways, and that they were grounded in the migratory capacities of human beings. The importance of symbols for this understanding lay in their function as passageways between various levels of the social world. Most fundamentally, symbols were seen to connect the everyday world with specific horizons of transcendent meaning.

Another general feature of human social worlds is temporality. All societies have a sense of the past, of corporate identity, whether that sense is preserved in written documents or in oral traditions;

all societies have a sense of the present order of everyday life and the importance of its mundane activities; all societies have a sense of the future, of corporate destiny, whether that image takes the form of utopian vision or the continuation of familiar traditions into the future. All social worlds exhibit temporality, but they differ in which dimension is most highly valued, culturally legitimated, and granted a powerful accent of reality.

In some societies it is the value and power of the past, of tradition, which illuminate the meaning of the future and shape what is believed ought to occur in the present. The future, in such societies, becomes largely a projection of the shared traditions of the past, so that present and future are seen as continuous with that which has gone before. In other societies the present may be the most absorbing and powerful reality that pervades the experience of people. In these groups the value of both past and future may be subordinated to the richness of immediate experience. And in still other societies the lure of the future may render the past and the present less significant. The cultural structure given to these three dimensions produces significant differences in the human experience of their reality.

The temporality of the social world is grounded, as was the phenomenon of multidimensionality, in the basic capacities of the human being. Humans exhibit a sense of internal time—their experience is articulated as past, a world of memory, as participation in a shared present, a common everyday world, and as future, an anticipation of things to come. It is important to understand that it is the relationship between an individual's sense of internal time and the cultural structure of the social world which renders human experience coherent or uneasy and even chaotic. As long as societies are relatively cohesive, the temporal dimensions of the social world and internal time seem concurrent. If a particular society values the past, for example, individuals in that society are likely to experience tradition as important; if a society values present experience or that which is imaged as future, these dimensions will likewise be reflected in the way individual experience is configured. Social crises may produce dissonance between the shared experience of a people and their internal sensibilities; in such situations there are struggles that may lead to a resolution of dissonance, social innovation, various processes of reinterpretation, or, at the extreme, the cultural disintegration of the group.

The temporal structure of human social worlds is more concretely apprehended in the way we relate to contemporaries, predecessors, and successors. The continuum of possible relations among contemporaries, from the intimate (companion) to the anonymous (enemy), is structured in different ways among different peoples. Plains tribes had their own understanding of these primary relations which constituted their social worlds. For example, among the Cheyennes and the Arapahoes, intimate relations pertained among blood relatives; but even parent-child relations, with their corresponding duties and obligations, could be extended to persons at great social distance. In such cases, individuals were expected to maintain appropriate attitudes toward these "fathers" and "mothers," even though social distance might be so great as to render appropriate behavior impossible (Eggan 1955, p. 50). And on the Plains, kinship was extended to animals, so that these beings are contemporaries maintaining quite intimate relations to the people; indeed, they are often companions, relating to individuals as "brothers" or "sisters."

Like the apprehension of contemporaries and companions, Plains cultures nuanced their sense of predecessors in particular ways. Not only were there shared memories of important men and women of the tribe, but there were also preserved in oral tradition accounts of the activities of predecessors who brought important cultural gifts to the people, or who granted individuals special powers. These predecessors have a symbolic status in the sense that they stand at the boundary of the world of the remembered past and also span that world, connecting it with orders of meaning that transcend memory. In addition to culture heroes and other persons who brought individuals special gifts, there are represented in the oral traditions the activities of creator figures who bring into existence the human beings and the order of nature. And, finally, there is the ubiquitous trickster predecessor who pervades the oral traditions with bawdy and often foolish acts, some of which end by contributing to the shape of the people's world.

Plains cultures also had some image, however vague, of their successors, and also some image of what form life might take after death. These images will not form a large part of subsequent discussions, even though they are important for other sorts of understanding. Rather, the effort of this chapter will be to show how Plains people came to understand the formation of their natural and social worlds. The rise of these orders is understood in terms of the activities of creator figures, culture heroes, and tricksters; these beings are important predecessors, often celebrated in ritual and mediated in the oral tradition. In the course of this discussion we will prepare ourselves to understand, in later chapters, dimensions of transcendence and the beings who populate these realms, as well as how they enter into the experience of persons in powerful ways and are reflected in the shared experience of the group through ritual and symbolic form. Now, however, we must turn to the oral traditions that provide an image of how the people and their institutions originated, as well as how the appropriate relationships among persons and other beings are to be understood. In the course of our entry into these traditions, we will begin to unearth and bring into view what seem to be fundamental cultural values, shared paradigms of value meaning, which arise out of a religious ground.

## The Blackfoot Cosmology

In Blackfoot traditions, the creator, the culture hero, and the trickster appear under the same name: Napi, Old Man.[1] We will focus first upon the activities of Old Man as creator and culture hero. In one version of the Blackfoot cosmology (Wissler and Duvall 1908, p. 19), Old Man is represented as sitting on a high mountain, surrounded by all the animals. Water surrounds the mountain as far as the eye can see, the consequence of a great flood which had been sent by the above-people because a supernatural baby had been killed by an Indian child. In this tradition we have either the notion of a preexisting creation which was destroyed by a flood, or the interpolation of a legend (the killing of the supernatural baby) in order to explain the flood. In either case, the re-creation of the world takes place through the agency of animals, the narrative appearing in the form of an "earth diver" motif, a familiar theme in North American Indian cosmologies (Hultkrantz 1979, p. 31; cf. Long 1963, pp. 188–93).

Old Man sent four creatures of the water to search for earth with which to make the world. Otter, Beaver, Muskrat, and Duck each took their turn diving for earth, and in the attempt the first three were killed. Duck was the last to dive and he also drowned, but in his paw he held a little piece of earth. Old Man saw the earth, took it in his hand and, after making feigning movements toward the waters three times, he dropped it in on the fourth movement. The earth spread upon the water, the above-people sent rain, and everything grew upon the earth. In this relatively sparse version, the animals are represented as sacrificing their lives for the sake of the earth and humans; and we confront the primal symbolism attaching to the number four—there are four water creatures and the Old Man creates the earth on the fourth movement (cf. Maclean 1892, p. 51; Maclean 1893, pp. 165–66).

In a more extended and elaborate Blackfoot tradition, the activities of the creator and culture hero are held together in a single narrative (Grinnell 1962, pp. 137–44). This tradition also includes echoes of trickster elements as well. The narrative opens with a vision of the fundamental harmony and mutuality among living things and their creator:

> All animals of the Plains at one time heard and knew him, and all birds of the air heard and knew him. All things that he had made understood him, when he spoke to them—the birds, the animals, and the people. (Grinnell 1962, p. 137)

Old Man is represented as coming from the south and traveling north, making animals and birds as he goes along, putting rivers in their places, and red earth at various places in the ground. After his work he rested, and where he lay is still impressed upon the rocks and the ground. Old Man created the grass for the animals, as well as an abundance of roots and berries. He also created the animals out of dirt, placing each one of them in an environment suited to its characteristics.

In addition to the animals, Old Man created a woman and a child out of dirt: "After he moulded the clay in human shape, he said to the clay, 'You must be people,' and then he covered it up and left it, and went away" (Grinnell 1962, p. 138). After four days, the images were able to rise and walk. After they were animate, the human beings walked with their creator down to a river, where he told them that his name was Napi, Old Man.

The woman whom Old Man had made is represented in this tradition as having a share in ordering life and death in the world of humans. After discussing the matter, Old Man proposed that they decide the case in the following manner: He will throw a buffalo chip into the water; if it floats, then when people die they will become alive again in four days. Then he threw a buffalo chip into the river, and it floated. But the woman disagreed, saying that she would throw a stone into the water and, if it floated, people would live forever, but, if it sank, people would die forever. Then she threw a stone into the river, and it sank. Not long afterward, the woman's child became sick and died; she pleaded with Old man to reverse the edict concerning death. But in response, Old Man said, "We will undo nothing that we have done. The child is dead, but it cannot be changed. People will have to die" (Grinnell 1962, p. 139).

In another version (Wissler and Duvall 1908, pp. 21–22), Old Man and Old Woman preexist and together give rise to the order of creation. They seek to come to an agreement about how people shall live, and, in the course of their discussion, it is decided that Old Man will have the first say but that Old Woman will have the second, that is to say, the *last* say. Old Man proposed that tanning hides be done quickly since it was such hard work; Old Woman disagreed, saying that such work should be long and difficult. These discussions go on concerning the location of the eyes, mouths, and genitals, as well as how many fingers the human beings should have (cf. Maclean 1892, p. 52). Then the narrative ends, fixing the order of life and death in a manner identical to the previous version.

In still another version (Wissler and Duvall 1908, p. 21), Old Man proposed that people should live forever, to which Old Woman disagreed, saying that there would be too many people on earth. Then Old Man proposed that people should die, but that in four days they should come to life again. Old Woman disagreed, saying that people should die forever in order that they would "be sorry for each other." Then the outcome is decided by throwing a buffalo chip into the water. Under normal conditions, a dry buffalo chip would float. But Old Woman, having great power, caused it to sink. As a consequence, people will have to die forever.

The first humans were poor and naked and had no way of surviving on the earth, and so Old Man gave them the conditions for civilization. He showed them how to gather roots and berries, and he gave them the animals and birds for food. He also showed them the different herbs, demonstrated their power, and specified their uses in human healing. In this series of acts, culture has been created and humans have become eaters of flesh. It is also at this point that the interrelatedness of the creation is disturbed by the appearance of ambivalence between humans and animals.

> In those days there were buffalo. Now the people had no arms, but those black animals with long beards were armed; and once, as the people were moving about, the buffalo saw them, and ran after them, and hooked them, and killed and ate them. (Grinnell 1962, p. 140)

In order to change this situation, Old Man taught the people how to construct and use bows and arrows. After arming the humans, Old Man taught them how to hunt, and from this time on humans were able to kill the buffalo for food.

Now that humans are carnivores, they must further become civilized, and so Old Man brought fire to them and taught them how to cook food. Old Man also taught the people how to make stone kettles to hold the food while it was cooking. Then Old Man revealed to the people something concerning the animals and other living things upon the earth:

> Whatever these animals tell you to do, you must obey them, as they appear to you in your sleep. Be guided by them. If anybody wants help, if you are alone . . . and cry aloud for help, your prayer will be answered. It may be by the eagles, perhaps by the

buffalo, or by the bears. Whatever animal answers your prayer, you must listen to him. (Grinnell 1962, p. 141)

These texts reveal to us a glimpse of the oral tradition as it struggles with basic tensions that have been opened up by creation. In some versions, relationships between humans, animals, and nature are portrayed as initially harmonious, but conflict or tension is soon introduced. Though the animals were given over to humans for their food, there is still the moral dilemma of eating creatures who possess consciousness and life in much the same fashion as humans. In this tradition the conflict is partly resolved through making humans dependent upon the animals in a new way. The animals were to become their powerful helpers. We shall see this dilemma come up in other traditions on the Plains, and we will come to understand, in subsequent chapters, how it is dealt with and partly resolved through ritual processes.

This creation tradition ends with Old Man continuing on his travels, moving north, with many of the animals following him. In the north, Old Man created more people and animals, teaching these people how to drive buffalo over a cliff and how to kill those animals with stone mauls. After his work of creation was ended, Old Man rested. When he becomes refreshed, something of his trickster nature emerges, as he slides down a hill just for fun. In a final series of actions, Old Man marked off the tribal hunting grounds and gave instructions to the people that they should defend them against intruders. Finally his work was completed: The world has been made, culture created, basic relationships established, and fundamental values ordered.

These narratives weave together both creator and culture-hero functions within a single being; and the inclusion of trickster elements seems quite natural as the tradition unfolds. This suggests that multiple levels of significance are occurring within the narrative, and that one should not seek to reduce its meaning to a single, consistent theme. The tensions revealed in these narratives may actually express the way these people represented their experience of the world.

# The Crow Cosmology

The origin of the Crow world begins, as did that of the Blackfeet, with an earth-diver narrative. The creator figure is initially identified as the Sun, Old Man; and in some traditions the Sun is identified with Old-Man-Coyote.[2] One version of the narrative (Lowie 1918, pp. 14–15; cf. Simms 1903b, pp. 281–82) opens with Old-Man-Coyote alone on the primal water with some ducks. He decided to send the ducks down beneath the water for earth with which to create the world. After three tries which ended in failure, success came when the hell-diver, the poorest of all the ducks, brought up a bit of earth from under the primal sea. At this point in the narrative, Old-Man-Coyote is identified with Sun, and the earth is made by this being, traveling from the east to the west. When the creation was finished, Sun heard the voices of other powerful beings who seemed in a mysterious way to have become animate by their own powers. From one of the cardinal directions, the east, a wolf was heard to howl; and in the west, the voice of a coyote was heard. Of the coyote, Sun said, "That coyote has attained life by his own powers, he is great" (Lowie 1918, p. 15).

Out on the Plains, Sun met another living being, a medicine stone. The oldest part of the earth, this stone also had self-generative powers. Farther on, Sun met another being who appeared initially in the form of a person; moving closer, it became clear that there were several persons who had the appearance of human beings. One of these beings Sun identified as a Star who had come upon the earth. As the Star-human was approached, he transformed himself into a plant, the Tobacco. Of the Tobacco, Sun said, "From now on all the people shall have this, take it in the spring and raise it. It is the stars above that have assumed this form, and they will take care of you. This is the Tobacco plant" (Lowie 1918, p. 15). In this account sacral significance is granted to the earth, to certain forms of animal life, and to a particular plant. We shall see how important these motifs were for Crow ritual forms. After these events took place, Sun created grass, mountains, trees, and people.

In other versions of the Crow cosmology, Old-Man-Coyote is

joined by a companion, a little coyote (Lowie 1918, p. 17). Together they make the earth, the animals, and the people. In still another version, Old-Man-Coyote is represented as the being who arranged the forms of culture for the people (Lowie 1918, pp. 17–19). The animals were made and a general division of labor between men and women established. Humans in this account emerged from the hollow of trees; and when the buffalo were first created they lived in holes in the ground, like coyotes. Old-Man-Coyote taught the people how to make fire, how to construct weapons, and how to hunt game. The buffalo, however, were not initially to be found, and little coyote, the companion, finally discovered them in their den under the ground.

It is interesting to note that, as compared with the Blackfoot accounts, Crow descriptions do not exhibit the clear tensions between animals and humans after culture appears and humans are given the animals for food. It is clear, however, that the creator and the first animals stand in a kinship relation. With the stratum of traditions represented here, it is difficult to say whether tensions between humans and animals were present or not. This is the case precisely because we are in the presence of an oral tradition, a system of dynamic meaning structures which exhibited considerable pluralism. And it is also well to recall that these traditions did not take the form of a normative account, one which was controlled by a professional elite, even though it is true that there were persons who were probably more adept at recounting such narratives than others. In any case, there was no clear distinction between a class of priests or shamans and others when it came to the knowledge of how the Crow world came into being. These were sacred stories, to be sure, but there was no one official version. A final reason why we cannot be sure about the themes which are or are not present in the narratives has to do with the fact, alluded to earlier, that these traditions were collected from an oral tradition and then frozen in written form at a certain time. We cannot be sure that we have all of the traditions, or if the oral tradition changed after these versions were recorded. In any case, the themes that are present in these accounts will serve to illuminate Crow ritual life later in the analysis. What we have at this point is a glimpse of horizons of meaning

[47]

which were probably widely shared and which represented how many Crows apprehended the formation of their natural and social worlds.

# The Cheyenne Cosmology

One version of the Cheyenne cosmology seems to reflect their previous agricultural background in an interesting manner (Grinnell 1971, p. 242). In this narrative, the ancient Cheyennes were living under the ground, surrounded by darkness. As are plants, the human beings were attracted to the light and warmth of the world above the ground. One day a man saw a little spot of white which penetrated the darkness. As he approached the spot, it grew brighter and brighter until the man was surrounded by the full light of day upon the surface of the earth. Although blinded and frightened at first, the man became accustomed to the light and found the surface world pleasant. He returned to his people and finally convinced some of them to leave the darkness of the underworld and come to live on the surface of the earth. Such was the beginning of the Cheyennes, an origin narrative which has much in common with Mandan traditions.

In the earth-diver version of the cosmology (Grinnell 1971, pp. 242–44; cf. Dorsey 1905a, pp. 34–39), we meet the creator floating on water along with preexisting water birds of various kinds. After the earth has been created out of mud brought up by one of the birds, the creator then made two people who, though in the form of humans, were clearly more than human. The woman was placed in the north, where it will be cold and difficult to live and grow things; and the man was placed in the south, where life will be pleasant and where an abundance of things will grow.

The woman of the north, according to this tradition, controls the Winter Man, that great power which brings snow and cold. The man in the south, represented by Thunder, is the power who brings the rain and causes things to grow in the spring. The Cheyenne year was punctuated by a conflict between Winter Man and Thunder. At the end of the summer, Winter Man comes from the north and says to Thunder: "Move back, move back, to the place from which you came. I want to spread all over the earth and freeze things and cover everything with snow" (Grinnell 1971, p. 244). Then in the spring, Thunder comes from the south and says to Winter Man: "Go back, go back, to the place from which you came; I wish to warm the earth and to make the grass grow, and all things to turn green" (Grinnell 1971, p. 244). According to this tradition, the man of the south and the woman of the north never came together, nor did they grow old, although later people were created and populated the earth.

After the creator had made the earth, constituted the seasons, and made humans and animals, the entire creation is represented as an interrelated whole, characterized by kinship associations. "At that time," the tradition says, "the animals and the people lived together as friends" (Grinnell 1971, p. 252). For reasons which remain unexplained in the tradition, there came a time when buffalo began to eat humans and other animals. In the light of this development, which the creator seems not to have anticipated or caused, it is decided that all of the animals should have a great race in order to determine whether the buffalo should continue to eat people or whether people should eat buffalo and other animals.

All of the creatures of the earth gathered for the race. Each creature was painted with different colors, the markings which they carry down to the present time. In the race the humans had the birds on their side. Before the race, however, all supposed that either a buffalo cow or a coyote would be the winner. After having been painted, the buffalo formed one line and all the other remaining animals formed another. The buffalo chose a cow, Slim Walking Woman, to run for them, and the race began. Slim Walking Woman took the lead and a small bird was just behind her, but as the race progressed the buffalo cow began to tire, as did the small bird. The bird flew to the side to rest, and a swift hawk took its place. In the meantime, the magpie was flying along slowly and steadily. When the participants in the race had gone a long way toward the east, they turned and began to return to the starting point. On this leg of the contest most of the animals became exhausted and dropped out of the race. Even the swift hawk had to withdraw, but magpie

[49]

kept up his steady pace. At the finish line, all of the animals were far behind magpie, who won the contest with ease. As a consequence of this race, the buffalo became frightened of people. Whereas they formerly would attack at the appearance of humans, now they would run away.

As we have seen with other Plains traditions, in the Cheyenne account the interrelatedness of creation is disturbed, although the cause is not specified. After the race, however, humans become carnivorous apparently for the first time: "This was the beginning of the eating of flesh by the people" (Grinnell 1971, p. 254; cf. also the story of Yellow Haired woman, pp. 244ff.). The relation between humans and animals is represented in this tradition in terms of three broad stages: original harmony, an imbalance of power in favor of the buffalo, and finally an imbalance of power in favor of humans. We shall have occasion to return later to this ambiguity in the traditions concerning the relation between humans and the animal world.

# The Arapaho Cosmology

The Arapaho cosmology embodies many of the same features, such as the earth-diver motif, which we have seen before. It differs in some important respects, however (Dorsey 1903b, pp. 191–212; cf. Dorsey and Kroeber 1903, pp. 1–6). This tradition opens again with a scene of primal water upon which a being in human form is seen to be walking about. Four days he walks, cradling in his arms an object finally identified as a Flat Pipe.[3] The being on the water remains deep in thought concerning what to do to secure a place for the sacred Pipe. Finally, the manlike creature decides to fast in order to arrive at an idea of what to do. After fasting for six days, he calls all of the preexisting creatures from the cardinal directions there to meet in council on the seventh day. After many and lively discussions, it is decided that earth should be obtained for the creation of the world. Six trials are attempted, but none of these trials is successful in bringing mud from under the surface of the primal water.

Only the being who possesses the Pipe and Turtle remain, and the decision is made that they should dive for the earth. The figure in human form merges with the body of the Sacred Pipe and then is transformed into a red-headed duck. Duck and Turtle make their dive, remaining under the surface of the water for seven days. On the evening of the seventh day, just as the sun is sinking below the western horizon, the two return to the surface. Both the Man–Flat-Pipe–Duck being and Turtle are successful in bringing earth from below the primal waters. The Man–Flat-Pipe–Duck then proceeds to create the world, casting portions of earth toward each of the four semi-cardinal directions, beginning at the southeast and ending with the northeast.

The imagery of this account is rich: Creation proceeds from the central, primal reality, the Pipe, and spreads out toward the four cardinal directions. These images suggest an original integrity and interrelatedness of creation. These qualities are confirmed as the narrative continues, representing the actions of the animals as they make the world ready for the coming of the humans. Turtle, for example, offers his body as a symbol of the earth, his four legs representing the cardinal directions, while the markings on his back represent a path and the texture of his shell the mountains and rivers. Other animals and plants also offer themselves for the creation—the kit fox, otter weed, and cattail. Especially important are the offerings of the eagle, who gives his holy feathers; the garter snake, who becomes the circumference of the world; and White Buffalo, who gives his body for food and clothing for the humans who are to come.

In the narrative these plants, animals, and birds are represented as being gentle of character and pure of motive, performing their sacrifice willingly for the sake of the creation. That White Buffalo will become food and clothing for the people appears as a consequence of his gracious gift and not as a result of some disturbance of the balance of power between humans and animals. The dimensions of kinship and interdependence represented in this account are thus very deep.

After an interlude in which Trickster appears, the narrative returns to a discussion of the Sacred Wheel, an object which we will discuss fully in connection with the Sun Dance. In the creation of the Wheel, the motifs outlined above continue. Plants, animals, and birds give willingly of their bodies so that the Sacred Wheel may come into existence. Its holiness seems to be grounded partly in the fact that it arises out of an act of cooperation between the animals and plants. After the creation of humans, a child becomes ill and the first Sun Dance is pledged. And again the birds, animals, and plants offer their bodies for the construction of the sacred lodge, confirming the horizons of meaning that relate to kinship and inter-dependence.

## Cosmological Motifs

Before extending our discussion of Plains social worlds, we need to expand somewhat upon an issue alluded to earlier. This issue has to do with the pluralism of the oral traditions. If these traditions were dynamic, if there was no sacred canon, and if what we have analyzed represents a frozen slice of a much broader and more complex cultural horizon, then to what extent can we argue that these narratives reflect the shared meanings of a deeply sedimented social world? It is clear that most of the recorded accounts that we have presented were gathered from prominent individuals, skilled story-tellers, and persons of religious and/or political leadership.[4] This may mean that we have more elaborate versions than we might gather from persons with less experience who occupy more ordinary positions in their societies. From what we know of the extent and importance of Indian story-telling, however, the major elements of these accounts were probably known by a large number of individuals in the tribes. Variations were widespread, to be sure, but the basic plot and the imagery of these accounts were probably deeply shared (Grinnell 1971, pp. xxiii–xxiv).

Indeed the imagery of these accounts suggests an interacting field of shared meanings which reveals to us something of Plains world views and cultural values. Certain of these images will be especially important for our later analysis. Most prominent and obvious in the previous narratives are the images of the center, from which creation proceeds toward the cardinal directions. The symbolic significance of the number four is carried on the surface of these images. Solar imagery, sunwise movements, and astral imagery have also been introduced and will become increasingly important as we move toward a view of the ritual life of the people. The constitution of the world of contemporaries as a world that includes not only human others but also animals and other beings is clear in these narratives, as is the moral significance of an initial kinship motif present in creation. The world of predecessors includes not only those humans who were once contemporary but also shared memories of important others who constituted the social world in significant ways.

A central ambiguity at the level of cultural values is also expressed in some of these traditions. This ambiguity has to do with the relationship between humans and the creatures of the natural world. The central problem seems to emerge when humans become dependent upon these creatures for their subsistence. The widespread belief in Native North America that animals possess consciousness, will, and soul is the ground of this problem (Hultkrantz 1953, pp. 483–97). The dilemma of feeding upon such creatures requires a cultural solution. We will see such solutions emerge in various forms of ritual enactment and especially in the great tribal festivals, such as the Sun Dance. And we will finally come to see not only how the earth and its creatures are imaged but also how fundamental moral attitudes and dispositions are shaped and sustained through ritual enactment and symbolic form.

Another theme, alluded to earlier, is clearly evident in these narratives: humans stand in a successor relationship to certain important animal predecessors who are represented as having participated in the formation of the world. And human beings in the present are viewed not only as heirs of these original relationships but also as able to establish and maintain relations with animals as contemporaries and even as intimate companions. Deep cultural values, such as reciprocity, interdependence, and kinship, along with the appropriate corresponding attitudes and obligations, are affirmed at the heart of these cosmological narratives. At the same time, however, a sense of tension and unresolved ambiguity is maintained.

## The Trickster Motif

In order to advance our understanding of Plains cultural values, we must turn finally to a consideration of Trickster, that enigmatic and fascinating figure which emerges within North American Indian traditions. We shall not review the interesting and sometimes tortuous arguments about this figure which have emerged in the various traditions.[5] Rather, we shall view the activities of Trickster as representing the polar opposites of the cultural values we are interested in examining. In this sense, Trickster's acts will be understood as functioning to reinforce the normative social order, or at least to suggest what it is, precisely by striking and often obscene oppositions. In sum, Trickster embodies a deformed world, a world opposite to that which is envisioned in the creation narratives. From this point of view, Trickster may be interpreted as a negative moral agent, a being of vicious as compared with virtuous character. We can approach these traditions through an examination of the value oppositions that are evident in Trickster's behavior: reciprocity/non-reciprocity, generosity/stinginess, truth/deception, kindness/brutality, and bravery/cowardice.

The Blackfoot Trickster appears in the traditions as Old Man; in the trickster episodes, Old Man, Napi, assumes quite a different character as compared with his activities as creator or culture hero. In order to expose his character and some of the cultural values that seem to be parodied, we will begin with a narrative which appears in similar versions among the Cheyennes and Arapahoes (Wissler and Duvall 1908, pp. 24–25; cf. Grinnell 1962, pp. 165–66; Grinnell 1971, pp. 301–2; Dorsey and Kroeber 1903, pp. 65–70). What is revealed here may thus be taken to typify many elements of a similar nature elsewhere on the Plains.

The story opens with Old Man traveling along one day accompanied by his companion, Fox. It was a hot day and Old Man's robe became too heavy, causing him discomfort. In order to relieve himself, he threw his robe over a large rock, making a present of the robe to Rock. As Fox and Old Man traveled on, a rain cloud came up and Old Man sent his companion back to retrieve the robe so that they would not get wet. Fox asked Rock for the robe, but he was refused. Hearing this, Old Man became angry, rushed upon the rock, and snatched his robe. As they continued their journey, Old Man and Fox suddenly heard a loud noise behind them. It was Rock, rolling along after them. Old Man and Fox began to run, but Rock gradually closed the gap. Old Man called upon both bears and buffalo bulls for assistance, but they were all crushed by Rock. Finally he called upon nighthawks for assistance, and they flew down toward Rock, breaking wind with deadly aim until Rock was completely destroyed. As Old Man continued along his way, he came to a nest of baby nighthawks. Discovering that their parents had gone for food, Old Man concluded that the mature nighthawks must have been the ones who assisted him and Fox in their conflict with Rock. Rather than showing kindness to the baby nighthawks, Old Man alleged that it must have been their parents who intervened and spoiled his fun with Rock. Turning upon the babies, he split their mouths back to their necks. The parent birds returned to discover what Old Man had done. Flying to find him, they finally had him in view; time after time they dove upon Old Man, defecating upon his robe. With each strike Old Man was obliged to cut off a piece of his robe until, finally, none was left.

This narrative illustrates the theme of an ambivalent relation to the animal world. The story unfolds in a universe where animals speak and where rocks possess consciousness and personality. The animals are represented both as being Old Man's friends and as reacting to him with hostility at times. Fox is represented as Old Man's close companion, and both bears and buffalo bulls willingly sacrifice their lives for Old Man's safety. The problem seems to lie with Old Man's character, which the story comments upon at length. In examining this level of the narrative, we seem to be in the presence of shared cultural values which are parodied in Old

Man's actions. The hypothesis which we wish to suggest is that the values that appear in Trickster's behavior are actually in conflict with the shared values forming the ethos of the Blackfoot social world.

Old Man is represented initially in the story as a generous character, since he gives the robe to Rock in such an apparently virtuous manner. His generosity is actually a pretense, since he wishes only to serve his own needs for comfort. When he becomes overheated, he feigns generous behavior through the gift of his robe; but when rain threatens, his selfish nature is revealed. And after Rock turns upon Old Man, his cowardice becomes apparent. Rather than face the consequences of his own actions, he is willing to sacrifice any creature's life to preserve his own. The major value conflicts at stake here seem minimally to be the opposition between truth/deception (Old Man is an inveterate liar), generosity/selfishness, reciprocity/non-reciprocity, and bravery/cowardice. The opposition between kindness/brutality also appears in his treatment of the baby nighthawks. The cultural affirmation of generosity, truth, reciprocity, kindness, and bravery, as well as the condemnation of their opposites appears in the consequences which flow from Old Man's action. The rock retaliates swiftly, as do the nighthawks. The hostility expressed by nature and animals to Trickster's behavior seems to give support to an ethos which is deeply marked by cultural values that are precisely the opposite of those mirrored in Old Man's activity.

Other traditions focus explicitly upon Trickster's deception of animals (Wissler and Duvall 1908, pp. 155–56). These narratives are similar to traditions which circulated among the Cheyennes, Arapahoes, and Crows (cf. Grinnell 1971, pp. 155–56). In these Plains traditions, though Trickster is initially successful in his deception, he usually is deceived himself. Animals are almost always represented as being kindly disposed to Trickster. They are his friends, as they were in the stories that image the creation of the natural and social worlds. As payment for their good disposition, they are treated to some form of deception, often involving a game, the consequences of which are to gain Trickster a good meal. One should not get the impression, incidentally, that these traditions are lacking in humor, suspense, and fast-moving action. Nothing could be less true, and one can imagine the delight with which some of them were received by groups of children. There is no doubt that they were very popular, and it is further probable that they functioned to give support to a shared ethos, a shared horizon of meanings representing appropriate relationships and behavior.

The theme of deception of animals is prominent in a Blackfoot story concerning Old Man and some squirrels.[6] Old Man was traveling along one day when he came upon a camp of squirrels who were engaged in a fascinating game. A number of the squirrels would lie down in a pit of hot ashes while another group would cover them up. When the squirrels in the ashes became too hot, the others would help them out of the pit. Old Man asked to be included in the game, but the squirrels refused, saying that since he did not know the rules he might be burned badly. They offered to demonstrate how the game was played, to which Old Man naturally agreed, but with one condition: all of the squirrels must be covered up at once. After discussing the matter, the squirrels agreed, with one exception. A pregnant female begged to be released from the game and Trickster agreed, thus, comment some traditions, saving the squirrels from extermination. Old Man proceeded to cover the squirrels with hot ashes. When they began to roast, they cried out for assistance. Rather than rescuing them, as the rules of the game dictated, Old Man piled on more coals and all the squirrels were roasted to death. The suggestive theme of the "last animal" which is prominent here will be dealt with subsequently.

Old Man laid the roasted squirrels on a scaffold made of red willows (since the meat was greasy, red willows have henceforth been greasy). After gorging himself, and with squirrel meat left to spare, Trickster lay down to sleep. Before he dropped off to sleep, he ordered his anus (some traditions say his nose) to awaken him at the approach of any danger. After one false alarm, Old Man slept soundly. Presently a lynx approached the meat and began to eat. Anus roared loudly, but Old Man did not awake and the remainder of his meat was consumed. When he finally awoke, he was furious and punished his anus by rubbing it with a piece of burning willow (this willow was hereafter known as stinking wood).

Old Man trailed the lynx and, when he discovered the animal, he broke off its tail and stretched its body, flattening its nose against a rock. He plucked some pubic hair from the lynx and stuck it on the animal's nose; then he held the creature over a fire, scorching it on both sides (this is how the lynx came to have its present form and markings). Old Man then lay down to rest, turning his burned anus toward the wind to relieve the pain. The pain continued, so he called for a stronger wind. The wind increased to storm velocity, beginning to blow Old Man across the hills and mountains. Try as he might, he could not stop himself, until finally he caught hold of a birch tree. After the wind died down, he turned violently upon the birch tree, charging it with spoiling his fun. In his anger, Old Man savagely scarred the birch tree with his knife, the marks of which can be seen to the present day.

A similar tale of deception is told of the Cheyenne trickster, Wihio (Grinnell 1971, pp. 286–90). Trickster was traveling along the bank of a stream when he came upon a village of prairie dogs. When asked where he was traveling, Wihio said that he was going to sing for some people. The animals begged Trickster to come and sing for them; he finally consented, provided the prairie dogs would dance. Arranging them in a circle, Trickster chose the fattest animals for the dance, instructing them that they must dance with their eyes closed. While the animals danced, Wihio took a club and began to kill the prairie dogs one by one. Finally, only one was left. Terrified at not hearing the sounds of his companions, the last animal finally opened his eyes. He barely escaped with his life, while Trickster proceeded to roast the remaining animals and have a good meal.

Wihio continued on his way and presently met a group of ducks. The narrative unfolds in exactly the same manner, and Trickster roasts all of the ducks but one, which he stuffed with strips of meat and buried in the coals to bake. As the meat was cooking, the wind began to blow, causing the trees to rub their branches together in an irritating manner. Wihio spoke to the trees several times, but with no success. Then he climbed up into the trees to try and separate the offending branches. The branches closed on his hand and he was caught fast. Meanwhile, a coyote appeared below him, smelling after his food. Trickster called out to the coyote not to eat his meat, but the animal proceeded to consume it all, including the meat stuffed in the duck which had been baking in the ashes. After his meal, coyote stuffed ashes in the cavity of the remaining duck and placed it back into the pit to roast. Trickster finally freed himself and retrieved the roasting duck which remained. After the first bite he discovered himself deceived and determined to kill coyote. After trying unsuccessfully to kill the animal, Trickster was left alone, frustrated and hungry.

These stories represent Trickster figures who are destructive to animals and other living things, who are deceptive, and who are also often violently self-destructive and foolish. The surface meanings of the tradition reveal this figure as a clown who is destructive to himself and others. Other Plains traditions illustrate similar themes concerning the trickster, his character, and his relationship to the natural and animal worlds. There are additional Blackfoot traditions concerning Old Man's deception of elk and deer (Wissler and Duvall 1908, pp. 27–29; Grinnell 1962, p. 158); Arapaho traditions concerning Trickster's deception of beaver, ducks, and elk (Dorsey and Kroeber 1903, pp. 57–62); and Crow traditions concerning the exploits of Old-Man-Coyote (Lowie 1918, pp. 17ff., 33–34, 36). In most of these traditions there is the theme of animals who are initially friendly, who are deceived, and who are killed as a consequence; in some traditions, the trickster is himself deceived and sometimes injured. The major value conflicts between truth and deception, between generosity and selfishness, between reciprocity and non-reciprocity, between kindness and brutality, and between bravery and cowardice are underlined in these narratives, despite the fact that they are often amusing and filled with suspense—good stories. The consistency with which these themes occur leads to the conclusion that we are in the presence of a shared ethos that is envisioned through the figure of the trickster. Rather than approving of the deformed world of the trickster, these traditions seem rather to affirm the normative values through embodying their opposites. The normative world of shared cultural values is underlined, supported, and legitimated in the experience of the listeners. And in some versions of these traditions, the raconteur actually points out which values are to be affirmed and which condemned (Grinnell 1962, pp. 159–64). The fact that children were almost always expected to be present at times when trickster tales were told suggests that this figure was a powerful socialization device in Plains cultures (Ramsey 1983, pp. 36–38).

The narratives up to this point have dealt exclusively with the relationship between Trickster and the plant and animal world. There are other traditions that portray his relation to the human world, which in the creation traditions he often has a hand in forming. In these traditions we reach a maximum tension between the creator figure in the cosmological accounts and the trickster figures, a tension that is heightened when we recall that there is often an ambiguity of identification between these two figures. In any case, trickster stories dealing with the human world illustrate value conflicts we have previously mentioned by highlighting Trickster's acts of deception, brutality, rape, and murder.

A Blackfoot tale typifies these qualities. Trickster came to a lodge in which there were two women and two babies (Wissler and Duvall 1908, pp. 33–34; cf. Dorsey and Kroeber 1903, pp. 101–105). The old women asked Trickster for some meat, and he left the camp pretending to hunt. Instead of hunting, Old Man pulled some hair from his robe and scattered it in the snow; then he rubbed his buttocks in the snow until they bled, leaving a sign which looked like a kill had been made. Returning to camp, Trickster told the old women that meat awaited them and that they should make haste to bring it into their lodge. While they were gone, Old Man entered the tent and cut off the heads of the babies, putting their bodies in the pot to cook and returning their heads to the cradles. The old women returned and said the coyotes must have stolen the meat. Old Man responded by telling the women that he had antelope cooking in the pot; then he told them the truth, that it was actually the babies who were cooking over the fire. At this point, Old Man ran off, disappearing into a hole in the ground. The old women were now helpless, and they sat on the ground mourning the loss of the babies. Old Man appeared in disguise and, after hearing their story, feigned anger and swore to kill Trickster. He entered the hole and made sounds of a struggle; after the struggle was apparently over, he emerged from the hole and said he had destroyed the evil one. He then told the women that they should go into the hole and bring out the body. The old women entered the hole and immediately Trickster blocked the entrance, building a fire so that the humans were finally suffocated.

This story of deception is overlaid with the motif of Trickster's wanton cruelty and brutality toward those to whom, in traditional cultural terms, he should have shown kindness and generosity—the elderly and the innocent children. Instead of exhibiting such qualities of character, Old Man shows himself to be a rapacious murderer. The narrative is unrelieved by a sense of counter-deception on the part of the humans. There is no way Trickster's deeds are balanced by a set of consequences which achieve a sense of justice in experience. There are other traditions, however, in which Trickster is made to pay for his deeds (Wissler and Duvall 1908, pp. 35–36; Simms 1903b, p. 284; Lowie 1918, pp. 43–45).

The sexual capacities and exploits of the trickster figure on the Plains are widespread and well known. In terms of his treatment of women, Trickster shows himself to be a being of insatiable desire which is often focused in an exploitative and brutal manner. Among the Blackfeet at the turn of the century, for example, Old Man was typically associated with sexual immorality. If a person exhibited such characteristics, Blackfeet would say that he "must be trying to be like the Old Man; he cannot be trusted with women" (Wissler and Duvall 1908, p. 10). This view of the trickster continues down to the present among some individuals. For example, a contemporary Blood woman said of the trickster: "Napi was the first man to use and abuse women for his own fun and pleasure" (Hungry Wolf 1980, p. 139). In addition to his generally degenerate character, Trickster is often associated with the transgression of deep tribal taboos against incest (Dorsey and Kroeber 1903, p. 82; Lowie 1918, pp. 41–43), and against sexual relations with one's mother-in-law (Dorsey and Kroeber 1903, pp. 75–77; cf. Dorsey and Kroeber 1903, pp. 86–89; Lowie 1918, pp. 49–51).

Trickster's genitals are typically of enormous size and seem to possess a life of their own. A Blackfoot tradition illustrates some of the themes which occur in this sort of story (Wissler and Duvall 1908, pp. 34–35; cf. Dorsey and Kroeber 1903, pp. 73–74). One day, so the story goes, Old Man came upon a young woman asleep in a lodge. Even though she was the daughter of a chief, Trickster boldly entered the lodge and put excrement on her dress. The smell awakened her, and she begged Trickster to clean her dress. After offering him many presents, which were refused, the young woman finally offered herself. Seeing the size of Trickster's genitals, the woman asked him to tie a stick across the organ so that penetration would not be too great. To this Old Man agreed, but, when they came together, he removed the stick and the woman was torn to pieces. When the chief returned and saw the condition of his daughter's body, he concluded that this could only have been the work of Trickster. Old Man was accused of the deed but feigned illness.

The chief decided to have a trial in order to flush out the guilty party. Everyone would be required to jump across a ditch, and the one who fell into the ditch would be considered guilty. As Old Man was proceeding to the trial he met a bird and persuaded it to trade genitals with him. When the bird tried to jump the ditch, he naturally fell into the chasm. As the bird was about to be killed, he told the people what had actually happened. When the people turned upon Trickster, he proposed a further trial—he would bring the young woman to life again. After all was made ready, Old Man had two women stand at the door on the inside of the lodge where the healing was to occur. They were armed with stone mauls. Outside the door stood two men armed with spears. As the healing ceremony began, Old Man put two pieces of fat on the fire. When they were hot he took them out of the fire and swinging the pieces of fat around his head, he splashed hot grease into the eyes of all present. As Trickster rushed out the door, the two women struck each other on the head with the mauls, and the two men outside speared each other. The humans were killed, and Old Man escaped with his life.

The treatment of women as portrayed in these traditions fails to represent the normative cultural values of Plains peoples, even though the stories are often told within the context of obvious humor. Indeed, when we discuss the various aspects of the religious life of these peoples, it will become clear that the position of women is often very high indeed. We can only conclude from this that the cultural values embodied by Trickster are a deformation of normative value meanings which ought more appropriately to inform the relationships between men and women, as well as among humans generally. Even though persons sometimes behaved in the manner of the trickster, this behavior is not legitimated by these traditions; rather, it is contrasted in striking and often colorful ways with a dialectical vision of the normative social order.

As is the case for most human groups, normative cultural values are distinguishable from what occurs at the level of moral practice. Here the trickster narratives reveal tensions between cultural values and actual behavior. In some cases there are actual contradictions between these two levels. Among the Blackfeet, for example, though Trickster's behavior with women was generally disapproved, it often received approval at the level of practice—at least for men. Girls were taught to value virginity and to anticipate faithfulness to their marriage vows, whereas boys were often encouraged to follow Trickster's example. When speaking of young men, one interpreter says, for example: "His efforts at debauchery are not only tolerated but encouraged by his family and should he lead a married woman astray is heralded as a person of promise" (Wissler 1911, p. 9). Along with other Plains tribes, the Blackfeet experienced moral tension between what they envisioned as good and what they sometimes encouraged in practice.

Also revealed in these narratives is a deep ambivalence involved in being human *and* a carnivore. There is clearly a tension, manifest in the creation narratives, between the necessity to eat and the killing of animals, which are believed to possess consciousness, will, and soul. And there are ambivalent elements manifest in Trickster's continual hunger, his deception of animals by exploiting aspects of their nature (their generosity, kindness, and gullibility), and his wasteful hunting techniques. That Trickster is a foolish and even a dangerous hunter appears in the theme of the "last animal" which runs through the narratives. As a consequence of an escape, often brought on by a momentary lapse in Trickster's character, an animal survives to continue the species. Clearly, the hunting techniques of Trickster are not affirmed; rather, the foolishness and potentially disastrous consequences of such activities are underlined in these stories.

Another possible dimension of meaning surrounding Trickster's character and activities may have been to represent to the people behavior that violated in fundamental ways the taken-for-granted world of ordinary experience. If common sense is viewed as a cultural system (Geertz 1983, pp. 73–94), that is, an organized system of shared meanings about the way things are done, Trickster clearly violates this system in ways that are at the same time humorous and obscene. What person in his or her right mind would punish their anus, or match wits with a powerful rock, or be so wasteful of food, or violate kinship relations so deeply? While the moral dimensions of the trickster narratives have been emphasized, those very dimensions may be part of a deeply taken-for-granted world of common sense. This world is also mirrored in the oppositions associated with Trickster's behavior.

Horizons of shared meaning concerning how the world was formed open up further understanding of Plains peoples. These meaning structures expressed a fundamental temporality; they portrayed the origin of the world at the hands of predecessors who stood at the juncture of ordinary experience and transcendent horizons of meaning. In these traditions, the culture hero/trickster performs a symbolic function by spanning more than one horizon of meaning, bringing into ordinary experience a sense of transcendence. The creator figures in these traditions also function symbolically, since they are often portrayed as originators or "first-workers" in a primordial sense.

It was through the shared understandings of how the natural and social worlds came into being that the people achieved a sense of identity. That sense of identity varies from group to group precisely because the predecessors who constitute the world themselves have different identities. While the contours of Plains social worlds have some continuity at the formal level—there are creators, tricksters, and culture heroes—there is also a level of uniqueness that distinguishes groups from each other precisely because each of these figures assumes a distinct identity in the different oral traditions.

The formation of the natural and social worlds has also involved in these traditions the constitution of certain appropriate forms of relationships. These relationships are not limited to humans but extend as well to the realm of nature, its forms of plant and animal life. We have sought to show how some of these creation narratives struggle with a fundamental problem concerning the natural world: Humans are portrayed as being kin to plant and animal beings, and also in a relationship of uneasy ambiguity. This ambiguity is sometimes apparently related to the emergence of the human as carnivore. The traditions do not solve these tensions, but they are identified and portrayed in various ways.[7]

With the appearance of the trickster, there is a portrayal of the antithesis of a normative order of cultural values. Trickster is also placed in a symbolic role since he clearly possesses more than ordinary powers. In his own way he stands in the world of ordinary experience and also transcends it, though often in destructive ways. Trickster heightens the tension that potentially and sometimes actually marks relations among humans and among humans and the world of nature. Trickster represents a deformed world in which both humans and other creatures would finally be destroyed, probably as a consequence of their own actions. The shared sense of the world as a vast kinship structure, including both humans and animals, is threatened by Trickster's anti-structure. The normative order of Plains social worlds has been legitimated by means of striking moral oppositions.

What we must now come to see is how the normative order of the world is not only legitimated but also mediated and infused with a sense of experiential reality through participation in ritual forms. In moving to this level, we bring more clearly into view the religious foundations upon which the cultural values we have discussed find their ground. We must see, in short, how the sacred powers at the heart of experience and in the world are evoked. When these matters are clearer, then we can grasp how religious and moral experience might have been formed among the peoples of the Northwestern Plains.

# CHAPTER 4

# Evoking the Sacred

THE POWER OF SYMBOLS lies in their complex associations with one or more dimensions of transcendent meaning. They evoke in human experience a sense of these horizons, thus illuminating, enriching, and deepening the dimensions of the shared everyday world. The monuments, architectural forms, and representational art of humans are often the most obvious occasions for such experiences of transcendence. Monuments evoke memories of founders, heroes, or religious leaders; architectural forms often are haloed with cosmic significance; and figures scratched in stone, painted on the body, or otherwise formed may not only suggest the activities of humans and animals but signal the presence of sacred beings, such as creators and culture heroes.

A living symbol or system of symbols requires a continual interaction among three primary dimensions: There is the symbolic object, whatever it is; there are the horizons of meaning with which the object is associated; and there is the human interpreter in whose experience meanings and object so evocatively coalesce. This triadic pattern is also present in the social world in the form of common symbolic objects, shared meanings with which they are associated, and the common sense of transcendence evoked in the experience of an interpreting community. As long as symbols live in a culture and in the experience of persons, they retain this evocative capacity. When they die, they lose their connection with transcendent meanings, returning to the world of ordinary significance. Rather than symbols—a shrine, an altar, or the representation of a sacred animal—they become wood, stone, or skin.

Symbols and symbol systems may not only die but may also change significance, becoming associated with different horizons of meaning. The shrine for one deity may become the shrine for another; the altar central to one form of worship may become the altar central to another form of worship; and the sacred being of one religious experience may become the sacred being within the context of another religious experience. Social crisis, secularization, or other types of social change may induce such shifts in symbolic meaning structure, and such shifts may call forth processes of reinterpretation by individuals or within interpreting communities. But as long as symbols live in a culture and in the experience of individuals, changes in meaning produce only changes in the locus and significance of transcendence. Only if symbols die, does a sense of a loss of transcendence occur. And even in these cases, such temporary losses generate hungers which seek their satisfaction in new or renewed symbol systems.

This understanding of symbols illuminates the nature of ritual in human communities. In a primordial sense, ritual is the incarnation or enactment of symbols in the world. Through word, song, dance and mimetic movement humans become representations of transcendent meanings—living symbols. Through enactment, the images of visions or dreams, the ecstasies of prayer or revelation, are embodied in the everyday world. Such embodiment, such ritual enactment, illuminates the world of ordinary experience from

[67]

within, raising it for the moment to the plane of the extraordinary, thus deepening and enriching it for the duration of the ritual. Ritual also enables humans periodically to renew a sense of transcendence in experience through successive reenactments. These rhythms in individual experience and the lives of communities accent the reality of transcendent dimensions of meaning. The significance of individual experience and the sense of destiny of the community are interpreted or reinterpreted through the prism of ritual reenactment. Ritual finally makes possible the mediation of symbol systems across generational time. Each generation has to incorporate or appropriate the symbol system of predecessors; and appropriation may sometimes mean changes in the nature of the meanings which were once associated with the symbols in the experience of predecessors. But such changes do not mean a disappearance of the generative power of symbol systems and their inexhaustible horizons of transcendent meaning.

This expanded view of symbols and ritual will illuminate our understanding of religious and moral dimensions of Plains social worlds, since these dimensions are fundamentally horizons of transcendent significance. We will examine in this chapter symbolic objects and ritual processes that were alive in these societies about a century ago, some of which continue in modified or reinterpreted forms even to the late twentieth century. Our task will be to discern the patterns of meaning that are associated with ritual and symbolic form, insofar as this is possible. These patterns appear both at the levels of individual experience and shared experiences in the social world.

We begin our investigation with the phenomenon of "medicine bundles" as they appear in Plains cultures. When we speak of these objects, as well as the men and women who are qualified to own and manipulate them, we wish to highlight their symbolic reality in the experience of the people and their communities.[1] Medicine bundles, then, will be interpreted as complex symbolic realities which are associated with various dimensions of transcendent meaning. The ritual that surrounds these objects powerfully evokes a sense of these dimensions of meaning at both the level of individual experience and in the shared experience of the social world.

[68]

# Blackfoot Bundles

A sacred object of considerable symbolic significance among the Blackfeet was the pipe bundle. The traditions related to the origin of this bundle do not appear in the form of a sacred canon, although there is widespread agreement that the pipe derives ultimately from Thunder.[2] Because the significance of pipe bundles essentially inheres in the ritual and its associated meanings, it is possible to have several such objects with similar origin traditions. In fact, at the turn of the century there were some seventeen of these bundles distributed among the three divisions of the Blackfeet (Wissler 1912, p. 136). We will first examine two origin traditions in order to grasp the general meanings which surround the bundle and which are evoked symbolically through the recollection of Thunder's traffic with the human beings.

The first tradition represents Thunder as an ambivalent character; he brings the rain which makes things grow, but he is also an inveterate stealer of women (Grinnell 1962, pp. 113–16). The narrative opens with Thunder entering the lodge of a man and woman and striking them down. The man was knocked unconscious but not killed, and the woman was abducted. When the man returned to his senses, he looked for his wife; when he could not find her, he concluded that she had been stolen by Thunder. He mourned her loss and determined to set out for Thunder's lodge to bring her back. All the animals laughed at him for undertaking such a journey. Wolf said,

> Do you think we would seek the home of the only one we fear? He is our only danger. From all others we can run away; but from him there is no running. He strikes, and there we lie. (Grinnell 1962, p. 113)

But the man persisted, finally arriving at a strange stone lodge in which lived the chief of the Ravens. Raven Chief told the man that Thunder's power was unequal to his own and that he would help him recover his wife. Raven transferred to the man powerful objects to accomplish this purpose, a raven wing and an arrow, the shaft of which was made from an elk horn. Armed with power, the man approached Thunder's lodge, which was made of stone after the fashion of Raven Chief's. Entering the lodge, he confronted Thunder; hanging in the lodge were many pairs of eyes, the humans whom Thunder had stolen. Among the eyes, the man saw those of his wife. When Thunder arose to strike the man, he was repelled by the raven wing; he arose a second time, but the man shot the elk horn arrow through the roof, letting sunlight suffuse the lodge. At this point, Thunder conceded defeat, and the man took his wife's eyes, restoring her as a whole person. The encounter between the man and Thunder ended with the transfer of a sacred pipe. Thunder said:

> I am of great power. I live here in summer, but when winter comes, I go far south. I go south with the birds. Here is my pipe. It is medicine SACRED, HOLY. Take it, and keep it. Now, when I first come in the spring, you shall fill and light this pipe, and you shall pray to me, you and the people. For I bring the rain which makes the berries large and ripe. I bring the rain which makes all things grow, and for this you shall pray to me, you and all the people. (Grinnell 1962, p. 116)

In this version a human comes into a relationship with a powerful sky-being, Thunder. But this tradition seems to represent Raven as possessing Sun power, which overcomes Thunder. Also we are introduced to a powerful animal, the elk. A song is sung to this animal in the course of the opening of the pipe bundle (Wissler 1912, p. 142).

In another version of the origin of the sacred pipe, we meet a theme that is widespread in Plains folklore (Wissler and Duvall 1908, pp. 89–90). This is the motif of the haughty young woman who will not marry because she cannot find anyone good enough for her. This version of the origin of the pipe would also probably have resonance in the experience of the people. The plot involves a young woman who one day heard Thunder in the distance. Because she had been unsuccessful in finding an acceptable man to marry, she thought to herself that she would marry Thunder. In the course of time, the young woman did marry Thunder and went with him to his lodge on a high mountain. She gave birth to two sons and lived happily, although she was sometimes homesick for her own people. Thunder perceived her discomfort and agreed to send her home. She was to return with a ritual of power associated with a sacred pipe. Thunder and his wife came to the people and transferred the pipe, along with the songs and movements associated with the ritual. As he was leaving, Thunder instructed the people to pray to him in the spring; receding in the distance, Thunder disappeared, and the people heard first a loud peal of thunder and then a smaller one, which was Thunder's youngest son. Now, the tradition says, when Thunder threatens the life of the people, they pray that they will not be harmed, "For the sake of your youngest child" (Wissler and Duvall 1908, p. 90). And Thunder hears and heeds their prayers.

From the origin traditions we already know that we are in the presence of more than ordinary horizons of meaning. Humans are portrayed as having established, in one case through marriage, a kinship relation with the power which brings growth and life to all the animals, plants, and the human beings. In both versions, human beings are related to powerful contemporaries, Thunder and Raven Chief, who bring essential elements into the lives of the people.

A view of the bundle and its ritual will deepen our understanding of the complex meanings that were evoked in the experience of the people.

The material objects in the pipe bundle may typically include the following: At the center is the sacred pipe, often accompanied by a white buffalo headdress, both of which may be wrapped in red flannel. A number of other items may also be present, such as a smaller pipe for smoking during the ritual, as well as the skins of certain animals and birds, such as the owl, loon, swan, crane, muskrat, otter, fawn, and prairie dog. Tobacco will often be placed in the bird skins, and a rattle may be wrapped in the prairie dog skin. In addition, there are pouches containing paints, incense materials, and other items for use in the ritual. Many of these objects are painted red; and in earlier times pipe bundle owners painted their robes red, thus making them recognizable to all the people (Wissler 1912, pp. 137–39). As we shall learn, the sacred red paint was often associated with the power of the sun.

The contents of this bundle and others among the Blackfeet arose from two sources: the reported vision experience of the original predecessor who received the bundle, and the vision experiences of successive owners. Since there were several of the pipe bundles among the Blackfeet, some of which were of considerable age, there must have been many variations in the contents and even in the form of the bundles. The contents and form are important not in themselves, however, but rather as they become occasions for the appearance in experience of horizons of transcendent meaning. It is in their symbolic significance, enacted in ritual, that the bundle and its contents become luminous with sacred power.

Preparation for opening the pipe bundle, as well as other important bundles, includes the purification of both body and spirit (Wissler 1912, pp. 257–62). For this purpose a sweat lodge is constructed. The symbolism of purifying steam is probably associated with breath and smoke, both of which are sources of life and vitality. While in the sweat lodge, participants sing songs to Sun, Moon, and Morning Star, evoking a complex structure of meaning which will be discussed subsequently. Other levels of symbolic meaning are present as well, such as the hole in which the stones are placed; this hole is rectangular, representing the awful power of Thunder who, when he strikes, makes such gashes in the ground. The pipe bundle itself is often placed on the top of the sweat lodge, its stem pointing toward the east, the source of life flowing from Sun. And a buffalo skull is often placed on the west side of the lodge, recalling the sacred relation between the people and the buffalo. These complex associations will be more fully discussed later, but at this point we need to penetrate further into the details of the ritual.

The opening of the pipe bundle traditionally occurred in response to one of four conditions: the sound of the first thunder in the spring, to renew the tobacco in the bundle, during a ceremony of transfer to another person, or in response to a vow made by a person in time of illness or other personal crisis (Wissler 1912, p. 147).[3] The ritual itself was composed of a complex of song, dance, and symbolic behavior which evoked horizons of transcendent meaning. The analysis of a particular ritual enactment will illustrate some of these motifs (Wissler 1912, pp. 140–46).

The ritual opens with the recitation of the origin narrative, preparing the people to enter into the sacred significance of what is about to unfold. Sweet pine is placed upon a live coal, and the living smoke of the incense rises to fill the tipi with its fragrance. The smudge altar itself is square, representing the power of Thunder when he strikes the earth. The owner of the pipe bundle and his wife purify their hands in the rising smoke, and begin to sing the first of eight groups of songs. In each group there are a total of seven songs. The first group of songs gathers up symbolically all creatures and powers above the earth and all creatures and powers upon the earth.

> That which is above; it is powerful.
> That which is below; it is powerful.

> (Wissler 1912, p. 142)

We recall that it is through the power of the breath in speech or song that humans and transcendent powers communicate. At the end of the seventh song, a second cloud of sweet pine incense arises in the tipi. The bundle now rests between the owner and his wife, ready to be exposed in the presence of the people.

The second group of seven songs is accompanied by symbolic movements as the wife of the bundle owner interacts with the pipe. During the first two songs, the pipe is represented as speaking to the woman, asking to be exposed to view.

> You stand up; you take me.
> You untie me; I am powerful.

> (Wissler 1912, p. 142)

As the ceremony proceeds, "every knot and cord is sung off the bundle and the contents come out into view" (Wissler 1912, p. 250). Mimetic movements reflecting the behavior of antelope and elk and songs addressing the buffalo accompany the ceremony at this point. As each cord or wrapping is removed, it is attended by cosmic symbolism reflected in the woman's movements as she gestures three

[73]

times toward each object, removing a cord or wrapping on the fourth movement.

The third group of seven songs involves the owner of the pipe in a set of symbolic movements that reflect the cosmic movements of his wife. The sacred pipe is taken from its wrappings and the mouthpiece is pointed slowly toward each of the cardinal directions, evoking the powers of the four quarters and focusing their intensity at this particular place and time and for this particular purpose. When these horizons of meaning are evoked, they combine with the previously evoked powers of earth and sky, filling the experience of the people with a rich and complex sense of transcendence.

Prayers are interspersed during the course of the ritual. Indeed, from one point of view, the entire bundle ceremony may be regarded as a prayer composed of song, dance, and symbolic movements (Wissler 1912, p. 252). A typical plea by a pipe owner to Thunder will give some sense of the flavor which such occasions must have had:

> Thunder, we beseech you, we beseech you. Help me, help me. Help me in that for which I have called upon you, for old age, the ability to escape dangers. Have mercy upon me thunder. . . . Have pity on all children and all women, all the old men, and middle-aged men, and married men. Try to take notice of them; try to take notice of them. Grant them safety; grant them safety. We are glad to meet you again for the sake of fortunate days. For this, have mercy on me for I have chosen for myself many summer days that I may live happily; that I may see many snows. Try to show me mercy; take heed. (Wissler 1912, pp. 252–53)

Notable in this prayer are appeals for the realization of general values, such as protection from danger, long life, happiness, and fulfillment. We shall speak later in this chapter about these and other elements of a broader value paradigm which finds its ground in religious horizons of meaning.

The fourth through the eighth groups of seven songs proceed according to a similar pattern. The pipe is danced with; songs are sung and dances performed with the skins of all the birds and animals in the bundle; the two animals of central importance to the people, the horse and the buffalo, are ever present on the surface of the ritual; and the owner's face is painted, marking him off from the world of everyday life and identifying him with meaning structures evoked symbolically in the ritual. Prominent among the colors employed are red and black, probably symbolizing Sun and night, or Moon, two powerful sky-beings which are prominent in the sweat lodge ritual as well as the pipe ritual.

Details of the pipe bundle ritual vary within the interpretative framework of the oral traditions, and some meanings must have changed through time. The principle of continuity was always the association of the bundle with Thunder; his power, it was believed, would bring not only specific valuable states to the owner but also produce beneficent effects for the community. A glimpse of community celebration involving the pipe was recorded by one interpreter. In this camp the ceremony ended with the leader dancing with the pipe around the entire circuit of the camp, followed by several hundred singing and dancing men, women, and children. Here the power both of the pipe and of the creatures of earth and sky are suffused throughout the group, and the symbolic meanings evoked by the ritual must have reverberated in the experience of many persons (Schultz 1973, pp. 116–17). Through ritual enactment, the ordinary world is illuminated from within by a complex of transcendent meanings.

Important as was the pipe bundle among the Blackfeet, an even more ancient complex of sacred objects is collected in the beaver bundle. This bundle illustrates the symbolic richness of rituals among Plains peoples.

Stories of the origin of beaver power among the people are not only deeply sedimented and widely shared, they also appear in a variety of form and detail.[4] One version comes from the narrative of Mad Wolf, an important medicine man and the owner of a beaver bundle (McClintock 1968, pp. 104–12). According to Mad Wolf, the origin of beaver power may be traced to the time when Blackfeet were pedestrian stone-age folk on the Plains.

The narrative of origin concerns two orphan brothers, a plot motif which was widespread on the Plains. The younger brother, Old Robe, lived with his older brother and his wife. Because the older brother's wife was hostile to Old Robe, she considered how she might get rid of him. One day her husband returned to find her beaten and bloody. Old Robe was charged with the crime, and now the older brother began to think how he could get rid of his younger brother. Settling upon a plan, he invited Old Robe to accompany him to a large island in the middle of a lake, there to collect duck and geese feathers for their arrows. The brothers built a raft and traveled to the island where they began to look for feathers. Old Robe wandered off alone. When he came back to the shore, he saw his brother, far off on the lake, going toward the mainland. In despair, Old Robe wept, crying out to all the earth and water animals, as well as to the Sun, the Moon, and the Stars. It is interesting to note at this point that Old Robe's older brother has violated a kinship relation which the Blackfeet valued extremely highly.

As he was wandering about on the island, Old Robe came upon the lodge of a beaver. Presently a little beaver came out and invited him to come into the lodge. When he entered, he saw there a huge beaver, whose hair was hoary with age. This impressive animal, perhaps the chief of the beavers (cf. Grinnell 1962, p. 119), listened quietly and attentively to Old Robe's story. After hearing how Old Robe had been betrayed by his older brother, the Beaver Chief took pity upon him, inviting him to stay the winter in his lodge. During that winter, Old Robe learned many things: the use of herbs and paints, how to plant and care for tobacco, how to mark off the days, and many songs and prayers useful for healing various diseases. Finally the booming of the ice was heard on the lake, and all knew that spring was finally near.

When the beavers came up out of their winter lodge, it was almost time for Old Robe to depart. Asking what he wanted for a gift, the Beaver Chief continued to show affection and concern for Old Robe. In response, Old Robe asked the old beaver that his son, the little beaver, be allowed to accompany him to the camp of his people. After four refusals, the beaver chief finally agreed. The old animal instructed Old Robe how to gather the objects for a sacred bundle such as he had seen in the lodge during the winter. In addition, Old Robe learned all the songs, prayers, and dances which belonged to the bundle.

Finally the elder brother was seen coming to the island in order to look for Old Robe's bones. While the elder brother was wandering about the island, little beaver and Old Robe jumped on the raft and made their way toward the mainland, leaving the brother weeping on the shore. When Old Robe arrived at his camp, he related the entire story of his experience with the beavers. All of the people soon came to know that he had sacred power which would be of benefit to all. They were eager to learn, and so little beaver and Old Robe spent the entire winter teaching the people the songs, prayers, and dances which pertained to the beaver bundle.

When spring arrived, Old Robe invited all the creatures of the earth, water, and sky to offer their power to the bundle (cf. Wissler 1912, pp. 191–92). Myriads upon myriads came, giving Old Robe their skins, their prayers, and their dances for the sacred bundle. In a fashion that recalls the cosmologies, the animals gave of themselves and their power for the sake of the human beings, each creature saying, "You can have this song and also my body" (Wissler 1912, p. 191). After gathering all of the sacred objects, songs, and dances together, Old Robe fashioned the first beaver bundle. And every spring he returned to the island and the lodge of the Beaver Chief, bringing back each time a new sacred object to add to the bundle. Thus the beaver bundle grew to its enormous size.[5]

Another origin narrative associates beaver power with the sun (Wissler and Duvall 1908, pp. 74–75). This tradition opens with a scene on the bank of a large lake. A man and his two wives were camping beside the lake. One day the older wife went to the lake for water and saw beside the lake a young man, Beaver. Beaver invited her into his tent (sexual intercourse), to which she agreed. The husband was sad at the loss of his wife and went looking for her in another camp, supposing that she had been abducted. The morning after her disappearance, the younger wife was drawing water from the lake when she saw the older woman rising up from beneath the surface. The older wife said that her husband could obtain Beaver's power in payment for her abduction. In order to obtain this power, the husband was instructed to prepare a feast for all the water creatures and to pray that Sun, Moon, and Morning Star would also come to the feast. The feast was prepared, and these solar beings did come down. While Sun sat beside the husband and

[77]

Moon sat beside the older wife, the beaver bundle and its ritual were transferred to the human beings. Humans became associated, through kinship established by sexual relations, with a powerful animal and its sacred power. This power would become beneficial for all the people. Also the ritual associates the people with Sun, Moon, and Morning Star—powerful sky-beings. A similar version (Wissler and Duvall 1908, pp. 75–76) interprets the people's relation to beaver power as arising after the wife of a great hunter has sexual intercourse with Beaver and gives birth to a beaver child. Power is transferred after the beaver father observes how kind the hunter is to the beaver child. In both of these versions, humans come into relationships with transcendent powers through kinship established on the grounds of a sexual interchange.

The beaver ritual is preceded by a sweat lodge, which purifies the bodies and spirits of the participants.[6] During the purification period, the beaver bundle is often placed against the west side of the sweat lodge (Wissler 1912, p. 174). After purification, the participants retire to a tipi where the ritual will unfold. A smudge altar is prepared in the tipi, as is the case for the pipe ritual. The beaver altar is circular, however, symbolizing Beaver's den and probably also the Sun (Wissler 1912, p. 255). Sweet grass is placed upon a hot coal, and the fragrance of the sacred smoke fills the tipi as the first group of seven songs is chanted. The motifs in these songs are significant for later analysis, and they will be quoted at length. The reference to Napi in the verses below should be interpreted to mean the Sun in this context.

1.  Behold Napi comes into the lodge.
    He is a strong Medicine Man.
    He came in.
    I see him.

2.  The Heavens provide us with food.
    The Heavens are glad to behold us.

3.  The Earth loves us.
    The Earth is glad to hear us sing.
    The Earth provides us with food.

4.  Song to the "Prongs."
    (The prongs are sacred sticks painted red. They are forked, and

are used to take hot coals from the fire in the burning of incense.)

5. The Old Man (Beaver Chief), is coming in.
The Old Man has come in.
He sits down beside his medicine.
It is a very strong medicine.

The Old Woman (Female Beaver) is coming in.
The Old Woman has come in.
She sits down and takes the medicine.
It is a very strong medicine.

6. I take hold of the sacred Buffalo.
While I am walking, I walk slowly.
I stop with my medicine.
The ground where my medicine rests is sacred.

7. When summer comes, He (Buffalo) will come down from the Mountains.

(McClintock 1968, pp. 79–81; cf. Wissler 1912, pp. 178–81)

After a number of other songs and chants, during which the outer covers of the bundle are removed, the major part of the ritual unfolds. Two women are intimately involved in the substance of the ritual (Wissler 1912, p. 177; McClintock 1968, p. 88). In a series of mimetic movements, they approach the bundle, stopping three times. With the fourth body movement, they hook at the bundle as would a buffalo, untying the thongs which hold the outer covers in place (McClintock 1968, p. 88; cf. Wissler 1912, p. 176). As the sacred objects are exposed, the ritual moves to another stage in which songs and dances are performed for all of the items in the bundle. In some cases, there are different songs which pertain to the different types of animal within a species (Wissler 1912, pp. 176–77).

Because the ritual is very long and quite strenuous, it is broken by periods of rest and smoking, as well as by prayers made by those present. A typical prayer by a Blood chief will give the flavor of such utterances:

Great Spirit in the Sun! I am praying for my people that they may be able to have food and survive the coming winter. May all our

[79]

children grow and have strong bodies. May they live long and be happy. (McClintock 1968, p. 85)

Not all the dances and songs are of the same emotional intensity as that expressed through this prayer, however. Indeed, some of them are punctuated by gaiety and laughter. For example, the buffalo dance, which mimics mating buffalo, and the dog dance, which is a women's dance of great intensity and popularity, demonstrate that the spiritual life of the Blackfeet was marked by joy (McClintock 1968, pp. 99–100; Wissler 1912, p. 186). These dances come at the end of the ceremony, after some of the more symbolically charged dances of the main part of the ritual have occurred.

Typical of one of the major dances of the ritual is that of the beaver. This dance involves four women who imitate the movements and activities of this central animal. Accompanied by singing, the women mimic the beaver working on its dam, carrying branches, and swimming. They swim, as beavers, across a lake and emerge on the shore, looking this way and that, as would beavers anticipating danger (McClintock 1968, pp. 90–91; Wissler 1912, p. 183). This pattern is generally followed for each creature represented in the bundle. Songs emphasize features of the creature's behavior or power, and dances imitate the movements of these creatures or important aspects of their activities. The complexity of this bundle is so great that almost every object associated with it has social depth in the sense that it was related to a narrative of origin. Fragments of these origin stories are often reflected in the unfolding ritual (Wissler 1912, pp. 194ff.). It is little wonder that this bundle required such skill and knowledge, and it is not surprising that some of its aspects have been forgotten with the passage of time and especially with the disturbances produced by the conquest of the Blackfeet and its aftermath.

Large and impressive bundles like the beaver and the pipe were, in traditional culture, privately owned, yet they seemed to address values and states of affairs which related to the general tribal welfare. These larger bundles do not exhaust the phenomenon among the Blackfeet by any means. There were a large number of smaller, personal bundles which related more specifically to the life history

[80]

and vision experience of individuals. All of these arose as a consequence of a dream- or waking-vision in which a supernatural visitant transferred power to an individual. Of course, an individual could acquire one of these smaller bundles through transfer, as earlier described. In either case, whether the bundle related to the primary experience of the owner or was acquired by transfer, these bundles had more specific uses than did the larger collections of sacred objects.

Some interesting examples of such smaller bundles are war bridles, sacred objects which are suspended under the bit of a horse and which are believed to give protection in an encounter with an enemy or success in the hunt (Wissler 1912, p. 107). Or there are the widely distributed sacred medicine shields (Wissler 1912, pp. 117–25), a phenomenon which will be discussed at greater length in our treatment of the Crows. And, finally, there are rock bundles which have power to call buffalo.[7]

More impressive than these smaller bundles were the painted tipis among the Blackfeet. These structures were decorated according to instructions received in vision experiences. They had bundles and their associated rituals as well, and at the turn of the century there were over fifty different types of painted tipis distributed throughout the Blackfoot confederacy (Wissler 1912, pp. 221–22). Although the designs upon the tipis related to an individual vision experience, the symbolic figures actually painted upon the structures evoked a sense of common meaning. The presence of important animals, such as the buffalo, as well as the prominence of such sky phenomena as the Sun, Moon, and Stars, reinforced the shared sense of transcendence among the people. In addition to these bundles, there was another important and larger bundle, the natoas, which will be discussed in the sixth chapter. The natoas bundle, with its ritual, is essentially associated among the Blackfeet with the great tribal festival of the Sun Dance.[8]

On the basis of this analysis, we can say that there was a pervasive family-based practice of "bundle religion" among the Blackfeet in the mid-nineteenth century. One interpreter says, "So universal is the ownership of bundles large and small that almost every tipi has a regular smudge place that is used without fail at least twice a day" (Wissler 1912, p. 257). This is consistent with what we came earlier to see as the cultural expectation that experiences of vision would occur. As a consequence of such vision experiences, a rich and complicated ritual life emerged. And because the cultural accent of reality was granted so powerfully to vision and to the sacred objects which embodied vision, almost every individual and even the most destitute of families would seek a share in those experiences of transcendence which secured life values, family destiny, and even group survival.

## Crow Bundles

Most Crow bundles were associated with warfare. Even the bundle used in the Sun Dance, to be treated in the sixth chapter, was built around the sentiment of revenge against an enemy (Wildschut 1960, pp. 171–72). Some understanding of the Crow cultural context in the mid-nineteenth century will enable us to grasp why religious sensibilities were so focused upon the activities of war. In 1850, the Crow numbered somewhat over three thousand persons, living in about four hundred lodges. As compared with their neighbors, the Crows were a relatively small group, and yet they occupied some of the richest territory. They were also wealthy in horses, the number at the height of their power being perhaps as many as ten thousand (Lowie 1935, p. xiv). Despite their small numbers, and perhaps partly because of this circumstance, the Crows were fierce warriors. They were besieged on the east by the Teton Dakotas, on the north by the Blackfeet, on the west by the Flatheads and Nez Perces, and on the south by the Shoshonis. Surrounded on all sides by hostile forces, the Crows literally fought for their social existence. And although many predicted their extermination, they were able to survive (Wildschut 1960, pp. 172–73; Curtis 1909, pp. 3–4). Given this historical context, it is little wonder that their religious and moral sensibilities were reflected in a kind of "warrior religion" (Weber 1952, chap. 4). This motif was of course not absent among other tribes, such as the Blackfeet, but it achieved high visibility among the Crows.

Although it will be impossible to capture all of the richness and complexity associated with Crow bundles, some view of the shields, arrow bundles, and rock bundles will provide a glimpse into these dimensions of cultural meaning. One of the most striking things to notice is how, on the one hand, Crow bundles reflect the cultural focus upon war and, on the other hand, how the symbolic forms associated with the bundles evoke dimensions of meaning which are broader than particular cultural interests.

Shields represent in a dramatic fashion the Crow interest in the promotion of life values associated with the continued existence of the group. Because that existence was so often threatened, the quest for power to overcome enemies was very widespread.[9] Shields which possessed sacred power thus always arose as a consequence of a dream- or waking-vision. In the vision, moreover, persons sometimes received more than one shield, each of which was constructed according to the content of the vision. Although such shields were viewed as very powerful, they were, interestingly enough, seldom taken into battle. They were too bulky and heavy for the requirements of mobile warfare. Rather, a part of the shield, such as a feather, might be taken on the warpath. In other instances, a miniature reproduction of the shield was made and then fastened in the hair or suspended around the neck when the warrior went on an expedition. War shields were usually inherited by a son, although the wife of an owner might retain the shield in her possession after the death of her husband (Wildschut 1960, pp. 65–67).

The spiritual significance of these shields is suggested partly by their descriptive features. Because they arose as a consequence of vision, a special relationship between the person and the transcendent power was established. This relationship and the particular powers associated with the experience were symbolically represented on the shield. When a man took a part of such a sacred object into battle, he was actually accompanied by the powers granted in the original vision. The material object—a feather or miniature reproduction—had the symbolic authority of the whole. Some further illumination may be cast upon these issues by looking briefly at an experience which gave rise to a war shield.

Typical is the experience of the Crow warrior known as Hump

or Humped-wolf (Wildschut 1960, pp. 67–68; Lowie 1922, pp. 409ff.). When he was about eighteen years old, Humped-wolf was on a war expedition in which several persons were killed and he received a serious leg wound. He became separated from the main war party and wandered about upon the Plains. When night came he found himself alone, in the midst of a snowstorm, and without warm robes. Certain that he would freeze to death, Humped-wolf suddenly saw a black object on the Plains. Discovering the object to be a dead buffalo, he crawled inside the still warm carcass and started to drift off to sleep. Just before he lost consciousness, he heard a voice calling and a buffalo snorting. He got up and moved toward the mysterious voice when he was suddenly confronted by a strange person. This person opened his mouth, showing that he had no teeth, and told Humped-wolf that he would live to be a very old man, himself without teeth. Then Humped-wolf turned toward the east where he saw a buffalo bull followed by another buffalo. The buffalo bull transformed himself into a man and the other buffalo became a bay horse. The buffalo-man then transferred power to Humped-wolf, giving him at the same time a new name, Full-mouth-buffalo.

After this experience, Full-mouth-buffalo traveled toward his people, still cold but filled with considerable confidence. Just before dawn he saw another person, whom he knew to be the person of his vision. The person began to sing, and Full-mouth-buffalo saw a Crow warrior in combat on the Plains with a Dakota. The Crow began to sing as the two warriors closed in upon each other. The Dakota was armed with a knife, a bow and arrows, and a tomahawk. The Crow had only a shield and a lance. Three times the Dakota attacked, first with his arrows, then with his tomahawk, and then with his knife. All these weapons were useless against the power of the shield. Upon the fourth attempt, the Crow killed the Dakota with his lance. As the enemy fell, Full-mouth-buffalo looked and saw that the fallen enemy was a coyote, who said to him, "You shall be the same" (Lowie 1922, p. 410).

Full-mouth-buffalo constructed a shield which conformed to the elements of his vision experience (Wildschut 1960, p. 67). It had a green border on the left side, representing the summer, the time for war parties. Dark brown lines on the shield represented bullets or other projectiles bouncing off the shield. Owl feathers were tied to the center of the shield, as were eagle feathers. Among the Crows, the owl and eagle were great and powerful birds. The owl possessed the power of sacred vision, since it could discern the future; and the eagle was chief of the birds, flying the highest, and thus having a view of all that happened upon the earth. In addition, the shield had a representation of a buffalo, symbolizing the being on the Plains from whom Humped-wolf obtained his vision, his special powers, and new name.

An example of war bundles which illustrates motifs that are broader than the specific activities of battle appears in the Crow arrow medicine. These bundles were believed to bring their owners both success in battle and general good fortune. An origin narrative will illustrate these motifs.

According to one version the arrow bundle originated in the experience of a young man, an orphan (Wildschut 1960, pp. 48–50; cf. Lowie 1922, pp. 321–22). This young man fasted in a lonely place; cutting off the first joint of his index finger, he prayed to the Sun for power. On the first night of his suffering, Morning Star (the Sun's son) appeared in a vision in the form of a human being. With him Morning Star had a powerful arrow which he showed to the young man and demonstrated its uses. He instructed the young man to return to his camp and make seven arrows, each a different color, which would form the central objects in seven different bundles. (In one version the visitant is the Dipper, accounting for the prominence of the number seven.) Morning Star then taught the young man the ritual and songs appropriate to the bundles, and, before departing, he gave the young man the original sacred arrow. Thus the tradition holds that the first arrow was given directly by Morning Star and was not made by humans.

With the appearance of the Sun and Morning Star (also the Dipper), we come into the presence of horizons of meaning which have appeared in powerful ways in the Blackfoot experience as well. These cosmic figures mediate a sense of transcendence which obviously cannot be contained completely by the cultural focus upon war. Thus, a plenitude of meaning overflows the cultural structure, illuminating Crow experience through symbolic forms that are deeper than any particular set of human interests. This does not change the fact, however, that in Crow experience of the mid-nineteenth century, war bundles played a prominent role in the life of the people; and success or failure in battle was attributed to the powers irrupting in their dream- and waking-visions (Wildschut 1960, p. 173).

Other bundles among the Crows were associated with love, healing, and hunting. Some of these bundles, such as the rock bundles, had multiple powers (Wildschut 1960, p. 92). In addition, the rock bundles probably recalled motifs associated with the creation stories among the Crow. It will be remembered that in these accounts there appear beings who were animate before the creation of the world took place. One of these beings was the medicine stone, the "oldest part of the earth" (Lowie 1918, p. 15).

Important tribal bundles existed among both the Cheyennes and the Arapahoes, as did smaller personal medicine objects. The Cheyenne Arrow bundle as well as the Arapaho Flat Pipe Bundle and the Sacred Wheel will be treated in the next two chapters when we deal with the themes of social and world renewal. In the concluding part of this chapter we need to have more clearly in view the elements of religious and moral experience which are evoked in the bundle ceremonies we have discussed.

## Religious and Moral Experience

The general argument we have been pursuing is that religious and moral experiences are evoked symbolically through ritual. A closer look at the content of these rituals will particularize our view of concrete religious and moral experiences. In order to accomplish this purpose, it is necessary to bring into view certain background horizons that have been present in the traditions we have discussed (see Waterman 1914, pp. 6–7, for the notion of background horizons). Four of these dimensions have appeared in cultic activities surrounding bundles: solar/lunar motifs, astral motifs, animal motifs, and plant motifs.

It is impossible to systematize the oral traditions, bringing a hierarchical order to these four dimensions, for example. It is evident, however, that solar/lunar and astral motifs are quite prominent in the traditions. The Moon appears as the wife of the Sun, while Morning Star appears as the son of Sun and Moon. The Dipper and Pleiades are also prominent in these traditions. In the religious sensibilities of the people, these motifs appear in connection with narratives that represent these beings as fundamentally related to the human world. Solar, lunar, and astral figures are not ordinary humans, but rather sources of transcendent power. They are also apprehended as a part of the social world of the people. It is not entirely clear whether these beings are material symbols of transcendent powers, "masks of the gods," or whether they are themselves identical with these powers. In any case, the nature of their power is often ambivalent and, as was seen in the case of Thunder, may include dimensions of the malevolent as well.

Animal theophanies are also a dominant theme in the oral traditions. In some cases animal forms mediate powers to humans that are associated with their specific characteristics (speed, vision, cunning), and in other cases the powers mediated by animals are more generalized. In either case, there seems to be the perception of animals in the empirical everyday world as beings possessed of consciousness, will, and capacities to act on behalf of humans and their world. The most dramatic forms of their action appear in the experiences of dream- or waking-vision, in which animals become mediators of various transcendent powers. Indeed, a general motif that has emerged concerns the agency of animals in the mediation of power to the human world. Whether the animal beings appear in a vision or in the context of the waking world of ordinary experience is not as important as is the prospect that power may be communicated.

Although the plant motif does not appear as dramatically as it does among agricultural peoples, it is present in the form of the sacred tobacco plant. Among the Crows, the cultivation of sacred Tobacco is essentially connected with their myth of origin. The ritual of the Tobacco Society is a reenactment of the creation myth which renews the people and their world. We will show subsequently that the plant motif seems to be connected in these traditions with a more generalized sensibility concerning the sacredness of the earth itself.

The view that emerges is that these background horizons form religious attitudes and evoke certain moral sensibilities. Further, these motifs represent to the people transcendent horizons of meaning which appear in their visions and are sustained through their rituals.

The experience of vision typically involves the person at three levels: the visual, the auditory, and the behavioral. The experience arises in the form of the sensuous appearance of a transcendent being; that being speaks or sings to the person. In the speaking or singing, significant power is communicated; and the person is taught appropriate forms of bodily movement and bodily presentation, such as dance and body painting. The person who experiences the initial gift of power may be a culture hero, or an anonymous predecessor, such as a "poor youth" who is visited by transcendent personages and receives special powers. In either case, if the experience is the occasion for the rise of an important ritual object, such as a bundle, then the narrative of origin becomes an important background horizon which informs the meaning of the ritual.

The ritual associated with particular bundles calls forth other transcendent horizons of meaning. Beginning with the sweat lodge, in which sky motifs are usually dominant, the ritual unfolds in a pattern that represents significant aspects of the original auditory and visual experience as interpreted by the present bundle owner. After the story of the bundle's origin is recalled, bodily movements in the form of song and dance reinforce the sense of these transcendent realities in the experience of individual participants. The pervasive phenomenon of body painting signals that participants understand themselves to be entering another order of reality. During ritual time, participants recapitulate in appearance and action their relationship with beings who gave rise to the sacred bundle. As a consequence of these acts, transcendent power suffuses their present experience.

Ritual is not compulsive of the powers which transcend humans in any mechanical way. These powers have either adopted particular humans or have granted their power voluntarily. There is no sense of compelling the powers to appear by the force of the ritual. Ritual is rather the way experiences of power are reenacted, their accent of reality renewed, and their capacity to influence human attitudes and action extended through social time. The background horizons that are mediated through ritual amount to a particular way of apprehending the world. This apprehension is the nexus that we must now elaborate further in order to understand how religious experience in Plains cultures informs moral dispositions and provides a general frame for action.

The apprehension of the world by Plains peoples seems most fundamentally to be characterized by kinship. Solar/lunar, astral, animal, and plant beings are not viewed as separate from the human world. Rather, these beings form a network of kinship relations with humans and enter their world in powerful ways. The Crows illustrate this apprehension of the world. Their world is imaged as two clans. One great clan is composed of the sun, moon, stars, and thunder. It includes all of the animals of the earth, as well as all of the souls of those who have died. The second great clan includes the earth and all that comes from it—plants, trees, rocks. The spirits of water, wind, and fire are prominent in this clan, the wind being the breath of the world and the source of human life. The wind of the human soul returns to the Other Side Camp at death. Likewise, because the earth is the mother of humans, at death the body returns to her bosom (Wildschut 1960, p. 2).

In such a world, the preservation of appropriate relations and their reestablishment if they are disrupted become of prime importance. Relations may be disrupted by human or other than human action, but the basic belief is that they may be reestablished. Ritual is the primary means of establishing, maintaining, and reestablishing relationships. Fundamental interrelatedness is more than simply a description of how things are; it is also an understanding of how things *ought* to be (Geertz 1973, p. 127). Conflict that emerges in human relations or between the human world and the world of transcendent powers is a violation of the religious and moral order. Such violations must be rectified through ritual activity. This does

[89]

not mean that ambivalent feelings toward the powers do not emerge (Hultkrantz 1981, pp. 177ff., 157ff.). There were perceptions that transcendent powers could be malevolent toward humans, but the *fundamental* belief seems to be that relationships could be ritually restored.

General religious and moral attitudes are supported by this basic apprehension of the world. There is, for example, an expectant attentiveness toward the world and toward experiences of the inner life. This attitude is sustained by the powerful accent of reality which is granted to such experiences in Plains cultures. Humans expect these experiences to occur, and they are actively sought. This attitude of expectant attentiveness is described as religious precisely because what is anticipated are irruptions of sacred power in human experience. The general moral attitude evoked by this religious experience is a sense of care. Since at any moment sacred power may appear, persons were expectant and attentive; they also tended to "take care," to be in the proper frame of mind and ready to enter into the appropriate relationship with transcendent powers.

Another more specific religious attitude is the sense of dependence which Plains folk felt toward the sacred sources of their life: Sun, Moon, Stars, other significant predecessors, and various plant and animal beings. Human welfare at both the individual and social level was dependent upon the continued support of these beings. Furthermore, new forms of human well-being could emerge as a consequence of the approach of a sacred personage who might "take pity" upon an individual, granting power which then might become efficacious for the group. The moral dispositions that are related to this religious apprehension form a complex that includes a sense of humility in the presence of sacred powers and a sense of moral tension related to the perception that dependence upon the powers could be dangerous.

Following upon the apprehension of dependence, another religious attitude may arise which is more specific, especially if dependence is understood in the language of kinship. Occupying a kinship relation with various classes of transcendent beings evokes at the level of moral experience sensibilities concerning family duties and obligations. Kinship duties and obligations are heightened and made morally serious in this context, given the nature of the beings with whom the people were so intimately related. Considerable care was taken to ascertain the appropriate modes of behavior due to transcendent kin. Appropriate moral dispositions were sustained by the bundle rituals we have described.

A final religious attitude is a specific sense of gratitude for the benefits that transcendent beings bring to individuals and to the group. The language employed in the bundle rituals clearly embodies this attitude. At the level of moral experience the sensibility of gratitude overflows into activities of ritual celebration which form such an obvious part of the ceremonies we have discussed.

The religious universe portrayed in Plains cosmologies and evoked through bundle rituals also supports a normative understanding of the human moral agent. Negatively embodied in Trickster, this view is centered upon the deep value of reciprocity that informs kinship relationships. On the ground of this general value paradigm are nurtured the more specific values we have previously discussed: truthful speech, generosity, kindness, and bravery. These values shaped moral dispositions and provided a model for moral action. These attitudes and dispositions translate concretely into relationships with the beings whom humans meet in their everyday life—the animals, plants, and other phenomena of "nature." These relationships are focused most dramatically in ritual forms which are enactments in the world of basic kinship structures.

Even though this normative understanding often failed to be embodied in moral practice, it was still the dominant image of moral agency for many Northwestern Plains tribes. More specific understandings of proper relationships among family members and within the larger society were guided by this image. The qualities of character recommended by this image apply to women and men alike, although the virtue of bravery was often associated more with men than with women. The many examples of women's courage and their participation in battle indicate, however, that bravery was by no means an exclusively male virtue.

In the bundle rituals the world is apprehended as a reality luminous with sacred power. Human beings live with other creatures in a vast kinship structure and interact upon a multitude of levels.

The relation between humans and the world of luminous animals, plants, sky-beings, and the earth itself is normatively one of kinship. This sensibility is evoked, sustained, and reestablished in experience through the symbolic forms of ritual. Basic relations may be disturbed by human activities, or through the activities of transcendent powers, but it was believed that right relations could be recovered and that the human beings could flourish, enabled by the power and goodness which flowed into the world from the sacred sources we have discussed.

We have now come to understand something of how peoples on the Northwestern Plains interpreted the formation of their world and how their religious and moral universe was framed. We have also seen something of how experiences of transcendent power occurred and how such experiences were sustained through ritual processes. The next two chapters take up the themes of social and world renewal, which are associated with more complex tribal rituals. In these chapters there will be a more explicit focus upon the activities of important culture heroes who came among the tribes and instituted powerful ritual processes. These ritual processes provide additional layers of symbolic form which give depth to the religious and moral dimensions of the Plains world picture.

CHAPTER 5

# Renewing the People

On the Northwestern Plains, rituals of world renewal preserved the spiritual and physical well-being of the people. One cannot easily separate the ritual forms that more properly have to do with the cosmos from those that affect human relationships; indeed, to do so does violence to what are, at their core, world views which do not make such distinctions. It is possible, however, to speak of ritual forms which do tend to emphasize the renewal of the social world, although such forms are never separated from meanings which reach out to the cosmos as well. Two such ritual processes, illustrating the theme of renewing the people and the social world, are the Sacred Arrow ceremony among the Cheyennes and the Crow Tobacco Society ceremony. A discussion of these ritual processes will enable us to unearth meanings which have to do with the revivification of the social world and will prepare us to understand, at a deeper level, the meanings in the Sun Dance that invigorate not only the people but also the entire cosmos. These rituals also provide symbolic reinforcement for the moral and religious dimensions of the Plains world picture. Such reinforcement occurs through participation in a wider communal context which deepens the reality sense of cultural values and religious sensibilities discussed in previous chapters.

The horizons of memory that nurtured root symbolic forms borne in ritual processes present interesting problems in the case of the Cheyennes; thus, we shall deal first with these issues before moving to a consideration of specific rituals.

## Early Cheyenne Traditions

Recall that the migration of the Cheyennes from their previous agricultural existence and their development of Plains institutions and lifeways involved the assimilation of a people known as the Suhtais. One complexity of tribal traditions comes at the point of trying to sort out traditions that reflect the older, agricultural way of life from those that reflect more recent developments. Other complexities arise because the Suhtai traditions bear the memory of a particular culture hero while the Cheyenne traditions speak of a different culture hero. In some traditions, these culture heroes appear together; in other traditions, they are treated separately. As will become clear, the Suhtai culture hero brought to the people the Sun Dance, while the Cheyenne culture hero brought the Sacred Arrows.

As was noted in chapter one, the Cheyennes probably lived in ancient times in the area known as the Eastern Woodlands, perhaps in the general vicinity of Minnesota and Wisconsin. During this period of their lives they lived in permanent villages on the shores of lakes, subsisting on wild rice, waterfowl, and small game (Hoebel 1978, pp. 5–6). Oral traditions recall such a time (Grinnell 1972, vol. 1, p. 6), and there are reflected in the activities of important mythical personnages traces of this time in Cheyenne history. One such tradition concerns the narration of the deeds of E HYOPH' STA, or Yellow Haired Woman (Grinnell 1962, pp. 244–52; cf. Grinnell

1907, pp. 173–78). Recounting this tradition will provide insight into the way the narrative contains memories of an earlier time, as well as indications of migration and social change.

According to the tradition, Yellow Haired Woman appeared among the people before they knew of the buffalo, at a time when they lived on fish and other small animals. It was a time of crisis and desperation brought on by scarcity of food. Two young men were selected from the village to search for food, but after four days' effort they returned empty-handed. At this point the camp packed in readiness to move, and the two young men were sent out ahead, being told not to return to their people until they had found something to eat. After traveling for eight days they came to a high peak in front of which ran a large stream. They set off across the stream, but, when they had reached the middle, the younger man was suddenly grasped under the water and held fast. Calling to the elder man, the youth said: "My friend, I cannot move, something is holding me. Tell my people what has happened to me. Tell them not to cry for me. Some mysterious power holds me" (Grinnell 1962, p. 246).

As the elder youth wept on the bank of the stream, he saw coming down from the peak a man wearing a coyote skin on his back and carrying a sharp knife. The coyote-man swam out to the younger man and, diving under the water, cut off the head of the serpent which held the boy. Then he told the elder youth to go to the peak and find there a large rock, which was a door. This the elder boy did, finding in the peak an old woman. After cutting up the serpent and hauling the meat to the peak, the two youths, the coyote-man, and the old woman went into the opening. Once inside, the elder youth could see that the interior of the peak was like a lodge, on one side of which was a sweat house. Still in shock from his experience, the younger man was put into the sweat lodge, where the coyote-man performed a ritual of healing.

After the younger boy had recovered, the old woman put out food in white stone bowls and gave each a flint knife with which to eat. After they had finished eating, the young men saw a fair-haired woman sitting in the lodge. The coyote-man asked which youth would take the woman for his sister or marry her. After discussion, it was decided that the handsome woman should marry the younger man. Before they departed from the peak, the coyote-man evoked a vision of the four directions. As the young people looked toward each cardinal point they saw animals of all kinds, including the buffalo. They also saw horses, perhaps an interpolation from a later time after they received these animals from the Europeans. Then the coyote-man said to the youths that all they had seen in the vision, Yellow Haired Woman would bring to the people. Instructions were given to the young woman, among which was the warning that she should never express pity or concern for any suffering animal.

The three young persons returned to the camp, and the next morning the Plains were black with buffalo. The people killed all they wanted; a time of plenty was inaugurated. Eight years after Yellow Haired Woman came to the Cheyennes, she made a mistake. It was upon the occasion of the abuse of a buffalo calf by some young boys that she expressed pity for the suffering of the animal. The consequence was radical: "That day the buffalo all disappeared" (Grinnell 1962, p. 251). Saddened by this turn of events, the young woman decided to return to her parents, the coyote-man and the old woman. The two young men also decided to return with her and, after weeping with all of their relatives, they set off toward the peak and were never seen by the people again.

In addition to the reflection of an earlier time before the Cheyennes subsisted upon buffalo, there are other interesting motifs associated with this narrative. Its structure is familiar, being based upon the careers and exploits of two young men, a theme we have seen before. What is even more significant, however, is what appears to be the figure of the Master of the Animals in the person of the coyote-man. This figure has been less prominent in the traditions we have examined, when it has been present at all. Since the Master of the Animals is a common figure in Algonquian cultures of the Eastern Woodlands (Hultkrantz 1979, pp. 22–23), it is not unreasonable to suppose that the figure of coyote-man is a reflection of a time before the Cheyenne migration onto the Plains. Significant also in this narrative is the sedimentation of traditions that reflect the migration of the people and that interpret this migration through the structure of myth.

Another central theme in this narrative concerns the people's relationship with their food supply. The Master of the Animals in this tradition is represented as formulating the rule of "no pity" where the killing of animals was concerned. As compared with other traditions, which often represent animals as giving themselves for humans, in this narrative the animals are given over to the people by coyote-man through the agency of his daughter. The problem of killing sentient beings finds an uneasy solution in the rule of "no pity"; indeed, the rule seems designed to restrain what is portrayed as a rather natural disposition of pity on the part of Yellow Haired Woman. In any case, this tradition adds another dimension to our understanding of the complexity of oral traditions on the Plains. It will be interesting later in this chapter to compare this tradition with the view of the buffalo embodied in the Arrow Ceremony.

Other Cheyenne traditions employ the motif of the two young men and seem to reflect the agricultural period in their history when they were associated with the Mandans and the Hidatsas (Hoebel 1978, p. 7). In some of these traditions the young men are unidentified (Dorsey 1905a, pp. 39–41), whereas in others they are identified with the culture heroes of the Cheyennes and the Suhtais (Grinnell 1907, pp. 179–89). In some versions only one of the culture heroes is identified (Grinnell 1962, pp. 257–62). In all of these traditions, the major theme concerns how the Cheyennes receive the buffalo and the corn. The corn symbolism clearly relates to the period in their history when they were agriculturalists, spending part of the year, as did the Mandans and Hidatsas, in hunting forays on the Plains.

The most familiar narrative theme that appears in these various traditions concerns a mysterious spring named Old Woman's Water. As we penetrate into the narrative, it will become clear that the old woman in the spring plays something of the role of the Mistress of the Animals, perhaps again reflecting older Algonquian motifs. Typical details of these narratives concern the appearance of two young men in the Cheyenne camp (Dorsey 1905a, pp. 39–41). The two young men were dressed alike and were painted in an identical manner. Neither knew the other and each asked the other why they were dressed alike; both discovered that they had been instructed by the old woman in the spring to dress and paint themselves in a certain manner. After learning this, the two young men entered the spring and found themselves in a large cave. At the entrance of the cave sat an old woman cooking buffalo meat and corn in earthen pots. The old woman addressed the young men as her "grandchildren" and proceeded to feed them from the pots, which miraculously remained filled even after the young men had satisfied themselves.

After they had eaten, the old woman invoked a vision similar to that produced by the coyote-man in the previous tradition. Rather than looking in the four directions, in this tradition the young men looked to the south where they saw many buffalo, to the west where they saw numerous other animals, and to the north where they saw fields of growing corn. Then the old woman instructed the young men to return to their people: "All this that you have seen shall in the future be yours for food. This night I cause the buffalo to be restored to you" (Dorsey 1905a, p. 40). Then she gave them seeds of corn for planting and the cooked meat and corn to take to the people. When the people ate, the pots did not diminish until the last, when two orphan children finished the food.

In other traditions the two young men are identified as the Cheyenne and the Suhtai culture heroes, Sweet Medicine and Erect Horns (Grinnell 1907, pp. 183–85, 189–94). In some of these traditions the setting is at the spring, Old Woman's Water, and in other versions this motif does not appear. Common to these versions is the theme of the culture heroes bringing to the people both buffalo and corn. An interesting and perhaps significant element of these traditions concerns the names of the culture heroes. In one, for example, the names of the two young men are Red Tassel, evoking the image of maize in bloom, and Rustling Leaf, recalling the sound of corn leaves rubbing together in the wind (Grinnell 1907, pp. 183–85); in others, the two young men are identified as Standing on the Ground (Erect Horns) and Sweet Root Standing (Sweet Medicine). In one of these versions the two culture heroes bring buffalo and corn from the old woman in the spring (Grinnell 1907, pp. 189–94). The names, especially Red Tassel and Rustling Leaf, perhaps reflect the agricultural period in which both the Cheyennes and the Suhtais once participated (Ottaway 1970, p. 96).

These materials give us some view of the social processes by which two peoples gave rise to common traditions. Although social changes and previous agricultural lifeways are imaged in the narratives, it is not clear that these traditions informed significant ritual processes. Traditions that did mediate basic symbolic forms and that informed important ritual activities came, for the Cheyennes, from the culture heroes.

## The Sweet Medicine Tradition

As a ritual of renewal of the people and their world, the ceremony of the sacred arrows gained prominence among the Cheyennes and assumed, along with the Sun Dance assimilated from the Suhtais, the status of a holy tradition. The historical generation and development of this ritual and its mythic framework may have taken place sometime after 1805, when the Cheyennes and the Suhtais camped just east of the Black Hills (Ottaway 1970, pp. 96–97). The meanings that informed the ritual and the people's experience find their rich expression in the tradition of Sweet Medicine, the Cheyenne culture hero. An analysis of this tradition will prepare us to understand some of the ways the meanings evoked in the ritual of the sacred arrows must have shaped the experience of the people.

There are many versions of the Sweet Medicine tradition, and this account is drawn from some of the earlier and more extensive renditions (Grinnell 1908, pp. 269–320; Dorsey 1905a, pp. 41–46; cf. Grinnell 1971, pp. 263–78, Grinnell 1972, vol.2, pp. 345–81; cf. also Powell 1969, pp. 460–71). In all of these traditions Sweet Medicine appears among the people as a child possessed of more than ordinary powers. As a very young boy, he seems to exhibit superior insight and knowledge (Grinnell 1971, p. 263) and, when he becomes an adult, he demonstrates the capacity to change forms, assuming at times the nature of a human being and at others the nature of an animal or other creature (Grinnell 1908, pp. 303–13).

Legend holds that Sweet Medicine and his brother lived longer than ordinary human beings. Some traditions say that Sweet Medicine lived among the people for five generations:

> All through the summer he was young, like a young man; and when fall came, and the grass began to dry up, he began to look older; and about the middle of the winter he was like a very old man, and walked bent over and crooked. In the spring he became young again. (Grinnell 1971, p. 277)

By contrast, the same tradition holds that Sweet Medicine's brother did not reflect the rhythm of the seasons but rather remained a middle-aged person until finally he died, having lived longer among the people than his brother. This tradition must have been widely distributed among the Cheyennes at the turn of the century, and as the ritual forms associated with the arrow ceremony were enacted, memories of the culture hero must have been evoked in the experience of many of the people. The seasonal rhythms of growth, maturation, and decline imaged in the life of Sweet Medicine may also reflect a motif associated with the people's earlier agricultural existence.

In its oral form, the Sweet Medicine tradition probably exhibited many variations, but recounting one of the recorded versions will fill out in more concrete form some of the motifs mentioned above. The meanings embodied in this tradition formed some of the most important contexts of interpretation and self understanding for the Cheyennes during their high culture period; these meanings continue, though in modified form, into the present (Powell 1969, vol. 2). Though the tradition exhibits a typical complexity, interconnecting with other domains of meaning, a central motif appears in the ritual process associated with the arrow bundle. These ritual forms center essentially upon the renewal of the people's moral universe.

In the particular version recounted here we see the central figure not only as culture hero, bringing the people their holy traditions, but also as Sweet Medicine, the trickster and master of the animals

(Grinnell 1972, pp. 345–81; this version is essentially the same as Grinnell 1908 and was originally published in 1923). The tradition opens with Sweet Medicine's extraordinary birth and shows him as a young boy attending a shaman's dance, there to demonstrate his superior powers.[1] At this dance, Sweet Medicine decapitated himself with his bow string. After his father put his head and body together under a buffalo robe, he rose up whole, shaking the robe four times symbolically. After this impressive demonstration of power, Sweet Medicine was involved in the wounding (some traditions say killing) of an important Cheyenne chief in an altercation over a buffalo robe. At this point, Sweet Medicine exhibited many trickster features as the young men of the tribe tried to capture him. Eluding them at every turn, the culture hero-trickster changed form, becoming first a coyote, then an owl, magpie, blackbird, and redbird. After many such adventures and much deprivation among the people, the culture hero brought the buffalo back to the Cheyennes.

Four years after Sweet Medicine had settled permanently in the camp, he and his wife set out on a long journey. They traveled to a high butte in the Black Hills (cf. Ottaway 1970). Entering into the butte through a mysterious rock door, the two human beings found themselves in what appeared to be a sacred lodge. The first object they saw was a coyote skin; then, four arrows feathered with hawk feathers, all pointing in the same direction. As they proceeded, they saw four different arrows feathered with eagle feathers. These arrows also pointed in the same direction. A Person who was in the lodge asked the culture hero which arrows he preferred. Sweet Medicine replied that he liked the eagle-feathered arrows best. Soon other Persons appeared in great numbers, instructing Sweet Medicine and his wife in the meaning and use of the arrows. The coyote hide was formed into a quiver for the arrows, and the quiver was wrapped in the hide of a four-year-old buffalo which had been killed in a ritual manner. In contrast to the Blackfeet, the sacred arrow bundle was not subject to successive transfers but remained in the custody of one virtuous man (Dorsey 1905a, p. 11). This man was set apart in traditional times by his bodily appearance, his flesh being ritually scarred, as well as by other special symbolism, such

[101]

as color (Grinnell 1910, p. 545). When the arrow keeper became old or unable because of illness to perform his sacred role, the arrow bundle was passed on to a successor designated by the keeper. The successor could be a son or relative, but, if such a person could not be found, then any male might come forward and seek to qualify himself for this central ritual office of the tribe (Grinnell 1910, p. 544). Bundle keepers stand in a kind of "apostolic succession" which is traced back to the activities of the sacred predecessor, Sweet Medicine himself (Dorsey 1905a, p. 3; cf. Grinnell 1910, p. 544). Indeed, it is not too much to say that "The keeper of the medicine arrows was in a sense the director of the tribe's affairs" (Grinnell 1910, p. 344).

Remaining four years in the sacred lodge, Sweet Medicine and his wife learned the ritual and symbolic meanings associated with the arrow bundle. When they emerged from the mountain, they brought people the renewing power available through the sacred bundle and its ritual. In this version Sweet Medicine's wife played a central role, receiving with him instruction from the Sacred Persons and bearing the bundle during the journey back to the people. This is interesting since the ceremony tended finally to exclude women, especially from viewing the sacred arrows. At the turn of the century, however, the entire family of the arrow keeper was considered sacred, as was his tipi, since it held the holy bundle (Dorsey 1905a, p. 11).

## The Ritual of the Sacred Arrows

It is not clear whether the arrow ritual was performed on a yearly basis or on the occasion of individual or social crisis. Some interpreters indicate that, at least in historic times, the ritual was performed annually (Dorsey 1905a, p. 5); others argue that the ceremony "was not annual like the medicine lodge, but took place when occasion seemed to demand" (Grinnell 1910, p. 546). Whether or not the arrow ritual was an annual event early in Cheyenne history, it was certainly performed in later times with considerably regularity. Like other Plains tribes, the Cheyenne social organization encouraged separation of the people into smaller units during the winter months, while the summer months witnessed the appearance of tribal organization and ritual forms (cf. Stands in Timber and Liberty 1967, pp. 36–37, n. 7). Being a tribal ceremony, the arrow ritual probably occurred during the time of the summer encampment.

The structure of the ritual and its shared symbolic forms give some insight into the religious and moral meanings that filled the experience of the Cheyennes during their high culture period. Rich indeed was the symbolism of form and color; and in important ways it is possible to view the Sweet Medicine tradition as being a general text for the ritual. A more detailed examination of the ritual process will bring these points into sharper focus.

The theme of sacrifice, which will appear in a prominent manner in the discussion of the ritual, is embodied symbolically and literally in the flesh of the arrow keeper—at least this was the custom in traditional days. The symbolism of the cardinal directions was evident on the arms, shoulders, thighs, back, and loins of the man performing this sacred role. From these areas of his body strips of flesh were cut; and in each of these body areas the number of cuts equaled the symbolic number four, evoking the powers of the cardinal directions. In addition, a strip of flesh was cut from the outside of each arm, extending from each wrist and passing up over the shoulders, from there to extend down each side of the chest until the cuts met in the center of the sternum. At the point where the cuts met, a round piece of flesh was extracted and immediately above this cut another crescent shaped piece of skin was taken out. Powerfully symbolizing the sun and moon, these scars reminded the people of the virtue of the person who kept the sacred arrows and of their power among the people (Grinnell 1910, pp. 544–45).

As we have seen in the case of other Plains tribes, important ritual activities often arose as a consequence of the vow of an individual. The arrow ceremony was pledged by an individual who then visited the other Cheyenne bands, informing them that an important religious event would soon occur at the time of the summer encampment. Because the arrow renewal was seen to have profound meaning for the welfare of the entire group, there was considerable social pressure motivating individuals and family groups to attend.

If individuals or groups resisted, the warrior societies intervened. Such resisters were subject to punishments, such as the destruction of their lodge poles or lodge covers and even the destruction of some or all of their horses (Grinnell 1910, p. 546). After the pledger had visited the Cheyenne bands, he returned to inform the arrow keeper that all was in readiness and that the renewal of the people could begin. The entire tribe then moved to a preselected campsite, forming themselves in the shape of a new moon circle (Dorsey 1905a, pp. 5–10). This basic tribal circle is the embodiment of root symbolic forms which will be enacted in the ritual process during the next four days.

On the first day, after the camp circle has been formed, the pledger sets up his tipi in the middle of the crescent, positioned on its lower edge. Now the people are invited to bring the sacrifices they deem appropriate. After all have brought something symbolizing their request to the sacred powers, the offerings are gathered together and hung above the door of what has now become the "sacrifice tipi."

Also on the first day a site at the center of the new moon circle is selected and upon this spot a lodge is erected. This lodge has the same shape as any other conical tipi, but it is perhaps twice to three times larger, being formed out of two or more lodge covers and from fifty to sixty poles. It is not difficult to discern the deep symbolic significance of this great Medicine Arrow lodge, especially if the Sweet Medicine tradition can be said to form a text for the ritual. Viewed in this manner, the sacred arrow lodge is the symbolic representation of the mountain the culture hero entered, there to learn the mysteries that were to form the life of the Cheyenne people. Within the Medicine Arrow lodge symbolic acts extend the efficaciousness of an earlier sacred moment into present social time and space.

On the second day of the arrow ceremony, the pledger and three other men take the people's sacrificial offerings into the huge arrow tipi, depositing them in front of an altar which has been constructed. Present in the sacred lodge are men of proven shamanistic power. After community sacrifices have been offered, four men proceed to the tipi of the arrow keeper; after receiving from him the arrow bundle, these men take the sacred object back to the company of shamans. At this point the bundle is opened and the work of renewal of the arrows begins. Feathers in need of repair are replaced and worn sinew is renewed. During the period of renewal, the warrior societies establish and maintain strict order in the camp. Significant is the fact that no women are allowed outside the tipis as long as the renewal ceremony is in progress. More will be said presently about this sexual exclusivity.

On the third day of the ceremony the shamans prepare sticks, made of willow, each of which represents a Cheyenne family. All day, into the night, and during part of the next day these sticks are passed through the smoke of incense fires which burn continually in front of the altar. This symbolic act evokes the central meanings which inform the ritual activity. Through the power of these symbolic forms "the whole tribe, band, family, individual, change for the better. Their courage and life are renewed" (Dorsey 1905a, p.5). The moral quality of the social world and of individual experience is believed to be deeply affected during this day of the ceremony.

On the afternoon of the fourth day, when the arrows have been renewed, the pledger takes a pole upon which the arrows are secured and places it upright in a hole in the ground. Two of the arrows point toward the sky, while two point toward the ground, suggesting symbolic associations with the holy people from whom Sweet Medicine first received the bundle: the Listeners-above-the-ground and the Listeners-under-the-ground (Grinnell 1910, p. 543). Communal offerings are also placed beside the pole, and at this point every Cheyenne male in the camp comes to view the arrows and to observe their renewed state. After the arrows have been viewed by all the men of the tribe, the arrow lodge is taken down and an even larger tipi is erected over the pole to which the arrows are secured. This lodge is called the Prophet's lodge, recalling the memory of Sweet Medicine as culture hero. After this lodge has been erected, the arrow bundle is returned to the tipi of the keeper. Then all men of proven shamanistic power gather in the huge tipi, there to sing four sacred songs. These are the same songs which, according to tradition, were taught to the people by Sweet Medicine. After singing, the main participants purify themselves in a sweat lodge. The Cheyenne social world has been renewed, individual moral virtues enhanced, and the quality of the corporate life assured for the year to come.

In a ritual as complex as the arrow ceremony, it is inevitable that various meanings will be evoked in the experience of the people. Some of these meanings are associated with the historical experience of the Cheyennes, and others with important aspects of the social structure.

Two of the sacred arrows were traditionally associated with the buffalo and two with humans. This clearly reflects the relationship of the people with their food supply and the concern to maintain social existence in the face of enemies. In their historical context, the arrows may be viewed as a powerful means of controlling the buffalo as well as efficacious war medicines.

Traditions tell of times when the arrows were used as a means of procuring buffalo. On these occasions the arrows were pointed at the buffalo, making them confused and causing them to mill about aimlessly. Cheyenne hunters, who possessed no horses, could kill as many animals as the group needed. Animals killed through the power of the arrows were butchered in a ritual manner: every portion was taken except the head, the backbone, and the tail. These body parts were left intact, connected together as they had been during the animal's life (Dorsey 1905a, p. 2). Such ritual butchering may reflect continuity with older Algonquian hunting practices. These older motifs connect ritual acts, such as the disposition of the animal's bones, with the continuing availability of the game upon which the group was dependent (Speck 1977, pp. 123–24). If further evidence were available, it might be possible to see a connection between such practices and the image of the Master of the Animals. Although such associations are largely speculative at this point, some of the evidence points clearly in this interpretative direction. It is also interesting, in light of the Yellow Haired Woman tradition, that this view of killing animals attempts to maintain appropriate relationships with those beings whose life and flesh contribute to the people's welfare.

In relation to enemies, the arrows possessed power to assure victory for the people and their continued existence as a group. This belief is inconsistent with the historical evidence, however, for in the six known moves of the arrows against enemies, only two proved successful (Grinnell 1910, p. 571).[2] Empirical evidence did little to dissuade the Cheyennes of the power of the arrows, however. When the group had been injured by another tribe, they moved as a whole on the warpath, confident that the arrow bundle, along with the sacred hat given them by Erect Horns, would ensure their success. The song that the arrow keeper sang as he pointed the arrows in the direction of an enemy is a powerful summary of this confidence:

> There you lie helpless
> Easily (to be) annihilated.

(Grinnell 1910, p. 572)

Despite its complex association with nourishment and war, the arrow renewal ritual also centered fundamentally upon the moral renewal of the Cheyenne social world. Other important activities took place during this propitious time in the life of the group: the sick were treated in sweat lodges especially erected for this purpose, doctors renewed and mixed their medicines, and men found this an especially powerful time to renew their shields or to make new ones (Grinnell 1910, p. 548). The social bonds within the group were also strengthened:

> The occasion was one of kindliness and good feeling among them; feasting went on continually, and men, women, and children visited one another and renewed old friendships; while relatives saw their young kinsfolk whom they had never met before. (Grinnell 1910, p. 547)

One aspect of the social structure is clearly reflected in the arrow ceremony: it is sexually exclusive, being a male activity. Some interpreters have claimed that the sacred hat was a powerful female symbol, complimenting the arrows (Grinnell 1910, pp. 542–43); others have stressed the way sexual exclusion functioned to maintain male dominance over females, as well as to legitimate other structures of authority, such as chiefs, elders, and shamans (Hoebel 1978, p. 18). Some interpreters have rationalized the complementarity between male and female symbolism in an elaborate manner (Powell 1969, vol.2, p. 444). Still others have provided a Marxist analysis of the role of women in Plains cultures (Klein, in Wood and Liberty 1980, pp. 133–35).[3] We have noted some of the roles women played in cultural activities in earlier chapters, stressing their place in the mythology and in the vision quest, but it is necessary to provide some further view of this problem.

Although it is possible to acknowledge critical aspects of the subordination of women in nineteenth-century Plains societies, it is nevertheless true that women played important roles in the religious life of the people. The general point to be made is that women not only seek visions and engage in shamanistic activities but that they also are fundamentally linked with men in rituals of social and world renewal (Weist, in Wood and Liberty 1980, p. 260). Furthermore, the exclusion of women from direct participation in the arrow ceremony did not exclude them from the benefits of social and moral renewal. And, as we shall see, a woman plays a central role in the cosmic renewal which occurs in the Sun Dance. We shall return to these considerations in the following chapter. Now, however, we must turn to an analysis of the ritual through which the Crow social world was renewed.

## The Crow Tobacco Society

An ancient Crow ritual which focuses upon both the renewal of the social world and of nature revolves around the tobacco plant. Despite the almost universal practice of smoking on the Plains, the special tobacco plant that was nurtured and ritually harvested by the Crows was not smoked. This plant was especially sacred, and only the seeds were preserved to be planted again in the subsequent season.[4] The symbolism of planting and harvesting, deriving from their previous agricultural existence, survived in Crow social structures. The traditions that preserved the sedimented memory of their separation from the Hidatsas spoke of two brothers who took their different paths in life (recall the Cheyenne traditions). One brother was destined to live by Tobacco (Crows), while the other brother was destined to live by the Pipe, Corn, and Pumpkin (Hidatsas). As we shall see, the meaning that tobacco came to have for the Crows transcended the limits of strictly agricultural activities (Lowie 1920, p. 177; cf. n. 1).

Though the ritual process was believed to benefit all of the people, planting and harvesting of sacred Tobacco were restricted to a special group, the Tobacco Society. This society was unique to the Crows and was probably of ancient origin—older, even, than the Sun Dance (Lowie 1920, p. 195; Simms 1904, p. 331). It is also probable that the society was more exclusive in earlier times as compared with its size in the nineteenth century. Following an ancient Crow cultural pattern, subdivisions of the society arose as a consequence of individual visions. By the turn of the century, the society had grown quite large (Lowie 1935, p. 276; Lowie 1920, p. 135). Growth was also accompanied by another ancient Crow cultural motif, the notion of adoption. The motivation to adopt new members was quite powerful, and the ritual surrounding the ceremony very complex.

Because of the interests of earlier observers, descriptions of the adoption and initiation of new members received a great deal of attention (see Lowie 1920, pp. 132ff.). Important as this material is, we will focus more attention upon the ritual processes surrounding planting and harvesting, as well as upon the meanings that seem to be evoked by means of the ritual.

Two themes related to the adoption process need to be mentioned, however, since they bear upon elements of central importance to the analysis. The first theme concerns the birth imagery informing the adoption ritual. This imagery is consistent with the idea of the renewal of life, and it associates that renewal with fertility symbolism. The relationship between the persons adopting and the persons adopted was one of kinship, father and mother to children; both a man and his wife were adopted together. The typical phrase used by a husband toward his wife was infused with birth imagery: "In my company they caused her to be born. . . ." (Lowie 1935, p. 277). The second theme concerns the symbolism of the Tobacco Society adoption lodge, and especially the altar that occupied its center. The lodge was constructed of ten poles, joined at the top, and positioned so as to allow sunlight to enter from the east, a persistent solar motif. The altar was a rectangular plot of cleared ground, bordered by willow arches, outside of which were placed logs of equal length. The space inside the borders was covered with rows of juniper sprigs (Lowie 1920, pp. 143–44). The altar evokes an image of a fertile garden—perhaps symbolizing the garden in which the sacred seeds will be planted. At an even deeper level the meanings have to do with the renewal of the Crow social world as well as the natural context surrounding that world.

Some interpreters have argued that the Tobacco Society does not exhibit significant solar and astral imagery (Lowie 1935, pp. 295–96). The resonance of these images is apparent in the ritual, however. The presence of this material does not represent a secondary accretion, but rather what may have been primary in the oral tradition and in the experience of the people. We recall a strong association in the oral traditions between the sacred Tobacco and stars. The most obvious place where such associations appear was in the Crow creation account, which contained both solar and astral motifs (Lowie 1918, pp. 14–16). In this account the creator was identified as the Sun. Also in this version we met certain creatures who possessed supernatural power: the wolf, the coyote, and the rock, "the oldest part of the earth" (Lowie 1918, p. 15).

Another creature appeared in this oral tradition, first in the form of a human being and then in the form of a plant, the sacred Tobacco. Identifying this being as one of the stars, Sun said on behalf of the human beings (Crows):

> From now on all the people shall have this, take it in the spring and raise it. It is the stars above that have assumed this form, and they will take care of you. This is the Tobacco plant. Take care of it and it will be the means of your living. (Lowie: 1918, p. 15)

The narrator of this version connected the creation account with a story of a young man who was adopted by Sun and who brought the Tobacco Society to the people (Lowie 1920, pp. 188–89).

Additional origin narratives, despite their individual variations, all associate tobacco with astral motifs (Lowie 1920, pp. 177–89). In some of these traditions there are references to specific constellations, such as the Dipper, or to specific stars, such as Morning Star (Lowie 1920, p. 185). Those who heard these traditions recited must have experienced a sense of transcendence evoked by the symbolic forms borne in the ritual. The content of such experiences had to do with the concrete astral and solar symbolism we have discussed. As for the Blackfeet, such symbolic forms were echoed and reinforced in other areas of experience. For example, these motifs appeared consistently in the sweat lodge ritual associated with the Tobacco Society ceremonies (Lowie 1920, p. 141). Since symbolic forms are multivalent and since oral tradition was fluid, it is impossible finally to interpret precisely how these meanings appeared in individual experience. The general description of these meanings, however, leads to some sense of the flavor of Crow experience within the context of the Tobacco Society.

Preparation of the tobacco seeds for planting was done by a mixer, a man or woman who occupied a prominent place in the ritual process. The tobacco was prepared for planting by mixing the seeds with elk or buffalo dung and a variety of roots, flowers, and wild onions. Often a pipe was lighted, and sacred smoke was blown into the container with the seeds and other materials. The preparation of tobacco was usually done for each subdivision of the society by its own mixer, although in some instances subdivisions might share a single mixer.

The location of the garden was decided on the basis of a vision, though in an interesting manner in the light of previous analysis. In this case, the mixers gathered together and shared their dreams concerning appropriate locations. A decision emerged out of a kind of "vision concensus." After the decision was made, the tribe moved toward the location, which was usually at the foot of a mountain range. It is interesting to observe that the vision concensus also conforms to the general Crow attitude toward experiences of transcendence through dreams. Each individual had access to power. Thus, it was important to attend to all reports of such experiences, since all were potentially significant and none had presumptive authority over another. At the meeting of the mixers, then, any member of the group was permitted to report his or her dream concerning the location of the garden. Although dream interpretation was routinized to a certain extent, there was room for innovation, since vision was given an independent authority no matter where it appeared. In this case, however, the authority of individual dreams was restricted to a particular social group, the mixers. Presumably, individual dream experiences of persons outside this group would not have bearing on the choice of the garden site.

After the selection of a site for the garden, the entire tribe moved to a location nearby (Lowie 1920, p. 162). Now the members of the Tobacco Society, sometimes accompanied by other tribal members, began their symbolic movement toward the garden site. This procession was led by a woman who held before her the skin of a beaver or otter, water animals who had power to bring nourishment from the sky to the growing crop (Curtis 1909, pp. 65–66). Again there is an important symbolic association of women not only with fertility but also with tribal welfare in general. In the Tobacco Society itself, women functioned not only as mixers but also as singers, dancers, body painters, and as leaders of the procession to the garden site (Lowie 1920, p. 195).

As the procession moved toward the garden site, the group stopped four times, reflecting the symbolic significance of the cardinal directions (Lowie 1920, p. 165). Upon reaching the site, the ground was prepared and the seeds planted, each row being identified with a particular planting group. Miniature sweat houses were constructed at the garden site as a symbol of purification (Lowie 1920, pp. 172–73). These small sweat houses were believed to be more powerful than the larger versions, and the incense from their altars rose as a prayer for the growth of a good crop. This symbolism served to remind all of the people of the significance of events that were unfolding in the garden. In addition to the small sweat lodges, a larger one was also constructed at the garden site. Members of the Society regularly entered this lodge for ritual purification, and their experience was normally infused by images deriving from basic solar motifs (Lowie 1920, p. 173). In addition, young men were allowed to sleep at the garden site in the hope that power would be mediated to them through their dreams.

Between the time of planting and the harvest, several visits were made to the garden and reports brought back to the people. During this period the Tobacco Society had frequent dances in order to induce the plants to grow faster (Lowie 1920, p. 174). When the plants were ready, members of the Society returned to the garden for the harvest. Using pieces of wood rather than their fingers, they removed the seed cases, exposing their sacred contents. The power of these seeds was so great that the people believed contact with them might bring on rashes or other more serious ailments. After the harvest, the tobacco stems and leaves were mixed with meat and ordinary tobacco and thrown into a creek or river (Lowie 1920, pp. 175–76; Simms 1904, p. 335). The seeds were preserved to be planted the next year. Especially sacred were the seeds that bore the mark of a small white cross, evoking the image of Morning Star (Lowie 1935, p. 281).

Though the planting and harvesting were restricted to members of the Tobacco Society, the sacred plant was believed to be beneficial for all the people (Lowie 1920, pp. 191, 194; Lowie 1935, p. 176). Through the layered symbolism of birth and growth imagery, we are able to see horizons of transcendent meaning that were absolutely essential for Crow life. As the plant appeared above the ground and moved through its growth stages, the spiritual forms of Crow life were themselves renewed. In addition to the renewal of the social world, there is further evidence that the renewal associated with the sacred Tobacco included as well the restoration of all living beings, plant and animal alike (Lowie 1920, p. 190).

The renewal of the social world and the renewal of nature are fundamentally associated in the ritual process and its basic symbolic forms. In a profound sense, the garden symbolized the yearly renewal of life through the agency of a sacred plant. The flowering of Tobacco evoked an experience of the flowering of new life in the social and natural worlds. This interpretation recalls Sun's words spoken about Tobacco in the creation narrative: "Take care of it and it will be the means of your living" (Lowie 1918, p. 15).

The process of general renewal, both of nature and of the moral universe, engendered through the arrow ritual and the Tobacco ceremony, must also be viewed more specifically. As earlier suggested, such rituals embodied the symbolic forms which were constitutive of Plains cultures. And these symbolic forms gave rise to a world within which the complex interrelations among humans and transcendent beings were sustained through social time. The quality of these relations was culturally defined and was differently nuanced for each group. But cultural values associated with kinship are the general symbolic ground which seems widely shared. This interpretation will be given further support through an analysis of the greatest of all tribal rituals on the Northwestern Plains—the Sun Dance.

CHAPTER 6

# Renewing the World

THE SUN DANCE IS A COMPLEX of ritual and symbolic form which
evokes a common sense of transcendence in the experience of the
people. The ritual is focused upon the dimensions of meaning that
thematize cosmic renewal. When combined with the moral renewal
discussed in the last chapter, the Sun Dance evokes processes of
cosmic renewal that support and deepen shared symbolic forms.
    Although the Sun Dance and the motif of world renewal are
widely shared on the Plains, the way they are articulated and experienced is nuanced differently. Experiences of transcendence are re-
fracted through particular histories and among people who have
developed specialized institutional responses to their environment.
Only through an examination of these particularities can we come
to an understanding of the Sun Dance as a celebration that reflects

a relationship between specific historical experiences and themes in human communities which approach the universal.

It was at the time of the summer encampment, when all of the various bands of the tribe came together, that the Sun Dance was normally performed. A ceremony of great complexity, the Sun Dance was surrounded by a number of related and interlocking activities. For example, among the Blackfeet, some of the larger bundles were transferred during the summer encampment; persons who had various diseases were treated by doctors or shamans; and dances were performed by the various men's societies. The summer encampment was also a time of intense social activity. It was the time of the tribal hunt, when sufficient food had to be gathered against the winter months; it was a time for socializing and feasting, as well as a time for the rehearsal of ancient traditions; it was a time when courtships occurred and marriages were consummated; it was a time when youth aspired to imitate their elders as they listened to stories of daring deeds and of coups counted on the warpath; and it was a time for telling stories of origins and destiny, as well as a time when children and adults listened avidly to tales of Trickster's exploits and foibles. Among the Blackfeet, the great tribal encampment lasted for a period of from two to four months, culminating with the Sun Dance, after which the tribe split up into smaller units and moved off toward their winter camping grounds (Wissler 1918, p. 268).

The focus of this chapter will be upon experiences that will extend and deepen the understanding of moral and religious meanings introduced in earlier chapters. Again what we will seek to do is interpret ritual and symbolic form in relation to oral tradition, treating this complex as an integral whole, thus putting back together what earlier interpreters have often analytically separated. We will continue to seek to understand how moral and religious experience had a role in the formation of attitudes, dispositions, and forms of behavior. Finally, we will show that the Sun Dance ritually reconciles some of the moral tensions apparent in the cosmologies. Specifically, the moral ambiguities expressed in the creation traditions concerning killing and eating of animals are ritually reconciled.

# The Blackfoot Sun Dance

We begin our specific discussion with an analysis of the Blackfoot Sun Dance. This beginning point is appropriate because the Blackfeet illustrate a form that is fundamentally associated with a bundle and its transfer. The Crows also share this feature, but in their case the traditional Sun Dance focuses more on the theme of revenge rather than on renewal, as we earlier indicated. Cheyenne and Arapaho Sun Dance forms also involve bundles, but in the Blackfoot case the principle of transfer is prominent and the relationship between bundle, ritual, and oral tradition is very close. In the discussion of the Blackfoot Sun Dance, we will begin with external description, moving from this toward an examination of some of the religious and moral meanings evoked by ritual and symbolic form.

The role of a sacred woman in the initiation of the Blackfoot Sun Dance is central and essential (Wissler 1918, pp. 231–34). Indeed, if such a woman did not come forward, the Sun Dance could not occur; and yet in traditional times there was not a year when a woman qualified to perform this sacred role failed to appear. The woman who initiated the ritual process, and who played such a central role in its articulation, did so by means of a vow. The vow was made to Sun during a time of illness or other family crisis. The essence of the vow was a promise to sponsor the ritual if the crisis was resolved. A man might also make such a vow, but it usually took the form of a pledge to support his wife in performing her role as the sacred woman. After a woman or her husband had made such a vow, then the woman, in the company of a medicine man, announced her intent in the midst of the camp, thus making public her commitment.

> Listen Sun. Pity me. You have seen my life. You know that I am pure. I have never committed adultery with any man. Now, therefore, I ask you to pity me. I will build you a lodge. Let my son survive. Bring him back to health, so that I may build this lodge for you. (Grinnell 1962, p. 264)

The theme of marital virtue which appears in this prayer is the central and essential qualification, without which no woman can aspire to the office of the sacred person. From a certain viewpoint, it may be true that the elevation of marital fidelity supported important cultural values and the family as a social institution. But it is also true that such purity is only a special case of the general condition that humans must assume before they enter into experiences of transcendence. This theme appears clearly in the rituals of the sweat lodge and the vision quest, as well as in the purification that took place daily at the family smudge altar and periodically in connection with the handling of bundles. Despite tensions at the level of actual moral practice, the Sun Dance provided support for a normative understanding of the moral life and of cultural values.

After the vow was made, and in preparation for the enactment of the Sun Dance, the sacred woman and her husband gathered a ritual food which occupied a central place in the ceremony. This food was the buffalo tongue, and the preparation and gathering of the tongues had to be done in an appropriate manner. According to one description, the husband followed the hunters, and, when he found a hunter butchering, he would sit down before him, pray for him, and offer him a pipe. Then the hunter would give him the tongue. This process continued until, according to tradition, one hundred tongues had been gathered. The tongues were then ritually prepared by a group of women who had also made a vow. Their vow, like that of the sacred woman, thematized the notion of marital fidelity. After the tongues had been sliced and boiled, they were reserved for later use as sacramental food in the Sun Dance (Wissler 1918, pp. 235ff.).

The vow made to the Sun also involved the obligation to acquire, through a transfer ceremony, the natoas or Sun Dance bundle.[1] The economic aspects of this obligation were considerable, and such a burden upon the woman and her relatives could become onerous. Even though the opening of this bundle was a central part of the ceremony, and must be so treated, it is necessary first to have some view of the material objects which composed a typical natoas.

The most important items in the bundle were the headdress, which was worn by the woman, and a digging stick, which was painted with sacred red paint. The basis in oral tradition that informs these items will be discussed later. In addition to the two primary items, a typical bundle might include the skins of various animals and birds, painting materials, a badger skin for wrapping the headdress, a rawhide case for the headdress, and a robe or other covering for the entire bundle. The headdress might be constructed on a rawhide base which represented a lizard, a creature that has power to control the rain. On the front of the headdress there was often a weasel skin and a small bag containing tobacco seeds. The edge of the headdress might be decorated with strips of white weasel skin, and projecting from the base were often the plumes of the eagle or raven (Wissler 1912, pp. 209–11).[2]

After the various hunting bands had been notified about the Sun Dance and had gathered in a great camp circle, the summer proceeded routinely with its economic and social activities until the time "when the service berries are ripe" (Wissler 1918, p. 231). At this point, the entire tribe began a series of four symbolic moves toward the site where the Sun lodge was to be built (Wissler 1918, pp. 230–31). The general pattern seems to have been as follows: On the move of the first day, the sacred woman began a fast which signaled the beginning of the Sun Dance. On this day a hundred-willow sweat lodge was made by one of the men's societies, and the tongues which had been collected and ritually prepared were sung and prayed over. The move of the second day took the group closer to the Sun Dance site, and on this day the tongues were honored again in song and prayer. In addition, a second hundred-willow sweat house was constructed. The third day continued in much the same fashion, and on the fourth day, as had been the case on the third day, a final hundred-willow sweat lodge was constructed. The singing and praying which proceeded in the tipi of the sacred woman continued, as did her fast.

Having reached the Sun Dance encampment on the fourth day, the fifth day was filled with activity. On this day, following a prescribed division of labor, the bands cut poles and cottonwood boughs to be used in the construction of the Sun's lodge. The center pole was cut in a ritual manner, to be discussed later. In addition to this activity, the transfer of the natoas bundle was under way in the sacred woman's tipi. This transfer was performed by four persons: the sacred woman and her husband, called the son and daughter, received the bundle from the previous owner and her husband, known as the mother and father. Finally, at the end of the fifth day, at the approach of the setting sun, groups approached the site from the four quarters, raising the Sun pole first and then placing the rafters into their proper arrangement.

On the sixth day a structure was made within the Sun's lodge to house persons possessing special powers to control the rain. Now began a series of activities, such as dancing to the Sun, torture ceremonies, praying over and painting supplicants, and dancing by the various societies. These activities might continue until the eighth day, or even several days beyond that point. Though this is a very general view of the structure of activity, variations occurred among the Blackfoot divisions and also over time, especially after the people were confined to reservations (Grinnell 1962, pp. 263–68; McClintock 1968, chaps. 12, 14, 16, 21–23).

## Blackfoot Sun Dance Traditions

We must now bring into view the dimensions of meaning evoked in the symbolic acts which make up the ritual of the Sun Dance. On the first level we must seek to envision the elements of the oral tradition that inform the general structure we have described. In this process we shall begin to glimpse some of the dimensions of transcendent meaning which filled the experience of the people, shaping attitudes, dispositions, and patterns of behavior. In addition, we can extend our understanding of paradigms of religious and moral meaning which are reflected in certain elements of the ritual process. Once again, the dynamism of the oral tradition was such that there is no "standard version" of myths of origin, for example; but there are sedimented themes which seem to be widely shared among the people. Even in the present, after years of acculturation, many of the Blackfeet know large portions of these traditions. And there are also strong indications that the ancient ritual of the Sun Dance is undergoing a contemporary renaissance (Hungry Wolf 1980, p. 31).

In chapter four we indicated how some of the more important bundles among the Blackfeet are believed to derive from either sky-

or underwater-beings, such as Thunder and Beaver. According to some traditions, the natoas is the sky bundle par excellence, its ultimate origin being Sun himself. There are other elements of the tradition, however, which associate its origins with underwater creatures as well. This is natural since the natoas was once connected with the beaver bundle. Still other traditions associate the bundle with Elk. The symbolic associations evoked by the natoas bundle are quite extensive and finally include not only sky- and underwater-beings, but animals, the earth, and humans—the entire creation. These general observations will become clearer as we proceed to an examination of the traditions in greater detail.[3]

A persistent set of traditions accounting for the origin of the natoas bundle appears in the Elk Woman cycle (Wissler 1912, pp. 211–14; Wissler and Duvall 1908, pp. 83–85). These traditions attribute the origins of the bundle to a powerful animal, the Elk, who transfers the bundle and its power to a woman after having seduced her (recall the power of the Elk horn over Thunder). Whatever the reason for its persistence, the tradition does underline a prominent element in Blackfoot consciousness, which is the belief that Elk had power over women. Another tradition, that of the Otter Woman, associates the rise of the bundle with beaver power (Wissler and Duvall 1908, pp. 78–79). In this tradition, Otter Woman goes down among the beavers, who later transfer the natoas bundle to the woman and her husband. Both of these traditions associate the Sun Dance bundle with the power of important animals, and, in the case of the Otter Woman tradition, we see elements of the earlier association of the natoas with the beaver bundle.[4]

Another persistent and perhaps more extensive tradition associates the rise of the natoas with sky-beings—the Sun, Moon, and Morning Star. One such tradition concerns Cuts-Wood, a poor boy whose sister had married and who was now alone, without relatives. Because of Cuts-Wood's pitiful condition, Morning Star came down and became his childhood friend. They played together continually, and in their play Morning Star constructed a sweat house, the lodge for the sacred woman, the Sun's lodge, and the booth for the weather dancers. In addition to the play Sun Dance lodge, Morning Star sang the songs associated with the ritual. When Cuts-

Wood grew up, he and his sister built a Sun lodge among the people. He taught his sister the importance of marital virtue as the ground for her vow, as well as the centrality of the buffalo tongues to the ceremony. As a consequence, then, of a child's play with a transcendent being, the present ritual of the Sun Dance originated (Wissler and Duvall 1908, pp. 66–68).

An additional set of traditions which accounted for the rise of the Sun Dance and the natoas bundle concerned either the plot of a woman who married a star or the plot of a poor young man who traveled to the Sun's lodge in order to have a terrible scar removed from his face. In some versions the star-husband tradition is combined with the Scar-Face tradition (McClintock 1968, pp. 491ff.). We shall examine each of these versions separately and then see how they are combined in at least one instance. In all versions of this tradition, the prominence of the Sun, Moon, and Morning Star is obvious. Although elements of the natoas bundle are accounted for in these traditions, they concern as well the rise of major dimensions of the Sun Dance ritual. The Scar-Face tradition also has culture-hero significance among the Blackfeet. This significant predecessor brought some of the people's most sacred ritual forms. Also both the star-husband and the Scar-Face traditions establish a kinship relationship between sky-beings and the people.

The star-husband motif is widespread on the Plains and may have originated sometime in the eighteenth century, although it is difficult to estimate its age with precision (Dundes 1965, p. 457). In one Blackfoot version, the major themes appear in a particular configuration which is widespread in North American Indian folklore. This configuration includes four elements: a prohibition, the violation of the prohibition, the consequences that flow from the violation, and the attempt to escape from the consequences (Dundes 1965, p. 209). The fourth element does not appear as clearly in some of the traditions as do the other dimensions. With these elements in mind, let us examine a particular star-husband plot.

The narrative opens with the scene of two women sleeping outside (Wissler and Duvall 1908, pp. 58–61). They woke up early and saw Morning Star in the pre-dawn sky. One woman was so impressed with the beauty of this astral being that she expressed the desire to marry him. Subsequently, Morning Star appeared to the woman in human form, and she went away with him to live in the Sun's lodge. When they arrived, Moon gave her daughter-in-law a digging stick, telling her that she could dig any turnips she wished except a very large and impressive one (prohibition). That turnip, said Moon, is *natojiwa,* sacred or holy. At this point we have the foundation in oral tradition for the presence of the root digger as a part of the natoas bundle, as well as the association with a sacred plant. It is also clear why the etymology of the term *natoas* associates together the meanings referring to sun power and turnip (Wissler 1912, p. 209).

The daughter-in-law was fascinated by the large and impressive turnip. Finally she disobeyed Moon's warning, digging up the turnip with the assistance of a female crane, Crane-Woman (violation). After teaching the daughter-in-law the ritual and songs associated with the digging stick, Crane-Woman moved in a sunwise direction around the turnip. After three feints toward the sacred object, she dug it up on the fourth movement. Looking through the hole left by the turnip, the daughter-in-law saw the earth below and the lodges of her people. She returned to the Sun's lodge with the digging stick and the sacred turnip, telling her husband, Morning Star, what had happened. Angered by her disobedience, the star-husband said that she could no longer remain with the sky people but must return to her own kind (consequence).

Taking with her the son who had been born, she descended from the sky on a spider's web. Before leaving the sky, Morning Star told her that she must not let the child touch the ground for fourteen days, otherwise the child would be transformed into a fixed star (prohibition). Also the star-husband told his wife to make the sign of Morning Star on the back of her tipi in order to remind her of his command. After returning to earth, the young woman was careful to obey Morning Star's interdiction. On the thirteenth day, however, she left the baby with his grandmother, who did not understand the importance of the prohibition. The boy touched the ground (violation), was transformed into a star, and went to fill up the hole in the sky left by the removal of the sacred turnip (consequence). The narrative ends with the woman's death, many years later, as a consequence of an unnamed mistake which she made at a Sun Dance ceremony.

Another tradition that associates the rise of the Sun Dance with sky-beings is the Scar-Face narrative. There are many versions of this tradition among the Blackfeet, but the plot is rather consistent (Wissler and Duvall 1908, pp. 61–65; Wissler 1918, pp. 269–70; Curtis 1911, pp. 59–60; McClintock 1968, pp. 491–500; and Josselin De Jong 1914, pp. 80–82). The central character of this narrative was a poor young man who wanted to marry a beautiful chief's daughter. The young man was disfigured by an ugly scar on his face, but the young woman agreed to marry him if he could find a way to remove the scar. Scar-Face decided to journey to Sun's lodge in search of a cure. After a long journey Scar-Face reached his destination, where he became close friends with Sun's son, Morning Star. In a sweat-house ritual involving Sun, Morning Star, and Scar-Face, the boy's face was healed. He so resembled Morning Star that Moon mistook Scar-Face for her own son; thereafter, Scar-Face was known as Mistaken Morning Star.

After being healed, Scar-Face and Morning Star had a number of adventures which had the outcome of ridding the sky country of dangerous creatures. On one occasion, when Sun had warned the boys not to go toward the west, Morning Star was convinced by Scar-Face to disobey the command. In the west they were attacked by seven white geese. Scar-Face killed the geese, ridding the sky country of their danger. On another occasion the boys went west again, where they were attacked by seven cranes. Scar-Face also killed the cranes, and as a consequence Sun gave him a bundle containing a shirt and some leggings. Sun painted seven black stripes on the leggings as a sign that Scar-Face had killed the dangerous enemies.

When Scar-Face returned to his people, he constructed a sweat house and transferred the bundle of clothing which Sun had given him to one of his closest friends. This is the origin tradition of the weasel-tail suit, which was marked with stripes symbolizing the killing of the birds and which was to be worn only by those who had demonstrated their bravery. In addition, the tradition accounts for the origin of the sweat house from the Sun; and it identifies the

Sun Dance structure with the lodge of the Sun where Scar-Face received his miraculous cure. "After a time," the narrative con- cludes, "Scar-Face went back and became a star" (Wissler and Du- vall 1908, p. 65).

In another version of the Scar-Face narrative, additional details appear (Grinnell 1962, pp. 93–103). The basic structure of the tra- dition is the same, although in this case the young woman whom Scar-Face wishes to marry "belongs" to the Sun. In a vision she was told by Sun that she must not marry; this element is an additional factor causing Scar-Face to journey to the Sun. The narrative un- folds in much the same manner as the other versions, but it is more explicit in its association of the Sun Dance with Sun himself, and it provides considerable detail concerning the imagery surrounding other central motifs of the ritual. Sun indicates to Scar-Face, for example, that the buffalo is the most sacred animal and that the most sacred part of the buffalo is the tongue. Berries are to be considered sacred, marking out another part of the plant world and surround- ing it with transcendent horizons of meaning. Both the buffalo and berries are to be regarded and used with the respect due to sacred things. Sun also revealed to Scar-Face what must be done if any of the people were in trouble or need. In times of crisis, said Sun, they must vow to construct a sacred lodge.

> You shall build the lodge like the world, round, with walls, but first you must build a sweat house of a hundred sticks. It shall be like the sky . . . and half of it shall be painted red. That is me. The other half you will paint black. That is the night. (Grinnell 1962, p. 101)

After revealing these things, Sun healed the boy's ugly scar, giv- ing him two raven feathers which would be a sign to the young woman that she could now marry. In addition, Sun commanded that these feathers be worn by the husband of the woman who pledged the Sun Dance. Morning Star and Sun gave the young man additional gifts, and, as he was preparing to leave, Moon cried and embraced him as her own son. Following the Wolf Trail (Milky Way), Scar-Face returned to his people and married the young

woman who had formerly been pledged to Sun. Soon they constructed the first Medicine Lodge, as Sun had commanded.

> The Sun was glad. He gave them great age. They were never sick.
> When they were very old, one morning, their children said:
> "Awake! Rise and eat." They did not move. In the night, in sleep,
> without pain, their shadows had departed for the Sand Hills.
> (Grinnell 1962, p. 103)

The tradition ends with Scar-Face and his wife performing the role
of culture heroes, bringing the traditions of the Sun Dance to the
people. In this instance, however, the culture heroes die as human
beings rather than returning to the sky to become stars.

The last version of the Scar-Face tradition which we shall discuss reveals further nuances that show how dynamic were the oral
traditions among the people.[5] This narrative begins with the star-
husband tradition and then weaves it together with the Scar-Face
tradition (McClintock 1968, pp. 491–500). The details of the marriage of a woman, Feather Woman, with Morning Star are similar
to the previous traditions. In this version, however, Feather Woman
became pregnant and was derided by the people before she was
taken up into the sky on the spider's web. Upon their arrival at the
Sun's lodge, Moon gave Feather Woman a buckskin dress which
was trimmed in elk teeth; in addition she gave her elk-teeth wristlets
and a robe of elk skin which was painted with sacred red paint.
Clearly this tradition reflects the Elk Woman motifs of other narratives.

After Feather Woman's son, Star Boy, was born, Moon gave her
the sacred digging stick along with the warning not to dig up the
large and impressive turnip. As in the other versions, Feather
Woman disobeyed this command, and she and Star Boy were let
down to earth upon the web of the Spider Man. Before his wife
returned to earth, Morning Star gave her the sacred natoas headdress. This tradition has accounted for the major ritual objects included in the natoas bundle in a single narrative, as compared with
the origin of parts of the bundle being accounted for by several
distinct traditions. The story also shows how the constructive imagination of the raconteur shaped the content of oral tradition.

Feather Woman finally died, as did her parents, leaving Star Boy alone and very poor. As he grew older, a strange scar spread across his face and he was named by the people Scar-Face, in derision. Then the tradition continues with the theme of Scar-Face's journey to the Sun, his friendship with Morning Star, and their adventures together. Star Boy was finally appointed by Sun to take the ritual of the Sun's lodge to the people. Both Scar-Face and his wife returned to the Sun's lodge after they had been married on earth and had delivered the sacred traditions to the people. The Sun made Scar-Face just like Morning Star, so that they were very difficult to tell apart. When Scar-Face (Jupiter) rises first, he is often mistaken for his father, Morning Star (Venus). Thus, as in other traditions, Scar-Face is often called Mistaken Morning Star. From this time onward, the people could see first the appearance of Scar-Face in the dawning sky, then his father, Morning Star, after which they could anticipate the rising of grandfather Sun.

The Blackfoot apprehension of the world as revealed in these traditions continues the theme of kinship between humans and transcendent beings. The cosmic vision mediated in the solar, lunar, and astral imagery amounts to a kind of "sacred family," the Sun, Moon, and Morning Star. These beings established a relationship with humans, and the social world became connected in an organic way with a world of transcendent beings. Contemporaries with humans are not only those other humans with whom social relations are pursued; contemporary as well are the Sun, Moon, and Morning Star, along with other significant constellations, such as the Dipper and Pleiades. These figures were also experienced as significant predecessors, beings who performed important deeds in the past. Other important predecessors, such as the culture hero, Scar-Face, brought to the people their most important ritual forms. The traditions we have reviewed evoke in experience a reality sense concerning this culture hero and these transcendent beings; and their narration enables persons to maintain this sensibility over generational time.

In addition to the sacred family, there was also a whole range of sky-beings, principal of which was Thunder. Also included were such important birds as the eagle, raven, and owl. And among the earth-beings there were important animals, such as the bear, buffalo, wolf, and horse. In the plant world, tobacco and service berries, among others, were considered to be especially sacred. Among the important underwater creatures we have met the beaver and the otter, as well as various underwater monsters who had to be propitiated. Animals, then, are also the contemporaries of humans in a significant way; they possess forms of consciousness which are often more powerful than humans', and they mediate a variety of transcendent powers to humans. This perspective is illustrated in the comment of a spiritual leader of the North Piegans, Brings-down-the-Sun:

> At one time animals and men were able to understand each other. We still talk to the animals just as we do to people, but they now seldom reply, except in dreams. We are then obedient to them and do whatever they tell us. Whenever we are in danger, or distress, we pray to them and they often help us. Many of the animals are friendly to man. They are able to read the future and give us warning of what will happen. (McClintock 1968, p. 476)

## Blackfoot Ritual Processes

The ritual and symbolic forms through which experiences of transcendence are evoked are deeply conditioned by the surrounding contexts, both natural and social. Nonhuman beings are related to humans through forms of social interaction which are peculiar to the group; and certain animal beings become prominent in experience, but not others. This interdependence between context and experiences of transcendence characterizes human religious experience generally, however, and should not reduce the significance of the ritual and symbolic forms we have discussed. The universes evoked by these forms, when widely shared, establish a deep reality sense in the experience of the people. Such apprehensions of the world, though they vary through time and with group experience, are nonetheless authentic irruptions of transcendence. It is precisely in the content of such experiences that responses at the level of attitude, disposition, and behavior receive their particular texture and cultural flavor. A further examination of certain dimensions of the Blackfoot Sun Dance ritual will establish this point more securely.

An elaboration of the hundred-willow sweat house and its complex symbolism is a good place to begin. We remarked earlier upon the importance of the symbolism of steam and smoke, as well as upon the essential requirement of purification before humans evoke transcendent beings. Our focus here will be upon the ritual itself and its interrelated symbolic forms. In this manner we can see at closer range some of the ways in which attitudes and dispositions may have been formed, as well as how behavior may have been influenced.

The images evoked in the sweat-house ritual were primarily those of the sacred family, the tradition of Scar-Face, and the sacred buffalo. These images were mediated in color, architecture, movement, materials, and substances. If we begin with color symbolism, we immediately confront solar, lunar, and astral themes. The lodge was painted red on one side and black on the other, symbolizing the Sun and Moon. In addition, a buffalo skull, which reflected this same color symbolism, was placed on the top of the sweat house. One side of the skull was decorated with red spots and the other side with black spots; secured to the top of the sweat house structure, the skull faced east, adding another dimension to its cosmic symbolism. One interpretation holds that the black spots on the buffalo skull represented stars (McClintock 1968, p. 286). In any case, Sun, Moon, and Morning Star were addressed continually in the sweat-house songs and prayers.

Architecturally, the sweat lodge was in the form of a circle, a solar symbol, and was constructed to represent the dome of the sky or the lodge where Scar-Face was taken (Wissler 1918, p. 250). The structural symbolism is deeply reflective of a sacred space where particular events and experiences once occurred. The construction of the sweat house was an act which evoked the meanings of the oral traditions and recapitulated them in a manner which must have resonated deeply in the experience of the people.

Movement also played its symbolic role in the sweat-house ritual. Traditionally, there were four sweat houses built, one for each of the four camp movements toward the Sun Dance site. Some interpreters have indicated that these four structures were built so as to follow a sunwise movement; the first was built on the east side of the camp, the second on the south, the third on the west, and the fourth on the north (McClintock 1968, p. 290). Even in alternate interpretations, the solar motif was emphasized through a layered symbolism. One view, for example, is that the sweat lodges were constructed all in a line facing the east. Two were constructed behind the Sun Dance lodge and two were placed in front of the lodge. The Sun's lodge itself opened toward the rising sun, thus reinforcing the pervasive solar symbolism (Grinnell 1962, p. 265).

At the apex of the sweat lodge was placed the decorated buffalo skull with its solar, lunar, and astral symbols, associating this animal with the destiny of the people in a special way. Sage grass was placed in the nose and eye sockets of the skull, which symbolized the feeding of the buffalo (McClintock 1968, pp. 286–87; Wissler 1918, p. 250). This association of the buffalo with the ultimate power that animates all of creation recalls the version of the Scar-Face tradition in which Sun is represented as favoring the buffalo above all creatures and giving him to the people for their food. In this tradition the Sun indicated which of the animals was most sacred: "The buffalo is. Of all animals I like him best. He is for the people. He is your food and shelter" (Grinnell 1962, p. 101). We shall discover such buffalo symbolism again in our further discussion of the Sun Dance ritual.

Materials and substances are also symbolically interconnected in the sweat-house ritual. Prominent among these were the stones, some say a hundred, which recalled the tradition of the rocks as some of the oldest beings on earth. The earth dug out from the floor of the sweat house to make a place for the heated stones was placed on one side of the structure and symbolized the earth brought up from the primal waters by the animals (McClintock 1968, pp. 285–86). The rising steam from the hot stones, as well as the smoke from incense and pipe, were reinforcing symbolic substances that represented human communication with the powers of earth and sky. This complex layer of symbolic forms, when combined with the bodily attitude of the participants as they subjected themselves to these cleansing substances, must have deepened the

experience of transcendence evoked in the sensibilities of participants. The ritual associated with the transfer of the natoas bundle continues the motifs we have discussed and reinforces the total symbolic universe. The beginning of the Sun Dance was signaled by the
onset of the sacred woman's fast, an act which placed her symbolically at the border between the world of ordinary experience and
transcendent horizons of meaning. From this point until the cul-
mination of the ritual transfer, the tipi of the sacred woman became
a center of intense symbolic activity. The tipi was kept tightly
closed, and the woman and her husband were required to perform
their activities according to a number of prohibitions that signaled
their entry into ritual time. The daughter, or sacred woman, must
do nothing for herself, remaining silent in the tipi, her body covered
with a buffalo robe which has been painted with sacred red paint
(Wissler 1918, p. 242). The tipi, with its warm temperatures, mirrored the experience of the sweat house, and the red paint continued
the basic color symbolism.

The movement of the woman's tipi during the approach to the
final site of the Sun Dance encampment was also accompanied by
complex ritual activity. The travois upon which her tipi and other
ritual objects were transported was decorated with the sacred red
paint. In the movement of the camp, the lead was always taken by
the four persons involved in the transfer—the sacred woman and
her husband and the natoas bundle owner and her husband. They
proceeded at some distance in advance of the main body of the
people, their status embodied for all to see in the color symbolism
of the Sun himself (Wissler 1918, p. 243).

The transfer ritual was rich with motifs of the sacred family, as
well as the buffalo and other powerful earth- and sky-beings (Wissler 1912, pp. 215–19). In song each of these beings was evoked,
and in some cases the traditions that informed the ritual became
texts that guided the actions of participants. When movements were
made by the former natoas owner toward a small cottonwood tree
which had been stuck in the ground inside the sacred tipi, for example, the woman imitated the hooking movement and call of
the elk, recalling the tradition of Elk Woman. And the tradition

resonated with additional meanings as she sang of the sacred turnip and digging stick, while at the same time making the call of the crane (Wissler 1912, p. 218). Almost all of the animals mentioned in the traditions were recalled in song and mimetic movement. The figures of the sacred family appeared again and again in the course of the ritual. An example of such a song may be cited; in this song the Sun was referred to as Old Man and the Moon as Old Woman:

> Old Man, he says, make haste to mark me.
> Old Woman, she says, mark me in a different place.
> Morning Star, he says, mark me in a different place.
> Old Man, he says, paint me now (the yellow paint).
> Old Woman, she says, paint me with different paint
>   (the black paint).
> Morning Star, he says, paint me different (the sun
>   dog symbols).

(Wissler 1912, p. 216)

This song refers to the altar associated with the natoas transfer (Wissler 1912, pp. 256–57). The hole that was excavated for this altar was bordered by sods on three sides. On the top of these sods were laid sprigs of creeping juniper. This plant recalls a memory in the tradition which held that, before the gift of the natoas headdress, the sacred woman wore a wreath of creeping juniper about her head (Wissler 1912, p. 214). On a background of white earth, a dry painting was made.[6] A Moon figure was drawn with yellow earth, with a narrow black band in the center. The prominence of the Moon symbol identified the woman with a particular member of the sacred family. On each side of the Moon were two bands, one side marked in yellow and the other in black, symbolizing sun dogs. At the ends of the sod borders surrounding the altar were two circular smudge places. The one on the right represented the place of Morning Star, while the one on the left represented the place of Mistaken Morning Star. The symbolism of color and form further reinforce the apprehension of the world which was constituted by the ritual.

The ceremonial gathering and preparation of buffalo tongues, along with their sacramental consumption, was a feature of the Sun Dance which deepens the symbolic horizons. These elements opened up a religious horizon that elevated the buffalo to a sacred place not occupied by any other animal. The ritual associated the buffalo with Sun in a special way, and through these means the moral tensions engendered by the killing and eating of this animal were ritually reconciled. This reconciliation surrounded the buffalo with a religiously grounded horizon of meaning which engendered certain attitudes, dispositions, and behavior patterns. An attitude of respect for the animal was engendered, attempts to establish harmony with this animal were evident, and a general reverence for the animal was expressed in ritual and symbolic form. This general reconciliation extended to the entire earth and was expressed in such symbolic acts as the offering of sacramental food to the earth in the course of the ritual (Wissler 1918, p. 245).

The apex of reconciliation with the buffalo and the entire creation introduced the theme of the renewal of the world and was reached in the final ritual acts of the Sun Dance. We will focus specifically upon the symbolism of the Sun's lodge, the form of the dancing, and the sacrifice of flesh to the Sun which once characterized the Blackfoot Sun Dance. Many other elements could be shown to support and reinforce the apprehension of the world that we have imaged in this discussion. But these three dimensions will perhaps give sufficient representation of the argument we have tried to establish.

The architecture of the Sun Dance lodge, like that of the hundred-willow sweat house, was a material form that symbolized the final power in the Blackfoot universe. Its circular shape, its opening toward the east, and its center pole were complex and interconnected material forms that evoked specific horizons of transcendent meaning in the experience of the people. It is, however, the center pole which will receive the most attention in this context. While the Sun pole may have associations with the World Tree of other religious traditions, for the Blackfeet it also seems to symbolize the concentrated Sun power which flowed from its source above, through the pole, and horizontally out into the social and natural worlds. This flowing of Sun power into the world is coextensive with the renewal of the world and the people.

Renewal of the world and the people is also enacted in the form of dance before the center pole. All of the dancers employed face and body paints, some of which corresponded to their personal dream or vision experiences. Some of the dancers, however, reflected in their body painting the solar, lunar, and astral symbolism with which we have now become familiar (Wissler 1918, p. 259). In addition, the weather dancers were believed to have achieved through their dreams a special relationship with the Sun. Thus, they were able to pray for and bless the people in powerful ways, extending horizontally into the social world the power mediated symbolically by the Sun Pole.

Dancing was relatively simple, yet definite in its intent. The orientation was consistently toward the center pole of the Sun's lodge. As a special instance, we may consider the dance performed by those who tortured themselves for the Sun (Wissler 1918, p. 263). These dancers were decorated with solar, lunar, and astral symbols. Cuts were made over each breast and one in the back, through which skewers were thrust. The breast skewers were attached to ropes or thongs which were tied to the center pole; a shield was often hung from the back skewer. After embracing the center pole, the dancers leaned back against the ropes, seeking to tear their flesh, all the while gazing at the pole and blowing a whistle made from the bone of an eagle's wing. After the flesh was torn loose, it was offered to the Sun and the supplicant retired to the hills in search of a vision.

The sacrificial offering of flesh was more widespread than that which was specifically associated with the Sun Dance (Wissler 1918, pp. 265–67). Such sacrifices were generally associated with solar motifs, however, thus suggesting the widespread religious theme of the relationship of sacrifice to spiritual renewal and, by implication, to world renewal. Such sacrifices often took the form of cutting off a finger joint or bit of flesh and offering it to the Sun. In any case, for the Blackfeet, the renewal of their world was accomplished through the annual celebration of the ritual of reconciliation by which the Sun's beneficent power suffused both the natural and social worlds. The earth, the animals, the humans, and the world of transcendent contemporaries as well as predecessors were gathered into a single interrelated community. After the Sun Dance, life in the year to come was anticipated in an attitude of expectation and with a disposition of hope.

# The Crow Sun Dance

The theme of renewal of the world was less visible in the Crow Sun Dance as compared with the Blackfeet. Part of the problem of interpretation derives from the motif of "warrior religion," referred to earlier. The Crow Sun Dance thematizes the idea of revenge against an enemy (Lowie 1935, p. 297; Lowie 1915, p. 7; Curtis 1909, pp. 79–80). For this reason, it was not an annual ceremony, as was generally the case on the Plains; rather, it arose periodically in response to a vow made under the duress of the death of a kinsperson at the hand of an enemy. Between 1830 and 1874, for example, Sun Dance ceremonies were held perhaps only every three or four years (Lowie 1935, p. 297). The prediction that the Sun Dance would pass out of Crow experience with the decline of intertribal warfare and the pacification of the west proved untrue (Lowie 1935, p. 297). To the contrary, the Sun Dance was recovered and has persisted, although its ritual forms have changed in conformity with changing social conditions (Miller 1980; cf. Voget 1984).

The traditional Crow Sun Dance was an occasion for various types of ecstatic experiences. Despite the prominence of the motif of revenge, the ritual was also characterized by what may be more primordial images which are similar to those found among the Blackfeet. The particular concern with revenge may, then, rest upon a core of more general symbolic forms.[7]

The Sun Dance among the Crows involved a number of elements similar in form to the Blackfoot ritual but different in some of their fundamental meanings. In addition, there were elements that evoked meanings peculiar to the Crow experience. Central to the Sun Dance was a particular bundle, the most important object in which was an effigy. This figure was a material object that symbolized the enemy, fixing in the experience of the mourner a vision of revenge. During the nineteenth and early twentieth centuries, there were a number of these bundles in existence, although they were not all identical in form, and some were much older than others (Wildschut 1960, pp. 20–33). The older bundles did have similarities in form, and all of the bundles were apparently constructed of the same material, the skin of a white-tailed deer. Their construction was preceded by a sweat bath and the purification of the body in the smoke of sacred pine needles (Wildschut 1960, p. 27). The older bundles also had prominent headgears made from the feathers of the owl, the bird of sacred vision among the Crows. This power was further symbolized by two marks painted under the eyes of the effigy. More recent bundles were painted idiosyncratically, perhaps reflecting more closely the individual vision experience of the owner (Wildschut 1960, p. 33).[8] All of these bundles, like those among the Blackfeet, arose as a consequence of an experience of transcendence in dream- or waking-vision. Unlike the Blackfeet, the reported myths of origin are often not as complex or as lengthy. This does not mean, however, that their symbolic richness is necessarily diminished.

## Crow Sun Dance Traditions

One story of the origin of a Sun Dance bundle and its central object, the effigy, was narrated by Birds-all-over-the-ground (Lowie 1915, pp. 13–14). According to this version, the effigy and the Sun Dance ritual appeared to a poor young man whose name was Four Dance. Being very poor and an orphan, Four Dance went out alone to seek a vision of power. He fasted in a lonely place, and on the third morning of his fast a bird appeared to him and told him to look toward the west. There Four Dance saw seven men preceded by a woman who held a strange effigy in front of her face. The men were beating on a drum painted with the image of a skunk. As the young man listened, the group began to sing, and Four Dance was able to learn all the songs. Finally, the group appeared before the young man as he lay in his fasting place. The woman was dressed in an elk-hide robe and began to sing, holding the effigy before her. At the end of the fourth song, the effigy was transformed into an owl which flew to perch upon the faster's chest. Suddenly one of the men shot the owl, which entered into Four Dance's chest and began to hoot. At this point the young man had a vision of how the Sun Dance ritual should proceed, and he knew that the mysterious woman was really the Moon. The effigy itself was said to represent the Moon, and the lodge the Sun's dwelling. Although not explicitly stated, it is reasonable to suppose that the seven men represented the Dipper. Thus we see in this vision the richness of solar, lunar, and astral imagery, as well as the presence of powerful bird symbolism.

Perhaps an older origin tradition was narrated by Two Leggings, chief of the River Crows (Wildschut 1960, pp. 21–25; cf. Nabokov 1967). This story concerns the vision experience of an unknown person, whom Two Leggings called Prairie-Dog-Man. While accompanying his father on a hunt, his small son had been killed by a group of forest people. Prairie-Dog-Man wandered about alone in the hills, agonizing over the death of his son. Finally, he heard a voice telling him to build a lodge to the Sun. Although the voice was clear, the man had no idea of what a Sun lodge might be. He ceased to weep, stood up, and saw before him a group of prairie dogs, one of which transformed himself into a human being. The human figure spoke: "There is a living being who has come to see us. All come and gather here for you have made the structure of the sun" (Wildschut 1960, p. 22).

The prairie dog village was transformed into an Indian camp, and in its center Prairie-Dog-Man saw a Sun Dance lodge, with a man and his wife standing before it. As the vision unfolded, Prairie-Dog-Man observed a man carrying a pine tree with a willow hoop decorated with eagle feathers fastened to the top. Then there appeared a small owl which flew toward the hoop. Upon reaching the hoop, the owl was transformed into a Sun Dance effigy. When he awoke, Prairie-Dog-Man looked about; the people and their village had disappeared, and in their place was a field of skunk cabbage. Returning to his people, Prairie-Dog-Man built the first Sun Dance lodge according to the details of his vision.

## Crow Ritual Processes

The occasion for the Crow Sun Dance was a vow made by a man who had lost a close relative at the hand of an enemy. After wandering about on the prairie for some time, the mourner finally made his intent known by announcing that all the buffalo tongues acquired in the hunt should be given to him. To the chief he would say: "On this hunt I want you to have all the tongues kept, do not let the children have any, I want them all" (Lowie 1935, p. 298; Lowie 1915, p. 10). By this sign the people knew that there would soon be a Sun Dance. The ceremonial gathering of tongues was not, as it was for the Blackfeet, surrounded by meanings which interpreted them as sacramental food. They were a delicacy, to be sure, but they were used as food for important warriors as well as for those who performed other services for the mourner (Lowie 1915, pp. 10–11). For this reason, the supply of tongues required for the ceremony was often very large.

After the collection of tongues, the pledger had to acquire the services of one of the persons who owned a Sun Dance bundle. The Crow supplicant, unlike the Blackfoot, normally did not acquire the bundle by transfer. Rather, he established a relationship with one of the bundle owners, assuming the role of "son," while the owner assumed the role of "father." As a consequence of this relationship, the man pledging the Sun Dance acquired the services of the owner and the use of his bundle with its all-important effigy (Lowie 1915, pp. 12ff.). Again, the appearance of solar, lunar, and astral motifs on the effigies was not uncommon, and the owl motif was quite prominent (Lowie 1915, pp. 14–16, 18–19). Indeed, solar, lunar, and astral symbolism was scattered through the entire ritual process (Lowie 1915, pp. 26, 30, 33, 41, 44, 47).

The Crow Sun Dance had a place for the role of a virtuous woman, although this person did not play as central a role in the ritual as was the case for the Blackfeet. In the Crow Sun Dance, the virtuous woman had a central role in the ceremonial cutting of the first pole for the Sun's lodge. This cutting was done with the assistance of a captive, perhaps from the offending tribe, and a transvestite. The transvestite actually felled the tree after the woman had symbolically "notched" it with an elk-horn wedge. As the tree fell, it was ceremonially shot by warriors and many persons counted coup upon it, treating it as an enemy (Lowie 1915, pp. 30–32; Curtis

1909, pp. 69–70). After the first pole was cut, the remainder of the poles for the lodge were felled without ceremony and were hauled to the site where the Sun's lodge was to be built.

The form of the Sun Dance structure was also different from the lodge of the Blackfeet, although the circular shape was the same. Rather than being constructed out of upright poles to which rafters resting in the crotch of the Sun pole were attached, the Crow lodge resembled the shape of a tipi (Lowie 1915, pp. 39–40). At the top of the structure was a nest, perhaps representing that of an eagle. The structure was then thatched with willow branches and covered with as many as one hundred skins (Curtis 1909, p. 74).

The central focus of the Crow Sun Dance was the vision quest of the pledger, although a number of other men joined him in his search for transcendent power. Essential to the preparation for such experiences was the fasting of the supplicant. By the time he approached the Sun's lodge in order to dance, he was usually weak from lack of food. Nevertheless, he entered the lodge and, to the accompaniment of drum and song, he danced for a vision. Moving with his eyes fixed upon the Sun Dance effigy, the successful mourner finally fell into a trance, experiencing a powerful vision of revenge in which the enemy and perhaps other members of his tribe were killed. Several days might pass before the vision came, although in one case the faster did not have to wait for a vision, since one of the enemy was killed on the first night of the Sun Dance (Lowie 1915, pp. 48–49). In any event, the experience of transcendence achieved by the pledger was the signal that marked the close of the Sun Dance ritual.

Although the suffering of the pledger continued, others sought their individual ecstasy through vision. Painted white, these persons suspended themselves on thongs which were connected to breast skewers. Some of these sufferers were suspended inside the Sun's lodge, while others would tie themselves to poles which had been placed in the ground outside the lodge. Still others would drag buffalo skulls attached to shoulder skewers, and others might cut off the joint of a finger, praying, "O, Sun, I give this to you; send me visions and give me an enemy!" (Curtis 1909, p. 78). In the midst of this spectacle, with its sounds of shouting and singing, "Some of those who had been pierced began to growl like animals and froth at the mouth and utter strange cries, while others made prophecies and described visions they were seeing" (Curtis 1909, p. 79). The apex of ecstasy was reached when the pledger of the Sun Dance was transported in vision. After this event, the excitement of the camp subsided, and the people moved off, motivated by the expectation of a vision soon to be fulfilled.[9]

Two additional comments are necessary before turning to a consideration of the Cheyenne and Arapaho Sun Dance. The first comment underlines the importance of reuniting relevant elements of the oral tradition with an interpretation of ritual. The two were united in experience and to separate them creates an interpretative tendency toward reversing what may have been primary in the order of experience. Even though it is important to know, in a literary-historical manner, at what point in time some of the oral traditions arose, it is finally the meaning of these traditions as they resonate in experience which is the key to understanding ritual processes and their symbolic forms. To interpret these meaning structures from the point of view of the experiencing person requires that we recover a sense of the primacy of these elements in the oral tradition.

The second comment reemphasizes a theme that has recurred in this analysis: Nature (plants, animals, earth) is always apprehended through a fundamental religious sensibility sustained and mediated through ritual forms. Moral sensibilities, or experiences of value, do not represent an autonomous meaning sphere. Likewise, religion as a meaning sphere is not clearly differentiated from other dimensions of experience, as the typical western expectation would have it. In these traditions, a sense of value arises out of a fundamental apprehension of the world. Religiously grounded moral values appear as a part of a total religious paradigm of meaning rather than as a distinct horizon. In other language, moral and religious experience is never separated from other dimensions of individual and social life. This point is further illustrated in the meanings that informed the Cheyenne Sun Dance during the high culture period on the Northwestern Plains.

# The Cheyenne Sun Dance

The long westward migration of the tribe known to white people in historic times as the Cheyennes probably began in the late seventeenth century, as we saw in chapter one. Sometime after they crossed the Missouri, the Cheyennes (or as they knew themselves, the Tsistsistas, the "Human Beings") met another tribe. This group, known as the Suhtais, or Buffalo People, became associated with the Cheyennes. As late as 1830, the Suhtais still camped by themselves, but it was not long thereafter that the two groups were fully united.

It was from the Suhtais that the Tsistsistas received the tradition of a culture hero who established institutional forms different from those brought by Sweet Medicine. This culture hero, known as Erect Horns, brought the people the Sacred Buffalo Hat and the ceremonies of the Sun Dance. As the two groups became one people, the arrow ceremony, brought by Sweet Medicine, and the Sun Dance, brought by Erect Horns, became complementary sources of power. The unification of these traditions in the experience of a single people marked the final phase of the transition of the Tsistsistas from an agricultural people to a people of the Plains, dependent entirely upon the buffalo. The assimilation of the Suhtais also meant the assimilation of their traditions. Central to these traditions were ritual forms which focused upon the themes of renewal of both social and natural worlds. The Sun Dance was the largest and most impressive of these ritual complexes (Hoebel 1978, p. 9; Powell 1969, vol. 1, pp. 24–26). Erect Horns was the culture hero who brought this source of world renewal to the people.

## Cheyenne Sun Dance Traditions

According to one tradition, there was a time when the earth turned barren and dry; the animals died and the ancient Cheyennes were desperate for food (Dorsey 1905a, pp. 46–49; cf. Grinnell 1972, vol.

2, pp. 337–81). Facing starvation, the tribe moved toward the north, camping finally beside the banks of a beautiful stream. The chiefs of the tribe ordered the men to go in pairs to the women they found attractive in order to beg food from them. A certain young man possessing special powers begged food from a beautiful woman who was the wife of the tribe's chief. While he was eating, he told the young woman that he was soon to undertake a journey far to the north and that he wished her to accompany him. The young woman agreed. Taking her dogs to carry their supplies, they set out upon the long journey.

For many days they traveled, each evening erecting their tipi so as to face the east. Finally the young woman inquired of the man why he had not shown affection for her, since they had eloped together. The young man replied that it was forbidden for them to have intercourse before they had received instructions from the great Above Person. After they had met with this being in the Sacred Mountain, then the earth would be renewed and the human beings would be perpetuated through the agency of the woman. Until these events had transpired, it was forbidden for them to have intercourse. They traveled on for several days until they came to a forest, in the middle of which arose a great mountain thrusting to the sky; beyond the mountain they saw many waters.

As they approached the mountain, they saw a large rock, which they rolled back exposing a passage into the heart of the upthrust. After they entered the passage, the rock rolled back, closing them inside the mountain. Remaining in the mountain for four days, the young man and the woman received instructions from Above Person and from Thunder. By this means they were able to learn all of the songs and rituals that belonged to the Sun Dance. At the end of the instruction, they were promised that if the people would follow the commands, then all of the world would be made new. Even the heavenly bodies would move:

> The Roaring Thunder will awaken them, the sun, moon, stars, and the rain will bring forth fruits of all kinds, all the animals will come forth behind you from this mountain, and they will follow you home. (Dorsey 1905a, p. 48)

Before they left the mountain, Above Person gave the man a horned cap to wear during the Sun Dance ceremonies: "Put this cap on as you go from here and the earth will bless you" (Dorsey 1905a, p. 48). As they emerged from the heart of the mountain, all of the buffalo followed them, and before their eyes the whole world seemed to become new. They traveled for many days, and each evening when the man and woman would stop for the night the buffalo would also lie down to rest. In the morning the man would put on his sacred hat and sing the songs which he had learned. Then the buffalo and the other animals would rise up and follow him. Finally the man and the woman reached their people. The man instructed the people in the performance of the Sun Dance, telling them that if they followed the commands they should never be hungry again. When they saw that the young man was wearing a sacred horned hat, the people named him Erect Horns. From that time forward, the Cheyennes have performed the rites of the Sun Dance, and the man who pledges the Sun Dance still wears the sacred hat which was given to Erect Horns.

## Cheyenne Ritual Processes

At the turn of the century, the Cheyenne Sun Dance reflected the themes of rebirth and renewal in a dramatic manner.[10] The name given to the Sun's lodge was the New-Life-Lodge, representing the renewal of the world. It was through the ritual construction of this lodge that new life flowed into the natural and social worlds. The major participants in the Sun Dance represented the figures of the Erect Horns tradition. As was the case among other groups, the occasion for the Sun Dance arose as a consequence of a vow. The man who made the vow to sponsor the Sun Dance was known as the "reproducer" or "multiplier," since it would be through him that new life would flow into nature and the social world. Between the time of his pledge and the end of the Sun Dance, the pledger and his wife abstained from sexual intercourse, as did the young man and woman in the Erect Horns tradition. The holiness of the vow is also reflected in the fact that the pledger was painted with sacred

red paint from the time of the initial announcement until the time of the Sun Dance itself (Dorsey 1905b, pp. 58–59). In addition to the pledger, there was his wife, who occupied the role of the sacred woman of the tradition. Also involved in the ceremony was a chief priest, one who "Shows How," representing Above Person. Other principal participants were all of those who had pledged the Sun Dance before, known collectively as the "reanimators." Finally, there were a number of dancers who were involved in the ceremony (Dorsey 1905b, pp. 62–63).

After the pledger had made his vow, the people were informed that the Sun Dance would soon be held. Gathering from the various band encampments, the people made their way toward the construction site of the Sun's lodge. Since the Lodge of New Birth was believed to renew not only the earth and animal life but also the life of the people, all were expected to be present. So solemn was the occasion that recalcitrant individuals or groups might be subject to coercion should they refuse to attend the ceremony (Grinnell 1914, pp. 247–48). As the people arrived at the site, they formed a great camp circle which opened toward the east and which was said to be symbolic of a certain cluster of stars known to the Cheyennes as the Camp-Circle (Dorsey 1905b, p. 62).

After the people had gathered and the camp circle had been formed, the work of the pledger, sacred woman, chief priest, and his assistant began. This work was nothing less than the recreation of the natural and social worlds. At first the world was barren. This condition was symbolized by the movement of a tipi into the camp circle. This tipi, known as the Lone-tipi, was the center from which new life would proceed and was signaled by symbolic associations that indicated its function to the people. The Lone-tipi was known as the "Tipi-from-which-the-Rebirth-lodge-comes." Sometimes it was called the "Hill from which buffalo came," recalling the Erect Horns tradition. Astral images were associated with this structure as well, since it was often designated as the "Morning Star" (Dorsey 1905b, p. 69).

As a consequence of the ritual acts performed within the Lone-tipi, the barren earth would be renewed. The material symbols of this condition are powerful and unmistakable. The first act of the lodge-maker's wife, the sacred woman, was to clear the ground within the Lone-tipi down to the barren earth, leaving a border of grass around this circle approximately three feet wide. Fresh sage was placed upon the grassy circumference and then covered with blankets or robes upon which the reanimators and other major participants would sit (Dorsey 1905b, p. 72). The lodge was thus surrounded with meanings associating it with the barren condition of the earth which stimulated the journey of Erect Horns. The tipi itself had been made sacred through a gradual ritual removal from the world of everyday life. It began as an ordinary dwelling belonging usually to one of the members of the lodge-maker's warrior society. After it was selected as the lodge which would become sacred, it was redefined. It was taken one step out of ordinary reality by becoming first the warrior's tipi and then the priest's tipi (Dorsey 1905b, pp. 67–69). Then it was moved within the camp circle to a special place and the barren earth was exposed within its enclosure. This completed the ritual movement from the world of ordinary things into the world of sacred meaning.

Within the Lone-tipi a series of ritual acts unfolded which began the reconstruction of the world. One of the first of these acts, to be repeated five times, was the creation of an "earth" upon the barren space within the Lone-tipi (Dorsey 1905b, pp. 74–75). The chief priest took the thumb of the lodge-maker in his own hand and caused the lodge-maker to make symbolic movements toward the four directions, as well as movements toward the symbol of regeneration, the Sun. Then the chief priest traced with the lodge-maker's thumb a small circle about one inch in diameter upon the face of the barren soil. With his own hand the priest enlarged this "earth" to about twice its original size. Even though small, obscure, and insignificant, this small earth was the navel of the new world which was in the process of being ritually reborn. All present in the Lone-tipi signified the holiness of the occasion by smoking a pipe. Each time the pipe was passed, the stem was directed toward the tiny "earth." After the pipe had been smoked out, the ashes were deposited carefully in the center of the first "earth." The symbolic associations of smoke as the prayers of the people, the fire in the bowl as the power of the Sun, and the grains of tobacco as the beings of the world, must have resonated powerfully in the experience of the participants.

The first "earth" was formed on the second day of the Sun Dance preparation ceremonies. Later that same day a second "earth" was formed. This earth, which had symbolic associations with the renewal of the buffalo (Dorsey 1905b, pp. 79–80), was also traced out with the lodge-maker's hand, but with a series of symbolic movements that differed from the making of the first earth. A rocking motion with the hand represented a buffalo wallowing, and a small ball of buffalo hair was placed at the center of the second earth by the chief priest. Through these symbolic movements, the renewal of the buffalo began. This earth was larger than the first, and thus the renewal was visibly spreading. On the third day a third "earth" was formed, but this time outside the Lone-tipi (Dorsey 1905b, pp. 84–86). Again a pipe was smoked, ritually pointing the stem toward this earth. The ashes were also deposited at the center of this larger earth. Then on the same day a fourth "earth" was constructed inside the Lone-tipi (Dorsey 1905b, p. 89). The pipe was smoked again in the usual fashion and this earth was even larger, symbolizing the fecundity of the renewing power which was flowing into the world in an act of cosmic rebirth. Finally, a fifth "earth" was constructed within the Lone-tipi; this earth will be discussed presently in connection with rituals that surround the buffalo skull.

The meanings surrounding smoking and the pipe are so significant that they must be elaborated. In addition to the symbolic associations already mentioned, there are additional dimensions of meaning. These appear and surround a pipe contained in a bundle along with a buffalo chip, sweet grass, and buffalo sinew. This bundle was obtained by the lodge-maker from the person who vowed the previous Sun Dance. It would be kept in the possession of the current lodge-maker until the next Sun Dance was pledged (Dorsey 1905b, p. 69). After the making of the first earth, this sacred pipe was exposed (Dorsey 1905b, pp. 76–78). Taking the sinew from the bundle, five shreds were torn off by the assistant chief priest. These shreds were rolled into a ball by the lodge-maker and placed in the bowl of the pipe. Then a small ball of sweet grass was pressed into the bowl on top of the buffalo sinew. The bowl was loaded with five pinches of tobacco, placed symbolically at the four corners of the bowl and at the center. The bowl was then sealed with tallow and both the stem and the bowl were painted with sacred red paint. Reflecting meanings having primarily to do with the buffalo, this new pipe was now ready to occupy the renewed earth which was emerging into the experience of the people. The ritual surrounding the filling of this pipe occurred several times in the course of the Sun Dance ceremony.

The rituals occurring within the Lone-tipi were related to activities taking place in the wider camp. On the third day, the day when the third earth was prepared outside the Lone-tipi, the Sun's lodge was under construction. The renewing power proceeding from the Lone-tipi was flowing out into the world, and the reconstruction of nature was proceeding with the building of the larger Lodge of New Birth.

On this same day occurred another series of acts symbolically related to the buffalo. A buffalo skull was brought into the Lone-tipi and the fifth earth, mentioned above, was formed in front of the skull. This earth also represented a buffalo wallow (Dorsey 1905b, p. 91). On the next, or fourth day, the buffalo skull was ritually painted (Dorsey 1905b, pp. 96–97). First, plugs of swamp grass were constructed and inserted into the eye and nose openings of the skull. Then a black line was drawn along the median line of the skull, from the back to the front. On each side of the black line a narrower white line was drawn. Then the entire skull, including the grass plugs and horns, was covered with the sacred red paint. Finally, a crescent moon was painted on the left jaw in black, and on the right jaw a sun was painted in red. In this case, red probably symbolized the meanings associated with the earth, while white and black may have evoked associations with the day and night.

The sacred pipe was again filled with sinew and tobacco, painted red, and sealed with tallow. The ceremonies in the Lone-tipi ended on the fourth day with the painting of the lodge-maker and his wife (Dorsey 1905b, pp. 104–6). At this point they both began to fast, and as the Lone-tipi was abandoned, its sacred power flowed toward the emerging Lodge of New Birth. The objects which had been so carefully prepared, such as the buffalo skull, the pipe, and other items, were carried outside the tipi. The woman led the procession with the skull, the priests proceeding behind her with the other sacred objects which were deposited in a location near the Sun Dance lodge (Dorsey 1905b, pp. 107–8).

On the day that the Lone-tipi was abandoned, other important activities were occurring, central among which was the cutting of the center pole for the Sun's lodge. A typical speech to the center pole emphasized meanings with which we have become familiar:

> The whole world has picked you out this day to represent the world. We have come in a body for this purpose, to cut you down, so that you will have pity on all men, women, and children who may take part in this ceremony. You are to be their body. You will represent the sunshine of all the world. (Dorsey 1905b, p. 111).

After the tree had been cut, bundles of dogwood and cottonwood brush were placed in the crotch of the center pole, symbolizing the nest of the Thunderbird (Dorsey 1905b, pp. 116–17). In addition, the rafter poles for the Sun's lodge were painted with bands of black and red, symbolizing the division of the earth into night and day. The center pole was then raised and the lodge was completed.

After a number of other activities, the day ended with a ritual act which must be understood within the context of particular dimensions of meaning (Dorsey 1905b, pp. 130–31). The place of a sacred woman in the process of renewal was quite prominent and was reinforced by interpretations mediated through the oral tradition. A recapitulation and an extension of this regenerative power now became incarnate in the midst of the people through the action of the chief priest and the lodge-maker's wife. The chief priest, who represented the culture hero, and the lodge-maker's wife, who represented the sacred woman of the Erect Horns tradition, had intercourse together. Through this act the power of symbolic meanings became incarnate in the union of flesh, and the world was fertilized and prepared for reanimation and new birth. This is to be understood as a holy act, necessary for the rejuvenation of the natural and social worlds.[11]

The activities of renewal in the Lone-tipi, and the gradual emergence of the Lodge of New Birth, culminated in the construction of an altar which was the material form of the renewed world. Through the power of symbol, the materials of the altar and their particular forms were connected with sedimented meanings in the oral tradition. These sedimented meanings, so long as the symbols were vital, had the capacity to engender experiences of transcendence. Central among the objects possessing symbolic significance was the buffalo skull. After it had been carried into the Lodge of New Birth, a rectangular excavation was made in the earth in front of the skull. Five pieces of sod were then secured, two of which were placed on each side of the skull and one behind. These sods represented the four directions and the Sun. The sods were then broken up and shaped so that they formed a semicircle of earth around the skull. Into this semicircle were inserted five sprigs taken from small bushes. These sprigs were placed in the middle of the earth which corresponded to the center of each sod. Two cottonwood and two plum saplings were set in the ground, two on the south side of the altar and two on the north side, with the altar itself facing east. Then a dry sand painting was made in the excavation in front of the skull. On a background of sand, four parallel lines were poured—red, black, white, and yellow. Dotted lines representing stars were placed on each side of the solid lines. The solid lines symbolized "roads": The white line was the path of the lodge-maker and his wife; the red line was the path of the Cheyennes; the black line was the trail of the buffalo; and the yellow line was the path of the Sun. As is the nature of all symbolism, the meanings that may be associated with colors are multivalent and must be understood within particular contexts. Rainbow sticks made of willow and painted white, red, black, and yellow were curved over one another in the area between the skull and the sand painting. Finally, nine sticks were placed in a row on the south side of the altar and seven sticks on the north side. The sticks on the south side were painted red and black and represented the Cheyennes; those on the north side were painted white and represented all the enemies of the Human Beings (Dorsey 1905b, pp. 133–47).

The meanings that center upon world renewal and social renaissance were particularly focused in the altar. The natural materials, when shaped into their particular forms, embodied the cultural meanings. The coordination of form and color symbolism further invigorated these meanings, enriching the experience of the people. The altar as a whole represented the fifth earth, the world renewed, and the social order reconstructed. And the Lodge of New Birth may be seen as the material representation of the mountain from which the renewed orders of life have emerged.

Central to the symbolism of the altar was the buffalo, the animal upon which the people were dependent for food and shelter. The ritual celebration of the buffalo placed at the center of a renewed world was reinforced by and reflected in action. Food was sacrificed in the Lodge of New Birth, an act which recalled meanings related to the renewed world, and feasting occurred as a part of the celebration of nature's abundance (Dorsey 1905b, pp. 159–50). There was a general belief that food that had been exposed to the invigorating power of the Sun's lodge was especially blessed. It was consumed sacramentally in a manner which recalls the consumption of tongues among the Blackfeet (Grinnell 1914, p. 248). Even children were involved in acts that symbolized the renewed world. They made clay effigies of various animals, especially the buffalo, and deposited them at the base of the center pole (Dorsey 1905b, p. 181). These animals, made in pairs, represented the animals which Erect Horns brought with him out of the Sacred Mountain, as well as the animals which Sweet Medicine brought (Dorsey 1905a, p. 49). It was said that the center pole represented the unification of the two traditions of renewal. One fork of the pole represented Sweet Medicine and his tradition of the sacred arrows, while the other fork represented Erect Horns and his tradition of the Lodge of New Birth (Dorsey 1905a, p. 49). In the ritual of the Lodge of New Birth the traditions of the two people, the Tsistsistas and the Suhtais, were united into a single system of symbolic forms, evoking in the experience of the people common horizons of transcendent meaning. Also obvious in this ritual process were the renewal of the buffalo and a ritual reconciliation of the people with this source of their food supply. The human as hunter and the activity of hunting were ritually reinterpreted so that hunting and the consumption of other life forms assumed a status which approached that of other older hunting cultures—a "holy occupation" (Speck 1977, p. 72).

The power of the symbolic forms was extended and invigorated by becoming incarnate in the dancing which continued until the end of the ritual. Dancers oriented their movements always toward the material object that evoked a sense of renewed life, the center pole, and their action was dramatically traced upon the background of a complicated system of body painting (Dorsey 1905b, pp. 152ff.). An even more dramatic series of acts was sometimes undertaken by some of the dancers. These acts involved the sacrifice of the dancer's flesh and blood in order that the renewal of the world might come about and that the power at the heart of the universe would take pity on all human beings. This torture took a form similar to that which has previously been described. The sufferers were attached to the center pole by breast skewers; and others dragged through the camp a number of buffalo skulls which were tied to thongs attached to skewers in the sufferer's back (Dorsey: 1905b, pp. 175ff.).

At the end of the dancing, the sacred pipe was smoked once again in the Lodge of New Birth. The fast was broken and a sweat house was prepared. The chief priest and his wife, along with the lodge-maker and his wife, entered the sweat lodge to purify themselves in the sacred mist. These acts signified the passage of the bodies of the participants from the world of transcendent meanings back into the world of ordinary existence. It was expected, of course, that the renewing power of the Lodge of New Birth would continue in the world and among the people until the time of the next Sun Dance (Dorsey 1905b, pp. 164–66). When that time occurred, the sequence of events expressed in ritual form and bodily movement would unfold once again. And the purpose for which the ritual was enacted would be fulfilled according to the understanding of the Cheyennes:

> At the time of the Lone-tipi, when the earth is first created, it is just beginning to grow. As the ceremony progresses, this earth increases in size, and when the lodge itself is erected we build a

fire which represents the heat of the sun, and we place the lodge to face the east that the heavenly bodies may pass over it and fertilize it. (Dorsey 1905b, p. 186)

## The Arapaho Sun Dance

It now remains to provide a brief comparative description of the Arapaho Sun Dance. By the beginning of the present century the Arapahoes had permanently been divided into a northern and a southern population. Those in the south were confined to a reservation in Oklahoma, and those in the north occupied a reservation in Wyoming.[12] The sacred Flat Pipe, which was believed to be the agent of creation, remained in the possession of the northern Arapahoes. Although this pipe was venerated by all of the people, it obviously played a more direct role in the northern Arapaho Sun Dance than it did in the ceremony in the south. Both divisions of the tribe possessed the Sacred Wheel, however. This Wheel occupied a prominent place in the Sun Dance ritual. In the north, the keeper of the Flat Pipe played a central role in the ceremony, while in the south this role was occupied by a chief priest without benefit of the Flat Pipe (Kroeber 1907, p. 309). The painted tipi of the Flat Pipe keeper dominated the camp circle of the Northern Arapahoes, symbolizing the power which brought all of the people into existence (Kroeber 1907, pp. 281–82).[13]

The Sun Dance among the northern and southern divisions of the Arapahoes differed in some minor details at the beginning of the century (Kroeber 1907, pp. 301–8). These differences do not seem to be significant at the symbolic level, and the ritual will be described without further reference to the division of the people. Furthermore, since the Arapaho and the Cheyenne rituals show some significant similarities, the description will be briefer than was the case for other groups. Despite this circumstance, we will see that the themes of the Arapaho Sun Dance, though shared with other groups, have a uniqueness and flavor of their own.

Part of that uniqueness derives from the character of the sacred objects, such as the Flat Pipe and the traditions that surround it.

Some of the sacred objects, such as the Wheel, evoke meanings similar to those among other Plains peoples. For example, the themes of new birth, regeneration, and renewal of the world are present in the Arapaho ceremony, but they do not seem to be as centrally featured as they are among the Cheyennes. The overarching meaning seems rather to focus upon the offering of sacrifices to the powers upon whom the people were dependent—sacrifices of food, clothing, and flesh. This difference in emphasis is reflected in the name which the Arapahoes gave to the Sun Dance lodge: the Offerings Lodge.

## Arapaho Sun Dance Traditions

Further understanding of the nuances of the Arapaho ritual comes through an analysis of the origin narrative which grounds the Sun Dance and explains the significance of the Sacred Wheel. Even though the narrative of tribal origin was very sacred and was kept by the owner of the Flat Pipe, there are elements of the creation account which give us some insight into certain fundamental meanings. We know, for example, that the Sacred Wheel derived from the creator, or Flat Pipe. It was constructed out of materials, both plant and animal (Dorsey 1903b, pp. 205–8). The creation narrative represents the plants and animals giving their bodies for the creation of the Sacred Wheel. Among the animals, there were the eagle, badger, rabbit, and White Buffalo. Among the plants there were the cottonwood, cedar, willow, red bush, water grass, and rabbit weeds. The Wheel was constructed of a long flexible piece of wood representing the gentle garter snake who offered his body to be the circumference of the earth (Dorsey 1903b, p. 202). Four markings were made on the inside of the Wheel, representing the Four Old Men, the Sacred Persons of the four directions, and at these points on the Wheel were tied bunches of eagle feathers (Dorsey 1903b, pp. 13–14). Taken as a whole, the Wheel was a symbolic representation of the entire creation.

After the creation of animal and vegetable life, the creator made a woman and a child to serve as his companions. After some time the young boy became ill and the owner of the Flat Pipe (creator) announced to all the animals and birds that a great ceremony was to be held on behalf of his son. All of the creatures rejoiced at this news and came from the four quarters to congregate at a central place. According to this tradition, this was the first Lodge of the Sun to be pledged upon the earth. The ritual lasted four days and the lodge itself was constructed by the creator with the assistance of all the animals and birds. In the course of time, the people multiplied, and another young child became ill. The people asked the keeper of the Flat Pipe (creator) to teach them how to pledge the Lodge of the Sun for the sake of the young child. Again the lodge was constructed, this time the animals and birds giving their bodies as materials. The keeper of the Flat Pipe (creator) instructed the people in the ritual acts and paints which pertained to the Sun Dance (Dorsey 1903b, pp. 208–9).

## Arapaho Ritual Processes

The general pattern of the Sun Dance among the Arapahoes was similar to the Cheyenne ritual. There was the formation of a camp circle after the vow to sponsor the Sun's lodge had been made. The major participants represented supernatural beings, such as the Sun, Moon, Wheel, and Mother Earth. One of the participants represented the Arapaho people as a whole (Dorsey 1903b, pp. 24–25). These major figures gathered together in a structure known as the Rabbit-tipi in order to prepare themselves and the sacred objects that would be used in the Sun Dance. The Rabbit-tipi corresponded in function to the Lone-tipi among the Cheyennes (cf. Dorsey 1903b, pp. 37ff.). In this structure both material objects and persons were gradually removed from the world of ordinary life and entered into the world of transcendent meanings.

The altar within the Sun's lodge seems to have represented the earth as it was renewed and refreshed. The Arapaho altar included the elements of the sods, the dry painted excavation in front of the buffalo skull, saplings and brush which were inserted into the ground and the sods, and upright sticks placed on each side of the altar. Behind the skull hung the Sacred Wheel (Dorsey 1903b, pp. 104–11). The activities within the Rabbit-tipi flowed outward, invigorating the emerging form of the Offerings Lodge, and the process culminated in the central symbolism of the altar which signaled a world and a people renewed.

Renewal and fertility symbolism also surrounded the headdresses worn by the lodge-maker and his wife. The belt and headdress worn by the lodge-maker's wife were painted red and were associated with the fecundity of the earth. The headdress worn by the lodge-maker was painted blue, representing the fertilizing power of the sky (Dorsey 1903b, p. 75). These symbolic forms become incarnate in the offering of the lodge-maker's wife to the chief priest at the Sun Dance. Whether intercourse occurred during the Sun Dances at the turn of the century, or whether the sacred woman simply exposed her body to the Moon, is not known for sure (Dorsey 1903b, pp. 172–78). In either case, the symbolic fertilizing of the earth was incarnated through the activity of the chief priest and the sacred woman and must be understood within the context of these particular cultural meanings.[14]

The central animal upon which the people depended was also renewed by the ritual. After the skull had been prepared, a buffalo robe was painted, one half black and the other half red. The skull and the robe together constituted a living animal among the people. This renewed animal, known as Young-Bull, was symbolically fed with buffalo chips and fervent prayers were offered on behalf of the people. As was the case for other groups, the buffalo was clearly located within a religious horizon of meaning. Attitudes, dispositions, and behavior toward this animal—as well as other creatures—were conditioned by this primary meaning context. Moral apprehensions were, in short, grounded in fundamental religious apprehensions and always appeared together in the experience of peoples on the Northwestern Plains (cf. Dorsey 1903b, pp. 71–73).

Unlike people who built for their gods permanent temples and other dwellings, the peoples of the Northwestern Plains allowed the material forms of the Sun's lodge to return to the natural elements. The earth altar was quickly worn away by wind and rain, the brush that symbolized the growth of a renewed world soon withered, and the timbers out of which the lodge was constructed rotted on the Plains. The Sun's pole would remain standing somewhat longer, reminding the people of the sacred acts that had unfolded at this place. But the material forms were simply the media through which transcendent dimensions of meaning symbolically irrupted into the experience of the people. As were the lives of the people and their world, these material forms were reconstructed periodically and renewing power was again released. During the interim, sedimented horizons of transcendent meaning were kept alive in oral tradition and a multitude of cultural expressions deeply imbedded in shared symbolic forms maintained through ritual processes.

CHAPTER 7

# A Kinship Among Beings

ON THE NORTHWESTERN PLAINS in 1850, a number of world views lived in the experience of the human groups that occupied that vast region. These understandings of the world were shaped by deeply shared symbolic forms sustained by ritual processes. Ritual enactment of sacred symbols in song, dance, color, and architecture informed the religious and moral experience of the people.

Although there were similarities among Plains institutions and world views in 1850, there were also important differences. These nuances arose as a consequence of creative reinterpretations of their oral traditions during the course of the people's migration to new homelands. The content of the oral traditions was shaped by the people's understanding of how their world was formed by specific creator, trickster, and culture hero figures. In addition, the ambience of their oral traditions supported legends, stories of sacred animals, and a host of other images which gave sense to their conscious lives, often irrupting powerfully in their dreams and waking visions. A rich inner life it was.

The method of this study has been to describe the shared meanings which constituted these world views. This task involved an exposition of the symbolic forms that illuminated them from within. In addition, a study of ritual processes has shown how deeply shared symbols gave shape to human experience and were maintained through social time. The study has also been informed by a number of hypotheses: We have developed a view of how symbols functioned in human social worlds; of how social worlds came into being and were maintained in experience; of how human experience was framed by temporality; and of how different orders of cultural life received various emphases.

In the light of these perspectives, *world* has been understood as a configuration of shared meanings which traced out in a people's experience their special sense of objects, events, and others—their understanding of the natural and social worlds. The humans have been seen to possess capacities for memory, for participating in a present order of experience, and for anticipating futures, their social worlds likewise being characterized by a sense of significant predecessors, by a shared everyday world, and by some vision of others who will come after them. Social worlds have also been seen as multivalent. Transcending the shared everyday world are worlds of memory, visions of projected futures, worlds of play, fantasy, and imagination, as well as worlds of dreams, religious experience, and a sensibility concerning what is good and true. Symbols have been viewed as those objects, events, or others which connected the sense of present experience with one or more of these levels of transcendent meaning. Symbols breach the everyday world, and they have been seen to function in both individual experience and in the collective experience of the group. The cultural flavor of social worlds has been understood to arise out of the way various possibilities for experience were ordered. That is, cultures differ in the value they assign to dreaming, imagining, and religious experience, as compared with thinking, practical action, and working. Social worlds have also been seen to be maintained through social time by collective rituals which focused a people's basic symbolic forms and established a sense of their shared reality. Ritual, finally, has been understood as a field of symbolic forms which was enacted and embodied in various ways.

Interpreting Plains cultures and their moral and religious dimensions in the light of the foregoing perspectives has been—as are all such endeavors—partly an act of the interpreter's imagination. But the evidence presented for these views stands on its own, open to the critical assessment of others. Other interpreters will doubtless see additional elements in these traditions and will read the symbolic forms in perhaps a different way. My only claim is that this interpretation represents a plausible argument, one which is true to the evidence, as far as it goes. It is by no means intended to be comprehensive, and it is certainly not final. More work needs to be done on the relation between concrete moral and religious experience and the social structures within which these experiences were acted out and embodied; and more could be done in comparative studies of other Plains tribes. Despite these limitations, more can be said about what has been discerned in this study and about its broader significance.

A basic problem with which certain layers of these Plains traditions struggled was the killing of animals who were believed to possess consciousness, will, and other capacities that were often superior to those of humans. The extension of the principle of kinship to animals and other phenomena is clearly the ground out of which this dilemma arose. Kinship relations carry corresponding duties and obligations; these duties and obligations have to do with appropriate forms of behavior and attitude. Destroying the possibility of relationship through killing the kinsperson creates tensions that these traditions express in various ways. The problem is deepened even further when the killing of animals occurs in a cultural context which interprets these beings, along with other phenomena, within a structure of religious meaning. It is true that these cultures did not have extremely elaborate ritual processes surrounding hunting as compared with older hunting cultures, such as the Montagnais-Naskapi of the Labrador Peninsula. This circumstance is probably related to their recent evolution as big game hunters.

We did identify, however, certain contexts in which the hunter's dilemma is ritually resolved. Presently we will return to this point and seek to deepen its significance.

The ambiguities surrounding the killing and eating of animals imply a much more general understanding. A world in which social space is shared not only with other humans, but also with animal beings and kinspersons who are clearly more than human, is a world that is religiously grounded in a fundamental manner. There is no space in such a world that is unrelated to this religious ground. This does not mean, of course, that human activities within a shared everyday world cease. To the contrary, Plains Indians worked, played, loved, engaged in practical pursuits, and fought each other as did other human groups.

What marked these cultures, along with other Native Americans, is the extent to which a religious ground permeated all other cultural forms. We have been able to distinguish experiences of transcendence from ordinary experiences, and we have argued that the people themselves made such a distinction; these conclusions do not, however, rest upon a view that differentiates among cultural realities and assigns them their respective autonomy or that places them in opposition to each other. If the term secular, for example, is taken to mean this-worldly and temporal as opposed to the spiritual and eternal, and if these categories are viewed as radically discontinuous, this kind of distinction does not characterize Plains religious experience. In these cultures, the world of ordinary human experience was grounded in, surrounded by, and regularly breached by transcendent realities possessing religious and moral significance for the people. Ordinary experience was not viewed as fundamentally separate from transcendent realities but rather as arising out of, surrounded by, and interpenetrated by sacred powers. Migrations into the world of sacred beings was a regular, and potentially a daily, occurrence; for in their dreams the people often entered the threshold of the world of transcendent significance. The people also discerned in the movement of animals, the fire of a pipe, the steam of a sweat lodge, and the forms of their architecture the internal spiritual forms that gave them meaning.

The central importance given to dreaming and waking visions, whether occurring spontaneously or ritually sought, was clearly the cultural feature that made the people's experience open to transcendent realities in the way that it was. The extension of kinship to animal and plant beings, as well as to solar, lunar, and astral beings, was evident in their languages, to be sure. But the reality of the kinship relationship was sustained both by the continual appearance of these beings in their visions and by seasons of recollection in ritual. Individual identity and destiny were understood in terms of such experiences. And individual attitudes, dispositions, and behavior—the moral elements of religious experience—were shaped by their content.

The identity and destiny of the people were also shaped by memories, borne in oral traditions and enacted in ritual, of important predecessors, through whose actions and experiences the people received some of their most sacred objects and a vision of their moral universe. These creators, culture heroes, and tricksters often occupied a relation of kinship with the people; yet they stood on the boundary of the human world, relating to it in an intimate manner and transcending it as well. Even though the people's understanding of the relationships among creator, trickster, and culture hero figures remains somewhat unclear, the significance of these beings can be further elaborated.

Creation accounts in these traditions largely conformed to a variant of the earth-diver motif, although there are echoes, as in the Crow story, of themes perhaps more closely associated with an agricultural context. The world is typically brought into being through the activities of a creator figure who is assisted by the "first animals" who preexist with the creator in some fashion. In addition, there is preexisting water, deep beneath which is earth and out of which the world will be made. Unlike Western theological traditions of creation *ex nihilo,* out of nothing, Plains traditions have little problem with a creator who is surrounded by preexisting materials and beings. Even more interesting, by contrast with Western traditions, is the notion that some of these animals possess autonomous life powers. Recall the creator's remark in the Crow account: "That coyote has attained life by his own powers, he is great." So casual a remark from a creator figure about a self-actualizing animal must seem especially dissonant to Western Christian ears. The creator in these latter traditions has, as a consequence of layers of theological interpretation, achieved a position of radical monotheism. This creator is viewed as the source of all things; nothing preexists alongside the creator before creation, neither matter nor form, and certainly not beings possessing self-generating powers of life. Classically the Christian creator was also viewed as all-powerful, all-knowing, and a being of pervasive presence. Plains traditions, by comparison, speak of creators who are limited in their powers, who have to take thought concerning what to do, who consult with the first animals and take their advice, who make mistakes which they have to correct, who move through space like human beings, and who are assisted in their task by various plant and animal beings.

To experience the world in this manner must have given rise to a feeling that things were originally quite tentative. They could have been otherwise. Old Man of the Blackfoot account could have disagreed with Old Woman's proposal concerning death, for example, but he did not and we are not told why. The mystery of death is addressed by the tradition, but not given elaborate explanation. Mortality arises not as a result of a human fall, but rather as a consequence of an ancestral gamble. The people experience death, they grieve in its presence, they fear its approach, and yet they do not strike out at a creator figure who allows such a reality to come into being in such a seemingly frivolous manner. They seem rather to accept the original tentativeness as well as the fixed outcome produced by the interaction between Old Man and Old Woman.

To experience the world in this manner is also to view human life and its various natural and social contexts as arising out of a cooperative effort among beings possessing relative amounts of power. One is never quite sure which power is greatest, although creator figures tend to have some ascendency without possessing anything like absolute sovereignty. Careful examination of the narratives does indicate patterns that informed the people's understanding. Certain animals are represented as having significant power: the beaver, the coyote, the wolf, the elk, the raven, and the buffalo, among others. Sometimes animals are represented as mediating the power of another being, such as Sun or Thunder; but just as often the animals have power that is apparently self-generated and often quite specific. Rather than a clear hierarchy of power, beings possess various degrees of power; and the traditions do not make entirely clear what degree of power will be manifested in various contexts. For example, in some Blackfoot traditions, Sun appears to possess great power, while in others, such as the Scar-Face tradition, the sky country is populated by dangerous birds who have apparently defied Sun's power. And in other traditions there are tales of monsters and other horrifying beings who possess terrible powers.

In such a world, *power* is a primal category, but it is manifested in terms of the appearance of various beings, who then grant specific powers to the human beings, either to individuals or to the group. Through vision, an individual may receive power to doctor or to engage in shamanistic activities. Or through the vision of a predecessor, or the establishment of kinship, the people may receive founding powers. For example, in the narrative of the anonymous hunter whose wife lived with the beavers and who gave birth to a beaver child, the Blackfeet received the Beaver bundle. Through the efforts of Sweet Medicine and Erect Horns, the Cheyennes received the sacred arrows and the Sun Dance. As a consequence of the appearance upon the earth of the Stars, the Crow people came to possess a sacred plant which became the source of their lives. And the Arapahoes received from their creator the gift of a sacred Flat Pipe.

In the world of everyday experience, individuals were attentive and expectant, since at any moment, through dreaming or the irruption of a waking vision, power might be granted. Though people might seek power for specific purposes and might sacrifice parts of their bodies in its pursuit, an element of "luck" seems apparent in these traditions. It is also significant to note that the traditions often represent the recipient of power as a person of ambiguous social standing, a "poor youth." Beings of power typically took "pity" on such individuals and came to relate to them in special ways. In the normal course of events, then, Plains people viewed the world as luminous with various forms of power. The continual struggle of the individual was to acquire power and thus to establish a sense of identity and destiny within the group. The successful person was viewed as extremely fortunate and was treated accordingly by the group. Often such persons achieved positions of social visibility or political leadership. Experiences of power were legitimated by the group and often interpreted by persons who possessed ritual knowledge.

To live in the world as represented by some Plains accounts of creation is to live with an intuition of the original kinship between humans and animals, as well as between creator figures and the first animals; and it is simultaneously to live with an intuition of imbalance, of danger, and of potentially disruptive relationships. In such a world there is a deep struggle to interpret how humans came to be dependent upon animal life for their existence. This struggle is embodied in the images of conflict between humans and animals which exist alongside images of mutuality and kinship. Were more known about these traditions, we might better be able to discern how these interpretative struggles are related to the people's migrations from an agricultural past, where they were dependent upon plant and animal life, to an existence centered almost entirely upon hunting.

Plains traditions represent and interpret the emergence of the human being as carnivore. In some creation accounts of the Blackfeet, it will be recalled, buffalo are represented as having power over humans. Being themselves carnivorous at this time, these animals attack, kill, and eat the humans. This situation was changed by the creator, who armed the ancient Blackfeet. From that time forward the people had power over the buffalo. Whether this tradition is older than another narrative, where the creator and the animals are represented in a kinship relation, is not clearly evident. In any case, there is a tension in these traditions as they struggle to interpret hunting. It is interesting to recall that, in the tradition that represents the buffalo as having power over humans, the creator makes humans dependent upon animals in new and more complex ways after they are given over to the people for food. The animals then become sources of sacred power which appear to the people in their dreams and visions. In some Cheyenne traditions, this uneasy dependence of humans upon other life forms for their existence is interpreted in a contest narrative. The question of who shall eat whom is decided not by the creator but by the outcome of a great race among the animals. By contrast, in the Arapaho creation account, White Buffalo is represented as generously giving his body to be food and clothing for the human beings. Other animals and plants also contribute to the form of the world, garter snake giving his body as its circumference.

If it is true that these traditions view hunting as fraught with ambiguity and if this ambiguity has moral dimensions because killing animals is perceived as a deep violation of kinship relations, the interpretative struggle takes on deeper significance. The people sensed, and they reflected in their traditions, the moral and religious problems involved in life feeding upon life. Unlike moderns, who are largely desensitized to the meanings surrounding their food supply, Plains Indians were extremely sensitive to the meaning of killing beings who were, in a deep sense, kinspersons. It is little wonder, then, that this moral and religious dilemma is ritually addressed in the great tribal ceremonies, especially those which thematize the process of world renewal.

Four additional points may be made about Plains creation narratives. First, even though the ambiguous nature of hunting is explored here and in the figure of Trickster, there is no sense that the world as it is formed is finally evil. By contrast, the world is, for the most part, a place for human habitation which is generous and beneficent. There are dangers in the world, to be sure; and there are dangerous beings to contend with. There are also dangerous tendencies within the social world which require control. These traditions realistically interpret this mixed picture as the way things are, not as a consequence of a cosmic decline of creation or a doctrine of natural evil. For the most part, then, the world is arranged so that humans can enjoy it and flourish. If there is a functional equivalent of the notion of evil, it appears in Trickster's activities.

Second, events which give rise to the world and to human beings are viewed as having happened at some time in the past. They are not viewed as events which are coextensive with the beginning of time or which lie somehow outside of time. The beings who populate the traditions are predecessors and often ancestors of the people, not occupants of some "heavenly" sphere, vertically or ontologically transcending human life and the human world. These beings are transcendent, however, in the sense that the past transcends present experience. They are memorialized in the oral traditions, and their presence is made contemporary through ritual processes. They are also transcendent in another sense. Although creator figures often exhibit human qualities and although animal beings are represented as similar to those in present experience, their powers clearly go beyond those of the humans. Creators and the first animals constituted the world in a way humans cannot, and they grant a power without which the human beings and the human world would be greatly diminished.

Third, creation accounts, though possessing elements of similarity, are apprehended by the people as specific to the group. These narratives are clearly stories of the origin of the Crow, the Cheyenne, the Arapaho, and the Blackfoot worlds. Geographical features, when present in the narratives, are specific to traditional tribal areas; and the animals which appear in the traditions are animals most prominent in tribal ecological surroundings. Even though the accounts exhibit cultural specificity and image tribal identity, they all share a feature which is important for this analysis: Tribes of the Northwestern Plains apprehended their world in the light of a deeply religious context. Their traditions express the people's relation to the sacred sources of their lives, powers that transcended and at the same time were intimately related to their existence.

Finally, the deeper meanings attached to the understanding of kinship are revealed in these narratives. Plains peoples apprehended the meaning of kinship in the light of its representation in creation stories. There was not a time, for example, when kinship originated; the creator figures and the first animals were already in such a relationship. The order of human life, though tentative in many of its aspects, clearly reflects this primordial form of mutuality and interrelatedness. To put it in other language, the world in Plains experience was apprehended through a deeply shared organic metaphor. Even though this understanding of kinship reflected patterns that had developed in the human social world, it still expressed the people's sense of a pre-given moral order.

In addition to creator figures, Plains oral traditions speak at length and in great detail about Trickster. Our primary interpretation of the function of this being has been to view him as the negative guardian of a normative moral order. Trickster's behavior embodied the rejection of kinship reciprocities, as well as the antithesis of truthful speech, generous action, brave deeds, and kindness to other humans and animals. These positive values and their corresponding moral attitudes, dispositions, and patterns of behavior formed a general picture of the moral universe of these peoples. Also modeled negatively in Trickster's behavior is a normative view of what the people must have understood as a fully developed moral agent. In these traditions the mature moral life minimally exhibited loyalty to kin, truthfulness, generosity, bravery, and kindness. As an agent of socialization, the trickster figure was a negative model of the moral life. Stories of his exploits impressed upon children and adults the destructive aspects of his moral universe. Trickster as role model functioned through contrast, enabling the people to preserve the normative aspects of their world through seeking to avoid the deformed moral universe reflected in this enigmatic being.

The trickster cycle in Plains oral traditions suggests other areas of exploration beyond the apparent socialization functions and the etiological or explanatory elements that attach to these tales. A discussion of these additional levels of meaning will add to our understanding of this significant yet ambiguous ancestor on the Northwestern Plains.

Trickster perhaps symbolized for Plains people the mystery of human capabilities for destructiveness and folly. As the cosmos was apprehended as a deep mixture of creative and potentially destructive tendencies, often appearing in the form of contradictions, so the moral universe could exhibit such features. Trickster demonstrates not only that destructive tendencies could become dominant, but also what some of the consequences of such a social world might be. While creator figures exhibit human characteristics, Trickster is a predecessor closer at hand in the sense that his moral qualities and behavior were often apparent in the human social world. Individuals clearly exhibited various degrees of violation of family relationships, deception, egocentricity, and cowardice, as well as the many forms of brutality of which humans are capable. Given the character of tribal life, with its kinship system, its demand

[167]

for stable social organization, especially at the great tribal gatherings, and its requirement that tensions among individuals and social groups be kept in check, it becomes clear how destructive and dangerous were Trickster's moral qualities. As moral agent, Trickster symbolized a decline of the human being and the human social world to a level which, in the extreme, would not be recognizably human.

Trickster was also viewed as a being who is almost completely lacking in common sense, despite his shape-shifting and creative powers. The deeply routinized meanings concerning how life is to be lived, how tasks are to be performed, and how to relate to powerful beings are all violated by Trickster. He is a fool, provoking laughter and ridicule, as well as a vision of what the social world would be without shared systems of unquestioned meaning. In addition, Trickster may have given the people a vicarious sense of what it might be like to live outside their familiar moral order— hence the persistent attraction of this figure to Plains peoples.

Finally, in the behavior of Trickster are levels which suggest the meaning of being a human and a hunter of other living beings. Supplementing the creation narratives, these aspects of the traditions expose a halo of ambiguity surrounding Trickster's hunting activity. He is motivated by continual hunger, which is the biological ground that drives humans to consume other forms of life. His hunger is, however, insatiable and continually pressing, leading him to be wasteful and foolish as a hunter. Furthermore, Trickster deceives animals by playing upon aspects of their nature, such as their generosity, friendliness, gullibility, and trust. What is revealed here is an ambiguity which attaches to human hunting. It is an activity which requires knowledge of animal nature and animal habits, which knowledge gives the human power to deceive them and thus to snare and kill them for food. Such deception is based upon luring animals by playing upon their own natural characteristics and modeling human hunting activities in such a manner that they seem to fit into the animal world. Thus the animal is tricked, killed, and consumed so that human life may continue.

Trickster's exploitative hunting techniques are imaged as destructive and dangerous, should they become normative in the human world. The theme of the "last animal" which runs through these narratives suggests this foolishness and danger in a fascinating manner. Through the momentary lapse of Trickster's general character, a last animal, usually a pregnant female, survives to continue the species. Clearly the hunting techniques represented in these tales are not affirmed, but rather their foolishness and potential disastrous consequences for the people are powerfully represented. If there are conservationist tendencies at work in these cultures, as there surely are, then a part of their moral legitimation derives from the way Trickster is imaged in the oral traditions.

In the light of the foregoing analysis, more can be said about the apparent tensions between creator and trickster figures as they appear in the traditions. Both sets of narratives express a mixture of creative and destructive tendencies in human experience. This problem is religiously addressed as the people grope symbolically toward an interpretation of a world in which an abundance of food exists, yet starvation is an ever-present possibility; in which animals are spirit-kin, yet are killed and eaten; in which life flourishes in every being, yet death comes to all; and in which human relationships are deep and good, yet are threatened internally by outbreaks of individual and social chaos.

The tensions generated by these oppositions may lie at the basis of the uneasy alliance between trickster and creator motifs. If this is so, then we are in the presence of an interpretation which is both realistic and affirmative. Realistic and affirmative elements are present in the way these traditions refuse finally to resolve basic oppositions, either by means of a savior figure or by positing a better order after death—familiar options for many in our culture. Rather the mixture of creative and destructive tendencies is realistically acknowledged and at the same time the flourishing of human life is also affirmed. These traditions plumb the depths of human possibilities for folly and destructiveness, facing directly the ambiguities of human existence within the vast kinship systems of nature and society, and acknowledging that humans remain in an uneasy relationship to these systems and are capable of sinking below the human—and even the animal—should destructive impulses not be curbed.

If the people had a view of the relationship between creator and trickster figures, it may have been something like this: Creators were understood as constitutive figures, giving rise to the cosmos; trickster figures were associated more closely, though not completely, with the human moral universe.

The social worlds of people on the Northwestern Plains were shaped as well by the deeds of another class of significant predecessors, the culture heroes and other ancestors of the tribes. These predecessors were, in some cases, clearly human. In the figure of Sweet Medicine, however, we meet a being who exhibits not only trickster elements, but also other powers of life beyond the normal human being; and, in the Cheyenne traditions of Coyote Man and Old Woman's Water, we seem to be in the presence of a master and mistress of the animals. In other cases, such as those anonymous persons whose visions engendered important institutional elements central to tribal life, we are confronted by humans who endured important experiences of sacred power on behalf of the people. The etiological aspects of these narratives are clearly evident; but beyond these, the figures are often memorialized and his or her deeds are recapitulated in the rituals of the tribes. In a manner common to all societies, culture heroes and other predecessors were founders who added important dimensions to the people's world and contributed to their understanding of identity and destiny. As George Washington and Abraham Lincoln are memorialized in public rituals and contribute to the American sense of identity and vision of destiny, so did Sweet Medicine, Erect Horns, and Scar-Face. Similar social processes operated as well within the traditions of the other tribes on the Northwestern Plains.

Even though we have emphasized the function of tribal ritual for the maintenance of the Plains world picture, this sensibility did not fade during the seasons when tribal groups were separated into smaller hunting bands. During such times dreams and waking visions continually occurred to individuals. Similarly, collections of sacred objects which symbolically bore the meanings of the tribal world view were widespread among the bands. Among the Blackfeet, these objects constituted, during the entire year, the core of a pervasive bundle religion.

The larger bundles, such as the Blackfoot Beaver bundle, the

Arapaho Flat Pipe, the Cheyenne Arrow bundle, and some of the larger Shield bundles among the Crows were cared for during the year by their owners or keepers. During their winter dispersion, groups such as the Cheyennes and Arapahoes knew that their sacred tribal objects were properly cared for and that, when the group reassembled, their significant ritual processes would unfold once again. Among the Blackfeet, these sacred objects were experienced in perhaps more immediate ways during band separation, since the major bundles were duplicated and widely distributed among the various groups. Crow Shield bundles were likewise widely distributed. In addition, personal collections of sacred objects were widespread, and they reinforced in the individual's consciousness a sense of identity and destiny that was broadly coherent with symbolic forms constituting the tribal world views.

Given what we have seen in preceding chapters, it is significant how much individual and social effort was expended on ritual processes. If hunting was successful in any given year and a food supply and other essential items were secured, a great deal of leisure was available in these hunting cultures of the 1850s. Camp life was pervaded by various levels of social activity, not the least of which was the rehearsal of oral traditions concerning Trickster, as well as participation of the people in various sorts of ritual processes. The social effort required for the Sun Dance, the Arrow Ceremony, and the Tobacco Society rituals was in itself impressive. When added to the religious activities pervading the social life of the bands, the picture becomes one of peoples whose worlds were maintained through pervasive ritual processes.

The great tribal ceremonies were interpreted as rituals of social and world renewal. Although this concept was certainly at the center of their meaning, many other social and personal activities ensued during these great gatherings. At the deepest of levels, however, these rituals restored and repaired human relations and achieved a symbolic reconciliation with the world and its many beings. The renewal of their primary animal, the buffalo, was a pervasive motif at the center of these rituals. As a consequence of these yearly activities, there emerged in the experience of the people a deepened sense of a kinship among beings.

Such a world picture was one in which nature, as living

[171]

organism, was directly addressed; and as living organism, nature could become worn and tired, requiring the cyclic restoration brought on by the seasons and by the symbolic renovation accomplished in Plains tribal rituals. Likewise, the moral universe could become stained and tattered, threatened by the emergence of destructive tendencies; these tendencies were checked and their consequences removed from social life through processes of symbolic social renewal. Through these ritual processes, the life fire burning within the human beings and energizing all life forms was both celebrated and adored.

Vision, the gift of power, and the normative importance of kinship—these were elements that constituted central features of Plains social worlds, formed the horizons of their moral and religious experience, and deeply motivated their actions. To us these may be strange worlds. Yet if openings into these worlds have been made possible, then contemporary experience may be enriched by the power, presence, and vision embodied in these predecessor traditions. This enrichment of experience could engender a softening and even transformation of the more destructive aspects of contemporary society—where kinship is applicable only to the human world, where vast social structures dominate rather than interact with the nonhuman world, where vision is largely confined to human imaginings, and where power is often reduced to strategies of human manipulation or threats of collective violence.

# Notes

## CHAPTER 1: RETRACING TIME

1. In this work, I seek to show the importance of the phenomenological perspective for interpreting religious and moral traditions. For further elaboration of my views, see *The Human Center: Moral Agency in the Social World* (1981). This perspective also influenced an earlier work, although to a lesser extent; see *Mission Among the Blackfeet* (1971). The literature which informs these books is the phenomenological sociology of Alfred Schutz (see Schutz 1964, 1966, 1967a, 1967b, 1970; Schutz and Luckmann 1973).

The notions of meaning, symbol, social worlds, tradition, ritual, the multidimensionality of human experience, and other key concepts which inform the chapters that follow are constructed out of this literature. Thus, the perspective is "Schutzean," in the sense that it is inspired by Schutz; but it is constructive in the sense that the categories are reworked and applied to the Plains materials. On the basis of this theoretical perspective, I have sought to illuminate the nature of moral and religious experience among Northwestern Plains tribes.

2. The reconstruction attempted in this work presents a number of important interpretative problems: First, the "text" to be interpreted is the historical,

linguistic, and ethnographical record laid down at the end of the last century and in the first decades of this century. This record reflects, in more or less adequate ways, the dynamic oral traditions of the tribes themselves. The problem is how to discern the complexes of meaning which are both concealed and revealed in the work of these early observers and scholars. Second, because the interest of some of these researchers was focused in part upon the methodological and conceptual problems of the discipline of cultural anthropology, they often ignored the very cultural meanings with which the student of religion is most preoccupied. Third, their presentation of the material sometimes separated, for purposes of analysis, elements of the social structure, such as ritual forms and constitutive mythology, which belong intimately together. This analysis will attempt to reintegrate these aspects of Plains religious and moral traditions. Fourth, the assumption which guides the analysis is that the ethnographic record reflects elements of the oral tradition as that corporate memory must have existed in the middle of the nineteenth century. This view rests upon the fact that many of the informants were persons of advanced age when the materials were gathered. Some were children or youth in 1850 and could remember the nature of tribal life during buffalo days. And certainly their immediate predecessors would have mediated to them a sense of their tribal traditions from an even earlier time. It is not assumed—quite to the contrary—that these traditions represent an undisturbed sediment of prehistoric memory. Rather, the traditions are viewed within a context that included dynamic processes of social change affecting all the Plains tribes. Finally, I am deeply and sometimes painfully aware of what has been lost in the transition from oral narrative to transcription to text. I am also aware that a careful hermeneutic can recover certain of these meanings and bring parts of these traditions more clearly into view. Through such a process we may be able to encounter these peoples and their traditions in fresh ways.

Getting at a "people's point of view" cannot mean, of course, a reproduction of their cultural meaning. Rather, the task is *interpretative,* which involves a construction of ideal types on the basis of historical, linguistic, and cultural materials. In this manner the content of social worlds and social experiences are interpreted and their shared meanings are displayed. The relative coherence between idealtypical constructs and the shared meanings of any social world is what renders an interpretation illuminating and adequate. There is finally no way to *prove* adequacy, especially with historical materials. Relative approximations may be achieved, however, through detailed examinations of particular cultural contexts. Such examinations generate more general interpretations of their meaning. These general interpretations may then be subjected to the more particular cultural phenomena; this process of interaction between the particular and the general issues in an interpretation that can claim at least relative adequacy. This interpretative method obviously stands in the tradition of Max Weber's *verstehen* sociology and is deeply influenced by the constructive reflections upon Weber by Alfred Schutz (1967b), as well as by the work of Clifford Geertz (1973, pp. 3–30; 1983, pp. 55–70).

3. Two questions arise at this point: Why choose the period between 1850 and 1900 as the base line for description; and why are these four groups chosen while others are omitted? On the first point, it seems clear that major religious institutions, such as the Sun Dance, reached their highest level of development

during the middle of the nineteenth century (Liberty 1980, p. 164). The ethnographic record laid down at the beginning of this century thus describes ritual and symbolic forms which constituted the social worlds and experiences of transcendence among these peoples in a powerful and often enduring manner. On the second point, it is not my argument that the four tribes typify Plains culture and experience in an exhaustive manner. Rather, what I seek to achieve, through comparative case studies, is some understanding of the social worlds and religious lives of these four distinct peoples. Other important groups, such as the Sioux, have been excluded, but not because they are unimportant. Rather, part of the reason for their exclusion relates to the extensive study that has already been done on this group by other scholars, such as my colleague, Joseph Epes Brown. At another level, the decision to include only four tribes was partly practical, an attempt to limit the size and scope of the work; and it was also partly personal, owing to my greater familiarity with at least one group, the Blackfeet.

4. The point being made about the relation between religious forms, culture, and ecological contexts may be clarified by an example closer to American experience. Religious institutions and ideas in the United States reflect in part of their history the transition of people from a rural to an urban context. As urbanization set in, religious forms and institutional patterns both preserved older rural images and at the same time deeply reflected the social patterns of an emerging industrial and urban society. The widespread diffusion of bureaucratic social organization in the American churches is but one sign of this quite pervasive process.

5. On the Northwestern Plains, other factors besides the arid conditions and technology prevented the emergence of horticulture. For example, the number of frost-free days is only about 120, and the growing season is thus severely limited. By contrast, for the tribes of the upper Missouri, such as the Mandans and Hidatsas, nature was a gentler presence. Longer growing seasons enabled them to develop a subsistence base which included a mixture of horticulture and hunting.

6. Although some scholars may prefer the more technical term "bison," I have opted for the term of more general use, "buffalo." In this preference I have been influenced by the opinion of Roe (1970, pp. 3–4). Carling Malouf has warned against overemphasizing big-game hunting as compared with hunting smaller animals and gathering wild plant foods (personal correspondence). It is indeed true that the Plains Indian diet included numerous wild plants. And certainly small animals were hunted when buffalo could not be found. The amount of meat gathered from a single buffalo kill was, of course, much greater than several small animals. Furthermore, if the animals were very small (e.g., rabbits), it would require the labor of many hunters to equal the results of a single buffalo hunter's success.

7. A major source of social change was, of course, the fur trade. The trade diffused new cultural items to the tribes and contributed to increased competition among and within groups. Although the results were often expansive, there were also long-term destructive effects. Game was depleted, white population pressures increased, traditional authority structures were weakened, and cultural dependence upon western products became more widespread. For examples, see Wolf (1982, pp. 176–81) and Lewis (1940).

8. My usage of the singular, plural, and adjectival forms of tribal names requires some comment. In much of the earlier literature, and in some present

works, the singular, plural, and adjectival forms are comprehended in a single term: Cheyenne (sing.), Cheyenne (pl.), and Cheyenne social structure (adj.). I have chosen to revert to the following usage: Cheyenne (sing. and adj.) and Cheyennes (pl.). The Blackfoot case presents special problems. In some of the older literature, the usage followed the form I have proposed. Present members of the tribe often prefer the term "Blackfeet" to cover all usages. My choice to depart from this pattern is based upon consistency and not any desire to ignore the wishes of contemporary Blackfeet people. The reservation in the United States is officially designated as the Blackfeet Reservation, and this usage will be followed in the text.

9. Carling Malouf's research in western Montana has pointed toward the possible use of pictographs in connection with the vision quest (personal correspondence). He also argues that such cultural items as pottery, pipes, and medicine wheels indicate a probable relationship with the Mississippian culture of the southeast (see also Wolf 1982, pp. 68–70).

## CHAPTER 2: EXPERIENCING THE SACRED

1. The continuing importance of "dream colors" in Crow bead work was mentioned by a member of the tribe, Ms. Frances Alden. Such colors are either dreamed by the contemporary bead-worker or are colors which ancestors have dreamed and which have been transferred to contemporaries (personal conversation, April 23, 1981, Helena, Montana).

## CHAPTER 3: FORMING THE WORLD

1. The Blackfoot collection was made between 1903 and 1907. The translations were made by D. C. Duvall, a native speaker, and revised by Wissler. The method was to record oral events and then to translate this material in order to preserve as much as possible of the oral style. The three Blackfoot divisions are represented, although material from the Piegan dominates (Wissler and Duvall 1908, pp. 5–6). For this reason, the ambiguity between Old Man as creator/culture hero and trickster may have been less prominent in Blood and Northern Blackfoot traditions, but we have no way of knowing.

Wissler believed that Old Man had disintegrated in these traditions from a creative and originating figure to a trickster (Wissler and Duvall 1908, p. 9); Grinnell sees these characters mixed in the traditions but does not posit an evolutionary hypothesis (Grinnell 1962, p. 257). The analysis of the name, Napi, Old Man, is also interesting in Grinnell: Napi is a compound of Ninah, man, and the particle, api, which expresses a color. The particle is always in connection with another word and never by itself. Thus, Grinnell concludes, "Na'pi would seem to mean dawn-light-color-man, or man-yellowish-white" (Grinnell 1962, p. 256). Although he refuses to assign Old Man of the creation traditions to the category of "light personified," Grinnell's views are suggestive. It may be that the name itself is a linguistic signal of the deeper symbolic associations between Old Man in his role as creator and the sun.

The problem with which these earlier interpreters struggled was the relationship between Old Man, or Napi, and the Sun, or Natos. Wissler finds them clearly distinguished (Wissler and Duvall 1908, p. 10) and Grinnell finds them one and the same, although Old Man is for him the more ancient figure (Grinnell 1962, p. 258). Wissler finally takes the position that the figure of Old Man is probably very ancient and that Natos, the sun, is of a more recent origin (Wissler and Duvall 1908, p. 12). The tentative position that we will take on this issue is one which views the problem from another perspective rather than attempting to solve it within the parameters of the older debate. This view, introduced in the text, is that these traditions are structures of shared meaning and that they configure the experience of people in particular ways. It will become clear, as the total argument unfolds, that the symbolic representation of the sacred power at the heart of the universe most clearly, for the Blackfeet, is evoked by the sun at the time these traditions reached their formation in about 1850. Solar imagery and ritual processes that recall the creation are held together in the people's experience, irrespective of the question of which layer of tradition is oldest.

A work published after my book was in press is *The Sun Came Down* (1985), by Percy Bullchild, a full-blood Blackfeet. Subtitled, "The History of the World as my Blackfeet Elders Told It," it is a fascinating account which weaves Blackfoot traditions about creation, trickster, and culture heroes, as well as sacred bundles and the Sun Dance, into a single coherent narrative. While there are some interesting differences between Bullchild's rendition and earlier collections such as those of Grinnell and Wissler, what is striking is the deep continuity with the past. In this connection it is interesting to note that Bullchild's version affirms solar symbolism as most fundamental to Blackfoot religious life.

2. According to Lowie, the sun is the being which approaches the status of a "supreme being" for the Crows (Lowie 1922, p. 318). As was the case for the Blackfeet, among the Crows there was an ambiguity concerning the identification of the trickster/culture hero, Old-Man-Coyote and the Sun (Lowie 1922, pp. 318–19). Old-Man-Coyote also appears under the name of "First-Worker," a Hidatsa designation, recalling the earlier relationship between these two tribes (Lowie 1922, p. 320).

3. The central importance of the Flat Pipe in Arapaho culture will be taken up in the sixth chapter when we treat the Sun Dance. See also Carter (1938, pp. 69–202). For reasons that will be given later, the Flat Pipe assumed greater significance in the lives of the Northern Arapahoes, while the Sacred Wheel became central to the culture of the Southern Arapahoes.

4. Wissler had twenty-one informants in all, and many of them were probably prominent individuals, although it is somewhat difficult to locate them socially by means of the information he provides (Wissler and Duvall 1908, p. 6). It is probable, however, that the Blackfeet of former times had a shared view in general terms of how their natural and social worlds had originated (Wissler and Duvall 1908, p. 9). The Crow account of creation is taken from a narrative produced by Medicine Crow, a chief and visionary of the tribe. This version is a prelude to an account of the Tobacco Society ritual (Lowie 1918, p. 14n.). Grinnell's Blackfoot informants included prominent men, although his creation account source is not identified (Grinnell 1962, pp. xvi–xvii). Grinnell's report of a Mandan fragment in the Cheyenne account of creation was told to him by Ben

Clark, a white man who married a Cheyenne woman (Grinnell 1971, p. 242). And Dorsey's Arapaho data come mainly from sun-dance priests, and one in particular named Hawkan, through an interpreter (Dorsey 1903b, pp. 3–4).

5. The trickster figure in Plains oral traditions, as well as elsewhere in North American Indian traditions, is an enigmatic being and has occasioned much scholarly debate. One set of problems has to do with the association, in the same figure, of creation and the bringing of culture and obscenity, humor and malicious behavior. Although we cannot completely solve these issues, it will be helpful to review some of the major dimensions of the discussion.

For this purpose, a helpful survey has been provided by Ricketts (Ricketts 1966, pp. 327–50). In the nineteenth century, an important theory which explained the contradictory tendencies of the trickster was proposed by Daniel Brinton in his *Myths of the New World* (1896). According to Brinton, the Algonquian trickster figure emerged as a consequence of the influence of late accretions upon an original conception of a noble light deity. By a process of negative evolution, the god of light becomes the Great Hare of the trickster cycle. Brinton's view was questioned by Franz Boas, who took the position that trickster elements in the oral traditions were probably the oldest strata. Boas argued that the trickster was originally a self-centered, amoral character. As human thought developed, however, there evolved the notion of a culture hero who brought good things to humans. Furthermore, contended Boas, the more highly developed the oral traditions, the greater degree of separation between the figure of the trickster and the figure of the culture hero. In the less sophisticated traditions, the Janus-like aspects of the trickster's personality are comingled.

In his work on the trickster figure, Paul Radin also took the position that these materials represented a very ancient stratum. In his book, *The Trickster* (1956), Radin developed a psychological interpretation which viewed the trickster as a representation of primal human mentality, appearing in its undifferentiated state. In the career of the trickster we see the human psyche struggling toward differentiation, and thus full humanity. Radin's views are complemented by those of Carl Jung, who contributed the final chapter of the book. Jung's position was that the trickster is

> obviously a "psychologem," an archetypal psychic structure of extreme antiquity. In his clearest manifestations he is a faithful copy of an absolutely undifferentiated human consciousness, corresponding to a psyche that has hardly left the animal level. (Radin 1956, p. 200)

In an earlier work, less influenced by Jung, Radin made the argument that the trickster was more to be identified with the structure of popular belief, whereas the culture hero and the conception of a high god were the consequence of the activities of religious professionals, a class of shamans.

In developing his position, Ricketts uses the distinction between shamanistic activity and popular belief to argue that the trickster figure actually represents not the religiosity of priestcraft but the religious sensibilities of humanism.

> The trickster may best be understood as the personification of all the traits of man raised to the highest degree. Man is sexual; the trickster is grossly erotic. Man is driven by hunger; the trickster will do anything to obtain a meal. Man is slow to learn from his mistakes; the trickster repeats the same blunders again and again.

Man's lot is hard in this world, yet life has its pleasures and joys also; the trickster is continually being buffeted about, but he also has his fun and he always comes up laughing. (Ricketts 1966, p. 347)

Hultkrantz assigns the figure of the trickster to the category of "myths of entertainment" (Hultkrantz 1981, pp. 17–18). In his earlier work, Hultkrantz took the view that the high god of American Indian mythology could be distinguished from the culture hero/trickster figure (Hultkrantz 1979, p. 32). The supreme being often plays little part in the creation, the most active role being taken by the culture hero. The culture hero has been evolved, through the story-teller's art, into the trickster, who is the "degenerate symbol of the evil and distorted in existence" (Hultkrantz 1979, p. 33). In his activity as culture creator and transformer, the culture hero may exhibit more noble qualities, but in other cases he may intentionally bring into being conditions which are harmful to humans. Hultkrantz continues:

More than any other mythological figure he has thus come to represent the somewhat capricious, dangerous, often malevolent aspect of the supernatural. (Hultkrantz 1979, p. 33)

The trickster may also represent a tendency in human experience which incorporates the comic within the experience of the sacred but perhaps not with the intent that Hultkrantz indicates, which is "to ease the pressure brought on by the tense and solemn atmosphere" (Hultkrantz 1979, p. 35; cf. Makarius 1970, 1973).

In a recent work, Sam Gill interprets the trickster in a manner which connects him with an understanding of the importance of moral principles which shape and restrain human behavior. From this point of view, the trickster represents the desire of humans to be transcendent of morality, being able to express desires freely and completely, without harm or restraint. Thus, the trickster is characterized by gastronomic and sexual excesses that violate the normative structure of most societies. The trickster, however, is represented as being unable to violate the morals of society without consequence. He violates the rules, but he usually suffers in the aftermath of the expression of his boundless desire. Gill concludes, "In Trickster is embodied the human struggle against the confinement felt by being bound to place, even within the obvious necessity of such definition in order to prevent chaos" (Gill 1982, p. 28). Trickster shows the importance of the restraint and structure which are given to human life by the presence of moral principles and a shared moral ethos.

Claude Lévi-Strauss interprets the trickster as a figure who performs a mediating function between polar opposites, such as human and animal; as such, this figure is typically ambiguous and equivocal (Lévi-Strauss 1967, pp. 223ff.). And my colleague, Volney Gay, has interpreted Trickster as the "antithesis of the culture hero who provides order out of chaos, form out of emptiness, and laws and customs from disorder and lawlessness" (Gay 1983, p. 375). As such, Trickster is an anti-hero, a being of negative virtue who flaunts the normative order of cultural values. Finally, in an illuminating essay, Jarold Ramsey has provided an expansive definition of Trickster:

A Trickster is an imaginary hyperbolic figure of the human, irrepressibly energetic and apparently unkillable, whose episodic career is based upon hostility to domesticity, maturity, good citizenship, modesty, and fidelity of any kind; who in

Freudian terms is mostly id, a little ego, and no superego; who is given to playful disguises and shape-changing; and who in his clever self-seeking may accomplish important mythic transformations of reality, both in terms of creating possibility and in terms of setting human limits. From a structural standpoint, Tricksters are important mediative figures. (Ramsey 1983, p. 27)

My own position on these matters, articulated in the text, treats Trickster figures in Northwestern Plains traditions from the point of view of their contribution to the preservation of certain specific cultural values which form the moral universes of these peoples. Trickster performs this function, among others, through playing the role of a negative moral agent, through whose action the normative moral order may be viewed. Other horizons of meaning surround these trickster figures, some of which seem interpretable through theories such as have been described. The main point of this analysis, however, is to emphasize the role which Trickster has in maintaining, through oppositions, the shared moral universe of the people.

6. Oral traditions that portray the activities of Trickster are persistent and may be found in many forms down to the present. As late as 1963, for example, I heard a version of Old Man and the squirrels which was almost identical to that recorded by Wissler and Duvall around the turn of the century. The only difference in the story was that, rather than squirrels, the animals were gophers, and Old Man was accompanied by a fox. This story was told by Ms. Albert Wells, a Piegan.

7. This problem has been treated in a fascinating manner by Calvin Martin in his analysis of the impact of the fur trade on tribes in eastern Canada. See Martin (1978, chaps. 4 and 5).

## CHAPTER 4: EVOKING THE SACRED

1. The combination of the term "medicine" with "bundle" requires some clarification. Generally, the term medicine refers to a concept that needs to be deepened and nuanced. In his discussion of Blackfoot bundles, for example, Wissler has translated the word *sáam* as "medicine." Uhlenbeck, however, translates the term *natósi* as "medicine man." The meanings clustered around this term are also sun and moon. Furthermore, the idea of sacredness or holiness is carried in the term, *nátosini,* "medicine power." To refer to a person possessing such power, the term *natósiu* would be translated, "he has medicine power." In the light of this discussion, the term *sáam* might better be associated with doctoring than with the powers of the shaman or holy person. This interpretation is given further support by the way Uhlenbeck translates *sáam* as "drug" or "medicine" (Uhlenbeck and Van Gulik 1934). In the context of this chapter, then, the term "medicine bundle" will refer to a collection of sacred objects associated with specific levels of transcendent meaning; and a "medicine" man or woman will indicate those persons who are intellectually and morally qualified to perform the rituals associated with bundles.

2. There are other pipes among the Blackfeet. For example, there is the Black Wrapped Pipe, which is essentially used in connection with war; and there is the Catchers Society Pipe, which I take to be associated with the hunting of buffalo,

at least in its origins, although Wildschut identifies it with war-making activities (Wildschut 1928, pp. 419–33). Wissler also mentions several other pipes: The Worm-Pipe, which is associated with the power of fire; the Pipe from the Seven Stars, associated with the power of astral beings; and the Black-Covered Pipe, which is given by Coyote and is associated with food (Wissler 1912, p. 91).

3. On September 15, 1963, I observed the opening of a pipe bundle on the Blackfeet Reservation in Browning, Montana. The occasion for the opening was in response to a vow made by a man who was ill. The officiating priest was Dan Bull Plume, and he was assisted by Fish Wolf Robe, both of whom have subsequently died.

On June 6, 1982, I observed the opening of another pipe bundle on the Blackfeet Reservation. The occasion for this opening was the sound of the first thunder, signaling the appearance of spring. Some significant differences, as compared with my experience in 1963, were evident: In 1963 the opening occurred in a tipi; in 1982 the ritual took place in a ceremonial house owned by George and Molly Kicking Woman. In 1963 the bundle that was opened was owned by a Blackfoot; in 1982 the bundle opened was the possession of a white man, a descendant of fur traders. At the level of ritual form, however, there was considerable continuity between 1963 and 1982, as well as between these two ceremonies and the observations made by Wissler at the turn of the century. This indicates that a core meaning structure is being preserved and mediated to present experience by the activities of persons such as George and Molly Kicking Woman, who performed the central ceremonial roles in the 1982 bundle opening.

4. Wissler, for example, records versions of origin from the Northern Blackfeet, Blood, North Piegan, and South Piegan divisions of the Blackfoot Confederacy (Wissler and Duvall 1908, pp. 74–78; Wissler 1912, pp. 192–94).

5. Wissler indicates that almost all of the creatures in the Blackfoot environment are represented in the beaver bundle, with the possible exception of the mountain sheep, the lion, and the owl (Wissler 1912, p. 190, n. 1). During the time of Wissler's research, beaver bundles were found among all the Blackfoot divisions except the Blood. These bundles were apparently individually owned, even though owning and caring for such a large and complex bundle required considerable sacrifice. By 1924, Wildschut reports that beaver bundles were owned by several persons, the expense of single ownership being too great (Wildschut 1924, p. 139; cf. Wissler 1912, p. 175). This development may be related to the increasing economic and social meanings which bundles came to acquire, especially at the time of their transfer (Wissler 1912, pp. 272–78). In addition to the functions of the beaver bundle discussed in the text, it also was associated with the planting of tobacco and the calling of buffalo (Wissler 1912, pp. 200–4, 204–9).

6. As compared with the ritual of the sacred pipe, the beaver ritual is more complex and a great deal longer. For example, the pipe ritual includes as many as seventy songs, in addition to dances and other symbolic movements (Wissler 1912, p. 146), whereas for the beaver ceremony the number of songs runs into the hundreds. Wissler estimates, for example, that there are from two to four hundred songs associated with the ritual (Wissler 1912, p. 190).

7. In 1963, I acquired such a rock bundle from Clarence Butterfly, a Piegan. He was willing to sell me the bundle, but he was unwilling to transfer to me the

songs, paints, and other ritual knowledge associated with this sacred object. From the Blackfoot perspective, then, I received only a replaceable material object; its sacred power was clearly retained by Clarence Butterfly.

8. It was also believed that the natoas, or Sun Dance bundle, was associated originally with the beaver bundle, although later in time it became a separate entity with its own ritual forms (Wissler 1912, pp. 211–15).

9. Among the Blackfeet, shields were important as well. The designs on Blackfoot shields were generally representative of the buffalo, as well as the sun, moon, or stars (Wissler 1912, p. 117).

## CHAPTER 5: RENEWING THE PEOPLE

1. In the Sweet Medicine tradition there are probably interpolations of material which relate elements deriving from Cheyenne contact with Western culture. Examples of such interpolations are references to the horse and gun, as well as elements that may relate to contact with missionaries. A clear evidence of this latter motif appears in some of the narratives of the miraculous birth of the culture hero. In the clearest of these narratives one is able to discern parallels with the New Testament accounts of the birth and miraculous powers of Jesus (Stands in Timber and Liberty 1967, pp. 27–41).

2. Furthermore, in about 1830, the Pawnees captured the Cheyenne arrow bundle, stimulating a deep crisis in the life of the tribe. In response to this crisis, the Cheyennes constructed four new arrows. Traditions recorded at the turn of the century tell of the attempts by the Cheyennes to recover their sacred arrows (Dorsey 1903a, pp. 644–58; Grinnell 1910, pp. 550ff.).

3. A Marxist reading of the status of Indian women in the nineteenth century holds that their position actually worsened as a consequence of the expansive tendencies brought about by the horse, the gun, and the fur trade (Klein, in Wood and Liberty 1980, pp. 133–35). This argument is based on the hypothesis that during the eighteenth century the productive roles of women and men were relatively equal. During this period more women were believed to be involved in hunting as compared with later, when a division of labor developed which assigned women the task of processing the kill. Men were left almost totally dominant as hunters and enjoyed the status that accompanied this important activity. The ensuing economic inequities were responsible for corresponding inequities spreading throughout the society, including legal institutions, social institutions, and religious institutions. Although this view does make some advance over earlier functionalist perspectives, which tended to overemphasize harmony and social integration, its weakness lies precisely in its doctrinaire commitment to Marxist logic: Conditions of production are actually the most basic of human realities—the substructure—and the cultural superstructure reflects faithfully changes that take place at this more basic level.

4. This tobacco was most probably *Nicotiana multivalvis,* or "short tobacco." The variety smoked by the Crows was "long tobacco," or *Nicotiana quadrivalvis.* This latter variety was probably derived from the Hidatsas, from whom the Crows had earlier separated (Lowie 1935, p. 274). The planting of sacred Tobacco was also practiced among the Blackfeet and formed a part of the ritual activities surrounding the beaver bundle (Wissler 1912, pp. 200–4). Rather than involving

the activities of a society, however, the planting was done by the owners of the beaver bundles. It is interesting that Blackfoot informants claimed that tobacco planting came from *their* traditions and that the Crows and other tribes received knowledge of this sacred plant from them. Whether true or not, it is interesting that the Blackfeet believed the tobacco seeds were actually small dwarf beings about a foot tall. These beings must be well fed and appropriately treated. The dwarf motif was also present in Crow traditions, although these figures do not seem to appear in connection with the Tobacco Society (Lowie 1918, pp. 165–71). Among the Blackfeet, the ground was prepared by slashing and burning; the tobacco seeds were mixed with deer, antelope, and mountain sheep dung, as well as with service berries. After the planting the people moved symbolically four times away from the garden site. In the fall the people moved back to the garden, and the beaver men harvested the crop. The tobacco leaves were cut up, mixed with other ingredients, and distributed among the people. Unlike the Crows, the Blackfeet smoked their tobacco; and unlike the Crows, the themes of social and moral renewal are not as prominent in the Blackfoot ritual process.

## CHAPTER 6: RENEWING THE WORLD

1. The term "natoas" is linguistically derived from a combination of meanings which refer to sun power, on the one hand, and to turnip, on the other (Wissler 1912, p. 209). The reasons for this set of associations will be examined presently. In any case, the term may be used to refer to the entire bundle, but its more specific reference is to the sacred headdress which is a central item in the bundle.

2. As was pointed out, the natoas bundle was believed to have once been a part of the beaver bundle. Even at the turn of the century, beaver bundle owners were considered competent to conduct the natoas transfer ceremony. In earlier days the natoas bundle and the ceremonial clothing which went with it were owned by the beaver men. When a Sun Dance was performed, the sacred woman obtained the natoas and costume from a beaver man, a horse being the usual price for their use (Wissler 1918, p. 247 n.1). The natoas bundle was duplicated, as were other important bundles, and at the turn of the century there were more than eight of these bundles among the Blackfeet. These bundles were not identical, but their general form was consistent (Wissler 1912, p. 209). The material aspects of the bundles were subordinate to their symbolic meaning. Material aspects could be duplicated or replaced if the bundle was lost, buried with its owner, or destroyed. The meanings evoked by the symbolic context are mediated through ritual, song, and sacred movement rather than by the sheer materiality of the bundle.

3. The problem of selection, given the nature of the oral tradition, is a treacherous one indeed. The judgments by which the selection was made must be made clear. In interpreting and selecting the portions of the tradition that seem most representative, a judgment has been made that the traditions that were narrated by persons of acknowledged ritual knowledge are the richest and most illuminating. These persons are often medicine men or chiefs. In making this judgment, I am aware of the fact that there may be a distinction between popular belief structures and those represented by persons who are competent to lead the people in ritual acts. I assume, however, that the traditions rendered by such persons have a normative significance for the group and, at least in their broad outlines, are widely

shared. An additional judgment has been made upon the contexts within which the traditions were reduced to writing. Wissler's material, for example, was gathered with considerable care, but his interests were often descriptive rather than focused upon aspects of cultural meaning. Grinnell and McClintock supplement Wissler in significant ways, partly because they both established rather long and personal relationships with the Blackfeet. The materials of Josselin De Jong seem to my mind less helpful than the above-mentioned sources.

4. An additional set of traditions concerns the adventures of Scabby Round Robe, who received from the beavers powers relating to the beaver bundle, as well as elements relating to the Sun Dance bundle (Wissler 1912, pp. 192–94; Wissler and Duvall 1908, pp. 81–83).

5. This version was narrated by a respected spiritual leader of the North Piegans, Brings-down-the-Sun; it was recorded by McClintock in July 1905.

6. The appearance of dry painting also occurs among such Plains tribes as the Cheyennes and the Arapahoes (Wissler 1912, p. 257).

7. In this analysis we move beyond the view of one of the major interpreters of the Crows, Robert H. Lowie. Part of the problem of interpretation revolves around the way Lowie presented his data and, particularly, the meaning which he assigned to ritual forms. An illustration of the problematic character of his views appears in his notion of "ceremonialism." The very essence of ceremonial life, according to Lowie, is that it exists for its own sake and has no further meaning:

> Ceremony for ceremony's sake is, I think, the secret of ceremonial activity; hence the vagueness, if not total absence, of any intelligible purpose for much ceremonial activity; hence the stability of many objective features in the absence of any stable subjective associations with those features. (Lowie 1914b, p. 96; cf. Lowie 1914a, pp. 628–829)

This means that it is fruitless to seek for horizons of meaning that are correlates of individual or social experiences of religious and moral awareness. From this point of view, the Crow Sun Dance is not a religious experience at all. Rather what occurs is of the nature of what Lowie calls a "free show"—that is, a number of intrinsically unrelated ritual performances which have no specific meaning but which gratify participants through the very act of their performance (Lowie 1914b, p. 96; Lowie 1914b, pp. 628–29). This view does not comprise an adequate understanding of the Crow Sun Dance, even on the basis of Lowie's own data, as we shall show.

8. The age of these bundles is uncertain, although estimates place them as early as the mid-eighteenth century. For the Crows, however, "the important thing about a ceremonial bundle was not its antiquity but its record of successes— the true sign of a gift from powerful supernatural helpers" (Voget 1984, p. 79). Also Voget views the owl as "a harbinger of evil and even death" (82, n.), as compared with the interpretation rendered in this chapter.

9. The form of the Crow Sun Dance we have discussed represents a pattern which last appeared in about 1874. In the 1940s there was a revival of the Sun Dance among the Crows; this pattern was introduced by the Wind River Shoshones (Miller 1980, p. 94; Voget 1984). The revival built upon a motif in Crow spiritual life which was very ancient: the search for experiences of transcendence through vision. In addition, there were elements that were essentially different

from the earlier form. One of these elements had to do with the shape of the lodge, which became almost identical with that among the Blackfeet and other neighboring groups. The theme of revenge was also displaced, and the Sun Dance became a religious occasion when communication between humans and the transcendent powers of earth and sky was sought. At this point, another ancient motif appears, which is the establishment of kinship between humans and the sacred powers symbolized on the center pole of the Sun's lodge (Miller 1980, p. 95). This modern form of the Sun Dance conforms more closely to the theme of personal and tribal renewal which was characteristic of earlier Blackfoot ritual, and which was also central to the traditional Sun Dance among the Cheyennes and Arapahoes.

10. The description which follows relies primarily upon the work of George Dorsey, who witnessed the Cheyenne Sun Dance in 1901 and 1903 (Dorsey 1905b, pp. 57ff.).

11. The act of sexual intercourse as a means of transferring power probably was diffused historically from the Mandans and the Hidatsas and reflects the fertility symbolism of these agricultural societies (Kehoe 1970, p. 99). Its form among the tribes under discussion was shaped both by the social structure developed on the Plains and by the particular ritual processes we have discussed. While women were certainly less involved in political life than men, their symbolic role in rituals essential to tribal welfare cannot be overlooked (Weist, in Wood and Liberty 1980, pp. 259–60). In these respects, the power and participation of women were very great indeed.

12. The Cheyennes were also so divided, the northern division being located in Montana and the southern division in Oklahoma.

13. Among the Northern Arapahoes, the Flat Pipe was suspended in its bundle upon a stand constructed like a tipi and containing four poles. Food and other gifts were offered to the Flat Pipe by participants in the Sun Dance. At other times feasts could also be held in honor of the Flat Pipe. At these times, the bundle was opened and those participating in the ceremony were allowed to touch the pipe with the sole of the right foot. The food which was prepared for such a feast was considered sacred, and it brought benefit to all who partook of it (see Carter 1938, pp. 73–101). Fertility symbolism is perhaps associated with the Flat Pipe, along with other meaning horizons. In such a context it may indeed carry the meaning of the "penis or root of man" (Dorsey 1903b, pp. 176–78). Such meanings must be viewed within the cultural context we have described and not reduced, for example, to a strict Freudian interpretation.

14. In the Arapaho case, the chief priest and the lodge-maker's wife represented perhaps the sun and the bison—obvious fertility symbolism; and the site of the ritual intercourse perhaps represented a buffalo wallow. As was also the case among some other groups, a root was transferred from the chief priest's mouth to the mouth of the woman during the act of intercourse. This root most probably represented the seed of renewal which would grow in the world and among the people (Kehoe 1970, pp. 100–1). The symbolism of the seed and the buffalo again signaled the amalgamation of traditions from an agricultural past and their reinterpretation within a new context.

# Bibliography

Albers, Patricia, and Seymour S. Parker
1971  "The Plains Vision Experience: A Study of Power and Privilege." *Southwestern Journal of Anthropology* 27/3, 203–33.

Benedict, Ruth
1922  "The Vision in Plains Culture," *American Anthropologist,* NS 24/1, 1–23.
1923  "The Concept of the Guardian Spirit in North America." *Memoirs of the American Anthropological Association* 29.

Berkhofer, Robert F., Jr.
1978  *The White Man's Indian.* New York: Vintage Books.

Brinton, Daniel G.
1896  *The Myths of the New World.* 3rd. ed. rev. Philadelphia: D. McKay.

Bullchild, Percy
1985  *The Sun Came Down.* San Francisco: Harper and Row.

Callicott, J. Baird
  1982  "Traditional American Indian and Western European Attitudes Toward Nature: An Overview." *Environmental Ethics* 4/4, 293–318.
Carter, John C.
  1938  "The Northern Arapaho Flat Pipe and the Ceremony of Covering the Pipe." *Bureau of American Ethnology Bulletin* 119.
Curtis, Edward S.
  1909  *The North American Indian*, 4. Reprint, 1970. New York: Johnson Reprint Corporation.
  1911  *The North American Indian*, 6. Norwood, Mass.: The Plimpton Press.
Dempsey, H.A.
  1956  "Stone 'Medicine Wheels'—Memorials to Blackfeet War Chiefs." *Journal Washington Academy of Sciences* XLVI/6, 177–82.
Dorsey, George
  1903a  "How the Pawnee Captured the Cheyenne Medicine Arrows." *American Anthropologist* NS 5, 644–58.
  1903b  "The Arapaho Sun Dance." *Field Columbian Museum Anthropological Series* 4.
  1905a  "The Cheyenne: Ceremonial Organization." *Field Columbian Museum Anthropological Series* 9/1.
  1905b  "The Cheyenne: The Sun Dance." *Field Columbian Museum Anthropological Series* 9/2.
Dorsey, George, and Alfred L. Kroeber
  1903  "Traditions of the Arapaho." *Field Columbian Museum Anthropological Series,* Publication 81, Vol. 5.
Dorsey, George, and James R. Murie
  1940  "Notes on Skidi Pawnee Society." *Field Museum of Natural History Anthropological Series,* 27.
Dundes, Alan
  1965  *The Study of Folklore.* Englewood Cliffs, N.J.: Prentice Hall.
Eggan, Fred
  1955  "The Cheyenne and Arapaho Kinship System." In *Social Anthropology of North American Tribes,* edited by Fred Eggan, 35–98. Chicago: University of Chicago Press.
  1966  *The American Indian: Perspectives for the Study of Social Change.* Chicago: Aldine Publishing Company.
Ewers, John C.
  1955  "The Horse in Blackfoot Indian Culture." *Bureau of American Ethnology Bulletin* 159.

1958    *The Blackfeet*. Norman: University of Oklahoma Press.
1967    "Was there a Northwestern Plains Sub-Culture: An Ethno-graphical Appraisal," *Plains Anthropologist*, 12/36, 167–74.
1969    "The Northwest Trade Gun." *Alberta Historical Review* 4/2, 3–9.
1975    "Intertribal Warfare as the Precursor of Indian-White Warfare on the Northern Great Plains." *Western Historical Quarterly* 6, 397–410.

Frison, George G.
1978    *Prehistoric Hunters of the High Plains*. New York: Academic Press.

Gay, Volney
1983    "Winnicott's Contribution to Religious Studies: The Resurrection of the Culture Hero," *Journal of the American Academy of Religion* LI/3, 371–95.

Geertz, Clifford
1973    *The Interpretation of Cultures*. New York: Basic Books.
1983    *Local Knowledge*. New York: Basic Books.

Gilbert, B. Miles
1980    "The Plains Setting." In *Anthropology on the Great Plains,* edited by W. Raymond Wood and Margot Liberty, 8–15. Lincoln: University of Nebraska Press.

Gill, Sam D.
1982    *Native American Religions*. Belmont, Calif.: Wadsworth Publishing Co.

Grinnell, George Bird
1907    "Some Early Cheyenne Tales." *Journal of American Folk Lore* 20, 169–94.
1908    "Some Early Cheyenne Tales II." *Journal of American Folklore* 21, 269–320.
1910    "The Great Mysteries of the Cheyenne." *American Anthropologist* NS 12, 542–75.
1914    "The Cheyenne Medicine Lodge." *American Anthropologist* NS 16, 245–56.
1922    "The Medicine Wheel." *American Anthropologist* 24/3, 299–310.
1962    *Blackfoot Lodge Tales*. Lincoln: University of Nebraska Press.
1966    *When Buffalo Ran*. Norman: Oklahoma University Press.
1971    *By Cheyenne Campfires*. Lincoln: University of Nebraska Press.
1972    *The Cheyenne Indians*. 2 vols. Lincoln: University of Nebraska Press.

Harrod, Howard L.
1971   *Mission Among the Blackfeet.* Norman: University of Oklahoma Press.
1981   *The Human Center: Moral Agency in the Social World.* Philadelphia: Fortress Press.

Hoebel, E. Adamson
1978   *The Cheyennes.* 2nd ed. New York: Holt, Rinehart and Winston.

Hultkrantz, Åke
1953   *Conceptions of the Soul Among North American Indians.* Stockholm: The Ethnographical Museum of Sweden.
1979   *The Religions of the American Indians.* Berkeley: University of California Press.
1981   *Belief and Worship in Native North America.* Edited by Christopher Vecsey. Syracuse: Syracuse University Press.

Hungry Wolf, Beverly
1980   *The Ways of My Grandmothers.* New York: William Morrow and Company.

Josselin De Jong, J. P. B.
1914   *Blackfoot Texts.* Amsterdam: Johannes Müller.

Kehoe, Alice B.
1970   "The Function of Ceremonial Sexual Intercourse Among the Northern Plains Indians." *Plains Anthropologist* 15, 99–103.
1981   *North American Indians.* Englewood Cliffs, N.J.: Prentice-Hall.

Kehoe, T.F.
1954   "Stone 'Medicine Wheels' in Southern Alberta and the Adjacent Portion of Montana." *Journal Washington Academy of Sciences* XLIV/5, 135.
1958   "Tipi Rings: The 'Direct Ethnological' Approach Applied to an Archaeological Problem." *American Anthropologist* 60/5, 861–73.
1960   "Stone Tipi Rings in North-Central Montana and the Adjacent Portion of Alberta, Canada: Their Historical, Ethnological, and Archaeological Aspects." *Bureau of American Ethnology Bulletin* 173, Paper 62.

Klein, Alan M.
1980   "Plains Economic Analysis: The Marxist Complement." In *Anthropology on the Great Plains,* edited by W. Raymond Wood and Margot Liberty, 129–40. Lincoln: University of Nebraska Press.

Kroeber, Alfred L.
1902  "The Arapaho." *Bulletin of the American Museum of Natural History* 18/1.
1907  "The Arapaho." *Bulletin of the American Museum of Natural History* 18/4.
1939  *Cultural and Natural Areas of Native North America.* Berkeley: University of California Press.
1948  *Anthropology.* New ed. New York: Harcourt Brace and World Company.

Lévi-Strauss, Claude
1967  "The Structural Study of Myth." In *Structural Anthropology,* 202–28. New York: Doubleday.

Lewis, Oscar
1942  "The Effects of White Contact Upon Blackfoot Culture: With Special Reference to the Role of the Fur Trade." *American Ethnological Society* Monograph No. 6. New York: J.J. Augustin.

Liberty, Margot
1980  "The Sun Dance." In *Anthropology on the Great Plains,* edited by W. Raymond Wood and Margot Liberty, 164–78. Lincoln: University of Nebraska Press.

Long, Charles
1963  *Alpha: The Myths of Creation.* Chico, Calif.: Scholars Press. Reprint 1982.

Lopez, Barry Holstun
1977  *Giving Birth to Thunder, Sleeping with His Daughter.* New York: Avon Books.

Lowie, Robert H.
1914a  "Ceremonialism in North America." *American Anthropologist* 16, 602–31.
1914b  "The Crow Sun Dance." *Journal of American Folklore* 27, 94–96.
1915  "The Sun Dance of the Crow Indians." *Anthropological Papers of the American Museum of Natural History* 16.
1918  "Myths and Traditions of the Crow Indians." *Anthropological Papers of the American Museum of Natural History* 25/1.
1920  "The Tobacco Society of the Crow Indians." *Anthropological Papers of the American Museum of Natural History* 21/2.
1922  "The Religion of the Crow Indians." *Anthropological Papers of the American Museum of Natural History* 25/2.
1935  *The Crow Indians.* New York: Farrar and Rinehart.
1954  "Indians of the Plains." *American Museum of Natural History Anthropological Handbook* 1.

Maclean, John
1892  *Canadian Savage Folk*. Toronto: W. Briggs.
1893  "Blackfoot Mythology." *Journal of American Folklore* 6, 165–72.

McClintock, Walter
1968  *The Old North Trail*. Lincoln: University of Nebraska Press.

Makarius, L.
1970  "Ritual Clowns and Symbolic Behavior." *Diogenes* 44–73.
1973  "The Crime of Manabozo." *American Anthropologist* 75/3, 663–75.

Malouf, Carling
1961  "Tipi Rings on the High Plains." *American Antiquity* 26/2, 381–89.

Martin, Calvin
1978  *Keepers of the Game: Indian-Animal Relationships and the Fur Trade*. Berkeley: University of California Press.

Miller, F.
1980  "The Crow Sun Dance Lodge: Form, Process and Geometry in the Creation of Sacred Space." *Temenos* 16.

Mooney, James
1907  "The Cheyenne Indians." *Memoirs of the American Anthropological Association* 1/6.

Nabokov, Peter
1967  *Two Leggings: The Making of a Crow Warrior*. New York: Thomas Y. Crowell.

Oliver, Symmes C.
1962  "Ecology and Cultural Continuity as Contributing Factors in the Social Organization of the Plains Indians." *University of California Publications in American Archaeology and Ethnology* 48/1.

Ottaway, Harold N.
1970  "A Possible Origin for the Cheyenne Sacred Arrow Complex." *Plains Anthropologist* 15, 94–98.

Paulson, Ivar
1964  "The Animal Guardian: A Critical and Synthetic Review." *History of Religions* 3/2, 202–19.

Powell, Peter J.
1969  *Sweet Medicine*. 2 vols. Norman: University of Oklahoma Press.

Provinse, John H.
1955    "The Underlying Sanctions of Plains Indian Culture." In *Social Anthropology of North American Indians*. Edited by Fred Eggan, 341–74. Chicago: University of Chicago Press.

Radin, Paul
1956    *The Trickster*. New York: Philosophical Library.

Ramsey, Jarold
1983    *Reading the Fire*. Lincoln: University of Nebraska Press.

Regan, Tom
1982    *All that Dwell Therein*. Berkeley: University of California Press.

Ricketts, Mac Linscott
1966    "The North American Indian Trickster." *History of Religions* 5/2, 327–50.

Roe, Frank Gilbert
1955    *The Indian and the Horse*. Norman: University of Oklahoma Press.
1970    *The North American Buffalo*. 2nd ed. Toronto: University of Toronto Press.

Schultz, J. W.
1973    *My Life as an Indian*. Williamstown, Mass.: Corner House Publishers.

Schutz, Alfred
1964    *Collected Papers, II, Studies in Social Theory*. Edited by Arvid Brodersen. The Hague: Martinus Nijhoff.
1966    *Collected Papers, III, Studies in Phenomenological Philosophy*. Edited by I. Schutz. The Hague: Martinus Nijhoff.
1967a   *Collected Papers, I, The Problem of Social Reality*. Edited by Maurice Natanson. The Hague: Martinus Nijhoff.
1967b   *The Phenomenology of the Social World*. Translated by George Walsh and Frederick Lehnert. Evanston: Northwestern University Press.
1970    *Reflections on the Problem of Relevance*. Edited by Richard Zaner. New Haven: Yale University Press.

Schutz, Alfred, and Thomas Luckmann
1973    *The Structures of the Life-World*. Evanston: Northwestern University Press.

Simms, S. C.
1903a   "A Wheel-Shaped Stone Monument in Wyoming." *American Anthropologist* 5/1, 107–10.
1903b   "Traditions of the Crows." *Field Columbian Museum Anthropological Series*, Publication 85 2/6.

1904 "Cultivation of 'Medicine Tobacco' by the Crows." *American Anthropologist* NS 6.

Speck, Frank G.
1977 *Naskapi: The Savage Hunters of the Labrador Peninsula.* New ed. Norman: University of Oklahoma Press.

Spier, Leslie
1921 "The Sun Dance of the Plains Indians: Its Diffusion and Development." *Anthropological Papers of the American Museum of Natural History* 16/7.

Stands In Timber, John, and Margot Liberty
1967 *Cheyenne Memories.* New Haven: Yale University Press.

Uhlenbeck, C.C., and R.H. Van Gulik
1934 *A Blackfoot-English Vocabulary.* Amsterdam.

Voget, Fred W.
1984 *The Shoshoni-Crow Sun Dance.* Norman: University of Oklahoma Press.

Waterman, T.T.
1914 "The Explanatory Element in the Folk-Tales of the North American Indian." *Journal of American Folklore* 27, 1–54.

Webb, Walter Prescott
1981 *The Great Plains.* Lincoln: University of Nebraska Press.

Weber, Max
1952 *Ancient Judaism.* New York: The Free Press.

Wedel, Waldo R.
1974 *Prehistoric Man on the Great Plains.* Norman: University of Oklahoma Press.

Weist, Katherine
1980 "Plains Indian Women: An Assessment." In *Anthropology on the Great Plains,* edited by W. Raymond Wood and Margot Liberty, 255–71. Lincoln: University of Nebraska Press.

Weltfish, Gene
1971 "The Plains Indians: Their Continuity in History and Their Indian Identity." In *North American Indians in Historical Perspective,* edited by Eleanor B. Leacock and Nancy O. Lurie, 200–27. New York: Random House.

Wheat, Joe Ben
1967 "A Paleo-Indian Bison Kill." *Scientific American* 216/1, 44–52.

Wildschut, William
1924 "Blackfoot Beaver Bundles." *Museum of American Indian Heye Foundation, Indian Notes,* 1, 138–41.

1928    "Blackfoot Pipe Bundles." *Museum of American Indian Heye Foundation, Indian Notes* 5/4, 419,433.
1960    "Crow Indian Medicine Bundles." Edited by John C. Ewers. *Contributions from the Museum of the American Indian Heye Foundation* 17.

Wissler, Clark
1908    "Ethnographical Problems of the Missouri Saskatchewan Area." *American Anthropologist* NS 10/2, 197–207.
1911    "The Social Life of the Blackfoot Indians." *Anthropological Papers of the American Museum of Natural History* 7/1.
1912    "Ceremonial Bundles of the Blackfoot Indians." *Anthropological Papers of the American Museum of Natural History* 7/2.
1914    "The Influence of the Horse in the Development of Plains Culture." *American Anthropologist* 16/1, 1–25.
1918    "The Sun Dance of the Blackfoot Indians." *Anthropological Papers of the American Museum of Natural History* 16/3.

Wissler, Clark, and D. C. Duvall
1908    "Mythology of the Blackfoot Indians." *Anthropological Papers of the American Museum of Natural History* 2/1.

Wolf, Eric R.
1982    *Europe and the People Without History.* Berkeley: University of California Press.

Wood, W. Raymond, and Margot Liberty, eds.
1980    *Anthropology on the Great Plains.* Lincoln: University of Nebraska Press.

# Name Index

Albers, Patricia, 31
Alden, Frances, 176 n.1

Benedict, Ruth, 24, 29, 31, 32, 34, 35
Berkhofer, Robert F., Jr., 5
Boas, Franz, 178 n.5
Brinton Daniel, 178 n.5
Brown, Joseph Epes, 175 n.3
Bullchild, Percy, 177 n.1
Bull Plume, Dan, 181 n.3
Butterfly, Clarence, 181–82 n.7

Carter, John C., 177 n.3, 185 n.13
Clark, Ben, 177–78 n.4
Curtis, Edward S., 10, 82, 112, 124, 135, 138, 139, 140

Dempsey, H.A., 19
Dorsey, George, 48, 50, 54, 59, 60, 61, 97, 98, 99, 101, 102, 104, 105, 106, 141, 142, 143, 144, 145, 146, 147, 148, 149, 150, 151, 152, 153, 154, 155, 178 n.4, 182 n.2, 185 n.10, 185 n.13
Dundes, Alan, 122
DuVall, D.C., 28, 41, 43, 54, 56, 59, 60, 61, 70, 71, 77, 78, 121, 122, 124, 125, 176 n.1, 177 nn.1,4, 180 n.6, 181 n.4, 184 n.4

Eggan, Fred, 9, 11, 13, 14, 29, 40
Ewers, John C., 8, 10, 11, 19

Frison, George C., 16, 17, 18

Gay, Volney, 179 n.5
Geertz, Clifford, 68, 89, 174 n.2
Gilbert, B. Miles, 17

130, 131, 132, 133, 134, 176 n.1, 177 nn.1,4, 180 n.6, 181 nn.2,4,5,6, 182 nn.4,8,9, 183 nn.1,2, 184 nn.3,4,6

Wolf, Eric R., 175 n.7, 176 n.9
Wolf Robe, Fish, 181 n.3
Wood, W. Raymond, 182 n.3, 185 n.11

# Subject Index

Creation. *See* Cosmology
Creator figure, 40, 41, 60, 64, 66, 157,
  161–62, 166, 169–70
  in Blackfoot traditions, 41–45, 54,
  164, 176 n.1
  in Cheyenne traditions, 48–50
  in Crow traditions, 46–48
Crees, 12, 14
Crisis, role in Blackfoot Sun Dance,
  117, 125
Crows
  as an agricultural people, 14, 108–9
  cosmology, 46–48, 86, 87, 89, 110,
  161, 177 n.4
  historical context of, 82
  hunting, 47, 138
  linguistic roots of, 13
  migration of, 13
  relationship to Hidatsas, 13–14,
  108–9
  renewal of social world, 108–14
  sacred bundles, 82–86, 117, 135–40,
  171
  social change, 13–14
  social organization, 14, 47, 48
  social structure, 108, 109
  Sun Dance, 109, 117, 135–40,
  184 nn.7,9
  Tobacco Society, 87, 108–14
  vision experience, 24, 27–28, 29, 31,
  32–33, 34, 35–36, 83, 84–85, 86,
  111–12, 136–37, 139
Cultural adaptation, 18–19
Cultural horizons and images,
  problems of interpretation, 4–5
Cultural values, 52, 53, 54, 55–56, 59,
  62–63, 65, 118, 158–59
Culture, relationship to morality and
  religion, 5–6
Culture area, Northwestern Plains as,
  7–8
Culture hero, 40, 41, 64, 66, 88, 157,
  161, 170, 178–79 n.5
  in Blackfoot traditions, 41, 42,
  44–45, 54, 122, 126, 127
  in Cheyenne traditions, 94–102,
  104, 105, 141, 148

  in Crow traditions, 24, 47, 177 n.2
  in Suhtai traditions, 94, 97, 98
Cuts-Wood, 121–22

Dakotas, 14, 34, 84
Dance. *See also* Sun Dance
  in Blackfoot traditions, 72, 74, 75,
  76, 77, 79, 80, 116, 120, 133–34
  in Cheyenne traditions, 144, 151
  in Crow traditions, 112, 113, 139
  as mediator of symbols, 67, 88, 157
  in Trickster traditions, 58
Death
  in Blackfoot cosmology, 43–44, 162
  in Crow cosmology, 89
Deception, 54, 56, 57, 58, 59, 60, 61,
  167, 168
Deer, 59, 136
Dependence, 90
Deprivation, 32
Destructiveness, 59, 167
Digging stick, 123, 132
Dipper, 85, 87, 111, 127, 137
Disease, 12–13, 76, 116
Doctors, 35, 105, 116, 163
Dog, domestication of, 9
Dogwood, 148
Dream colors in Crow beadwork,
  176 n.1
Dream interpretation, 111–112
Dreams, 158, 160. *See also* Vision
  experience
Drum, as mediator of power, 27, 136,
  139
Duck, 42, 46, 51, 58–59, 76

Eagle, 44, 51, 85, 101, 119, 127, 134,
  137, 139, 153
Earth
  and creation, 42–51, 161
  and natoas bundle, 121
  powers of, 74
  as provider, 78
  relationship to humans, 92
  renewal of, 142–55
  and rock, 86, 110, 130
  sacredness of, 88

of the Blackfoot natoas bundle and
  Sun Dance, 121–27
in Blackfoot traditions, 116
of Cheyenne Sun Dance traditions,
  141–43
of Crow Sun Dance bundle, 136–37
Origins, problems of interpretation, 5
Orphan, motif of, 75–77, 85, 97–98,
  121–22, 136–37
Otter, 42, 71, 112, 128
Otter weed, 51
Otter Woman in Blackfoot traditions,
  121
Owl, 71, 85, 101, 127, 136, 137, 138

Paint, 71, 76, 118, 119, 153
Painted tipi
  in Arapaho traditions, 152
  in Blackfoot traditions, 81
Painting, 71–72, 75, 119, 136, 147,
  154–55
of body, 88, 98, 112, 120, 133–34,
  139, 143–44, 147, 151
Pawnee, 34, 182 n.2
Personal bundles in Blackfoot
  traditions, 80–81
Phenomenology, 173 n.1
Piegan (Pikuni), 10, 26, 128, 181 n.4,
  184 n.5
Pine needles, 136
Pine tree, 137
Pipe, 36, 109, 111, 118, 130, 145, 146,
  160, 176 n.9. *See also* Sacred Pipe
Pipe bundle (Blackfoot), 69–75, 80,
  181 n.3
Pipe from the Seven Stars in Blackfoot
  traditions, 181 n.2
Plant motifs, 86–88, 89, 123. *See also*
  Plants
Plants, 89, 90, 91, 92, 128, 153. *See also*
  Tobacco; *individual plant names*
Pleiades, 87, 127
Plum tree, 149
Poor young man, motif of, 35–36,
  124–25, 136–37, 163
Pottery, 176 n.9
Power. *See also* Transcendent powers

animals as mediators of, 87, 162–63
beaver, 75–78
inheritance of, 31–32
quest for, 83, 136–37, 139, 163–64
and ritual, 88–89
sources of, 73, 74, 75, 77, 133, 141,
  161–63
of symbols, 66–67
transfer of, 29–32, 36, 69–71, 72,
  77–78, 81, 84–85
types of, 35
visions of, 23–32, 34, 36, 163
Prairie dog, 58, 71, 137
Prairie-Dog-Man in Crow traditions,
  137
Prayer, 33, 34, 44–45, 67, 71, 74, 76,
  77, 79–80, 117, 119, 120, 129, 145,
  155
Predecessors in Plains traditions,
  40–41, 53, 64, 68, 72, 88, 90, 102,
  127, 158, 161, 165–67, 170
Priests, 47, 144, 145, 146, 148, 151, 152,
  155, 178 n.4
Primal water, 42, 46, 50–51, 130, 161
Prongs, 78–79
Property. *See also* Reciprocity
  exchange of, 30–32
Prophet, 35
Prophet's lodge in Cheyenne
  traditions, 105
Puberty rites, 34
Pumpkin, 109
Purification, rituals of, 32–33, 72, 73,
  78, 105–6, 112, 118, 129, 136, 151

Rabbit, 153
Rabbit-tipi in Arapaho traditions,
  154–55
Rabbit weed, 153
Rape, 60
Raven, 69–71, 119, 125, 127, 162
Reciprocity, 53, 54, 56, 59, 91, 167
Redbird, 101
Red bush, 153
Red Tassel in Cheyenne traditions, 98,
  99

in Crow traditions, 46–48, 85, 110, 136, 177 n.2
in Plains traditions, 87, 89, 90, 162, 163
Sun Dance, 53, 94, 115–56, 171
in Arapaho traditions, 52, 117, 152–56
in Blackfoot traditions, 19, 27, 81, 115, 117–34
in Cheyenne traditions, 99, 117, 141–52, 163
in Crow traditions, 109, 117, 135–40, 184 nn.7,9
in Suhtai traditions, 94, 99
Sun dog symbols, 132
Sun Pole, 133–34
Sun's lodge
in Blackfoot traditions, 119–27, 133–34
in Crow traditions, 137–39
Swan, 71
Sweat bath, 136
Sweat-house ritual in Blackfoot traditions, 124, 129–31
Sweat lodge, 88, 119, 121, 160
and healing, 95, 107
and purification, 33, 72, 75, 78, 105–6, 112, 151
in Tobacco Society ceremony, 111
Sweet grass, 78, 146
Sweet Medicine, 98, 99–102, 105, 141, 150, 163, 170
Sweet Medicine tradition, 99–102, 104, 182 n.1
Sweet pine incense, 73
Sweet Root Standing in Cheyenne traditions, 98
Symbolic form and ritual, 116
Symbolic movement, 73–74, 112, 119, 129, 145, 146
Symbols
as mediators, 25–26, 38, 72, 158
as mediators of tradition, 1–2, 36–37, 68
nature of, 25–26, 66–68, 111, 149, 158
and religious and moral attitudes, dispositions, and sensibilities, 1–3, 53, 68, 88, 161

Symbolism
of altar (Arapaho) 154–55
astral and solar, 111
of the Blackfoot natoas bundle, 121
of Blackfoot painted tipis, 81
of buffalo, 130
of bundles, 68, 72, 121
of cardinal directions, 51, 53, 103, 112
of Cheyenne Lone-tipi, 144–48
of Cheyenne New-Life-Lodge altar, 149–50
in Cheyenne sacred arrow ceremony, 103, 104, 105
of color. *See* Color, symbolism of
of the Crow Tobacco Society adoption lodge, 109–10
of Crow war shields, 83–85
of dancing, 151
of fertility, 109–10, 112, 113
of form, 103, 150
of hundred-willow sweat house, 129–31
male and female, 108
of the number four, 42, 53, 103
of pipe, 146–47
of planting and harvesting (Crow), 108–14
of predecessors, 40
of smoke, 129, 130, 145, 146–47
of steam, 129, 130
of the Sun's Lodge, 133–34
of tribal circle, 104
of Trickster, culture hero, creator figure, 64, 65

Taboos, 61
Temporality, 38–41, 64, 158, 165–66
Teton Dakotas, 82
Thunder, 87, 89, 162
in Blackfoot traditions, 69–75, 121, 127
in Cheyenne traditions, 48–49, 142
Thunderbird, 148
Tipi rings, 17–18
Tobacco
in Blackfoot traditions, 71, 72, 76, 119, 128, 182–83, n.4
in Cheyenne traditions, 145, 147